DESIGN AND ANALYSIS OF COMPUTER COMMUNICATION NETWORKS

McGraw-Hill Computer Science Series

Tremblay and Bunt: *An Introduction to Computer Science:
An Algorithmic Approach, Short Edition*
Tremblay and Manohar: *Discrete Mathematical Structures with Applications to
Computer Science*
Tremblay and Sorenson: *An Introduction to Data Structures with Applications*
Tucker: *Programming Languages*
Wiederhold: *Database Design*
Winston: *The Psychology of Computer Vision*

McGraw-Hill Advanced Computer Science Series

Davis and Lenat: *Knowledge-Based Systems in Artificial Intelligence*
Feigenbaum and Feldman: *Computers and Thought*
Kogge: *The Architecture of Pipelined Computers*
Lindsay, Buchanan, Feigenbaum, and Lederberg: *Applications of Artificial
Intelligence for Organic Chemistry: The Dendral Project*
Nilsson: *Problem-Solving Methods in Artificial Intelligence*
Winston: *The Psychology of Computer Vision*
Wulf, Levin, and Harbison: *HYDRA/C.mmp: An Experimental
Computer System*

DESIGN AND ANALYSIS OF COMPUTER COMMUNICATION NETWORKS

Vijay Ahuja, Ph.D.

International Business Machines Corporation

McGraw-Hill Book Company

New York   St. Louis   San Francisco   Auckland   Bogotá   Hamburg
Johannesburg   London   Madrid   Mexico   Montreal   New Delhi
Panama   Paris   São Paulo   Singapore   Sydney   Tokyo   Toronto

To my respected parents
Dr. Yog Dhyan
and
Mrs. Shakuntla Ahuja

This book was set in Times Roman by Santype-Byrd.
The editors were James E. Vastyan and James B. Armstrong;
the production supervisor was Phil Galea.
The drawings were done by Danmark & Michaels, Inc.
R. R. Donnelley & Sons Company was printer and binder.

**DESIGN AND ANALYSIS OF
COMPUTER COMMUNICATION NETWORKS**

1234567890 DODO 8987654321

ISBN 0-07-000697-0

Library of Congress Cataloging in Publication Data

Ahuja, Vijay.
    Design and analysis of computer communication networks.

    (McGraw-Hill computer science series)
    Includes index.
    1. Computer networks. I. Title. II. Series.
TK5105.5.A39   001.64'404   81-11826
ISBN 0-07-000697-0   AACR2

CONTENTS

PREFACE

In this era of a growing confluence of communications and computing, it is becoming increasingly important for computer scientists, programmers, engineers, and network designers to understand the concepts used to design efficient and viable communication networks. Such concepts range from understanding the ever-growing variety of network components to observing total network behavior. There exists a need to provide a concise description of the various network components, strategies to put them together, and approaches to analyze and improve network behavior. It is our intent to familiarize the reader with the concepts and approaches required for the design and analysis of computer communication networks.

This book is intended for students and professionals who have some background in computer software or in computer or communication hardware. For those associated with networks, the book should provide an introduction to the fundamentals of computer communication networks and their analysis as well as an insight into diverse approaches and algorithms. The book provides both descriptive and analytic treatment of various aspects of network design. The emphasis is on the components of networks, such as transmission links and network nodes, and on network analysis problems, such as routing and flow control. It is hoped that this book will also serve as the textbook for a first course in computer communications in an undergraduate or graduate curriculum.

The book consists of eight chapters and an appendix. Chapter 1 provides an introduction to networks, including packet switching and circuit switching. Chapters 2 through 7 use several concepts in probability theory and queuing theory, and Chap. 8 presents these concepts together. Readers requiring a background in probability theory or queuing theory are suggested to review Chap. 8 before proceeding to study Chaps. 2 through 7.

Chapters 2 and 3 describe the network components. Chapter 2 treats transmission links, namely, terrestrial, radio, and satellite channels and optical fiber. It also includes treatment of various polling strategies for terrestrial links, and approaches for efficient utilization of satellite links and radio channels. Chapter 3 addresses the functions and design aspects of a network node. It also provides approaches used to estimate processor capacity, memory size, and frequency of overruns on message buffers. Chapter 4 describes various algorithms for the topological design of a network. Chapter 5 contains a description of network protocols for internode communications and for managing network resources. Chapter 6 addresses network congestion and deadlock problems, and describes several algorithms that control message flow in a network. Chapter 7 provides a description of various approaches for selecting and defining message routes in a network. Chapter 8 describes techniques to estimate network performance parameters, such as response time and throughput. It also includes an introduction to elementary concepts of probability theory that are used in other parts of the book. The appendix contains a description of some public networks, such as DATAPAC and TYMNET.

ACKNOWLEDGMENTS

The task of writing a book requires cooperation, contribution, and sacrifice on the part of numerous individuals. I wish to express my deep gratitude to the reviewers—George A. Deaton, Jr., IBM Corporation; John Spragins, Clemson University; Harold S. Stone, University of Massachusetts; and Safwat Zaky, University of Toronto—who contributed significantly to improving the quality of my manuscript. My employer, IBM Corporation, and its management, provided typing help and encouragement throughout this effort. A special thanks is due to my wife, Neeta, for her moral support, and to my children, for always offering complete cooperation to my unconventional working hours during evenings, weekends, and holidays.

Vijay Ahuja

CHAPTER
ONE

INTRODUCTION

CHAPTER OUTLINE

The further backward you can look, the further forward you can see.

Winston Churchill

1-1 NETWORKS—A PERSPECTIVE

Networks first appeared under the guise of time-shared systems in the late 1960s. In a time-shared system, each of the several terminal users has exclusive use of the system resources on a time-sliced basis. Operating systems, such as those for the IBM System/360, GECOS III for the Honeywell 600 series, and the Univac 1108, offered the options of time-shared systems. Some operating systems were entirely devoted to time sharing, such as the PDP-8 Time Sharing System (TSS/8). Time-sharing operating systems were followed by a variety of communication-oriented software packages. Several communication access methods, terminal system software, and interactive system software packages were introduced in the 1960s and early 1970s. Some of the well-known packages are those for the airline reservations, the information retrieval systems for libraries, and the general-purpose database management systems, such as the IBM Information Management System/360. The computer and communication industries were introducing asynchronous (start/stop) and synchronous (binary synchronous) line protocols. By the late 1970s, several types of terminals, terminal controllers, front-end processors, line concentrators, and related equipment had grown to a sizeable portion of the data processing market.

The early networking years saw new strides in connecting computing equipment to existing communication facilities. A courtship of the computing and communication technologies was taking place. Line multiplexers, such as the IBM 270X and 370X series, and modems provided a computer interface for several communication links. By 1972, several computer networks had emerged. Important characteristics of some of them are tabulated in Table 1-1. Experimental networks, such as the Distributed Computing System (DCS) in California and Triangle Universities Computation Center (TUCC) in North Carolina, were being developed by universities to serve their student communities. The DCS network uses a ring interface for each node, and connects all the nodes by a loop [7],* while TUCC is a centralized (star-connected) network serving three universities and other educational institutions in North Carolina.

* Bracketed numbers refer to the references at the end of this chapter.

Table 1-1 Early networks and their characteristics

	ARPA	CYBERNET	DCS	MERIT	OCTOPUS	TSS	TUCC
Organization	Distributed	Distributed	Distributed	Distributed	Mixed	Distributed	Centralized
Number of nodes	23	36	9	3	10	9	4
Communication interface	Honeywell DDP 516	CDC 3300 PPU	Ring interface	PDP-11	CDC PPU	IBM 2701	IBM 2701
Communication protocol	Message-switched	Message-switched	Mixed	Message-switched	Point-to-point	Point-to-point	Point-to-point
Message format	Variable length	Fixed length	Variable length	Variable length	Variable length	Variable length	Variable length

Source: D. J. Farber, "Networks: An Introduction," *Datamation*, April 1972, p. 37. Reprinted with permission of *Datamation* magazine. © Copyright by Technical Publishing Company, a division of Dun-Donnelley Publishing Corporation, a Dun & Bradstreet Company, 1978, all rights reserved.

In the mid-1970s, there was a phenomenal growth in nearly every aspect of communication networks. In the case of terminals, the early typewriter terminals were replaced by a wide range of function-rich terminals. The new terminals ranged from memory-less display units to the so-called front-end processors with disks, memory, tapes, printer, and display. Display terminals now include novel features such as color and multidimensions. Terminals or terminal systems have been developed for specific applications, such as text editing, office mail, banking, supermarket checkouts, point-of-sales systems, hospital systems, securities, production control, inventory control, computer-aided instructions and design, and the like.

An important aspect of communication network development has been the reduction in cost and improvement in speed and quality of transmission links. In the early years, terminals were connected through low-speed start-stop lines. Several innovations in communication technology have led to faster and more reliable links. Today, networks are using terrestrial links (with speeds on the order of megabits per second), satellite links, and radio channels.

The concept of a network node has grown from a simple communication line multiplexer to programmable minicomputers. Network nodes now provide several additional functions, such as message- or packet-switching, routing, flow control, network monitoring, and management. The concept of offloading the host processors has culminated in a new class of network nodes—the *front-end processors*—that also provide data management and transaction processing functions.

Concurrent with the above developments, several groups started to investigate various problems in connecting terminal networks to more than one host computer. The objective of one of the groups was to provide resource sharing by interconnecting several host computers. In early 1969, a contract for the Advanced Research Project Agency (ARPA) network was awarded to Bolt, Beranek and Newman, Inc. (BB&N), a Massachusetts-based engineering firm. The ARPA network, or ARPANET, grew from a small four-node net in 1969 to a network providing computing to about 100 computers by 1975 [10, p. 305], Figure 1-1 shows the ARPANET topology in 1969; Fig. 1-2 shows a more recent topology [12].

Networks can transmit messages by *circuit switching* or *store-and-forward message switching*. In circuit switching, networks transmit messages over a group of temporarily dedicated links on the message route, which are allocated simultaneously for message transfer. In store-and-forward message switching, the networks store and then

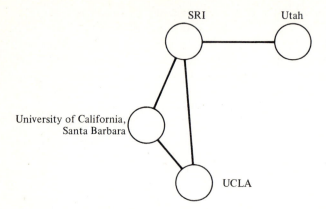

Figure 1-1 ARPANET—December 1969. (From L. Kleinrock, *Queueing Systems*, vol. II: *Computer Applications*. Wiley, New York, p. 306. Reprinted with permission.)

move the message over each of a group of shared links on the message route. Circuit switching results in a fixed message transmission delay, while message switching involves variable message transmission delay. In the case of some networks, messages are first segmented into smaller units or *packets*. The packets traverse the network independently until they reach the destination node, where they are reassembled into the original message. The maximum packet size is fixed, thereby allowing ease in managing storage and transmission. This approach, *packet switching*, has been adopted by several networks, such as ARPANET [3, 4] and TELENET. Table 1-2 compares the characteristics of some of the prevalent packet-switched networks in 1975.

While the computer industry developed various types of network software and hardware, the academic community was busy addressing itself to some of the classical problems in network design and analysis. Network topology (establishing connectivity between the nodes and assigning link capacities) must satisfy the network load, network transit time, and reliability requirements. Pioneer work was done in developing the ARPANET topology. Several protocols are being developed that permit orderly exchange of data between network nodes. Algorithms and protocols to prevent network congestion and deadlocks are being investigated. A number of routing strategies that prevent congestion and impose minimal processing overhead have been proposed and implemented. Some studies [5] have proposed a hierarchical technique for routing messages in networks with a relatively large number (such as 100 or more) of nodes. Algorithms were also devel-

Table 1-2 Characteristics of some packet-switched networks

	ARPANET	CIGALE/CYCLADES	CTNE	DDX-1	EIN	EPSS	NPL	RCP
Country	United States	France	Spain	Japan	Europe	United Kingdom	United Kingdom	France
Membership	Private	Private	Public	Public	Private	Public	Private	Public
User input	Multipacket	Packet	Packet	Packet	Packet	Packet	Packet	Packet
Maximum speed	200 kb	48 kb	n.a.	48 kb	130 kb	48 kb	n.a.	4.8 kb
User capabilities								
Terminal-computer	Yes	Yes	Yes	Yes	n.a.	Yes	Yes	Yes
Computer-computer	Yes	Yes	Yes	Yes	n.a.	Yes	Yes	n.a.

Source: D. Wood, A Survey of the Capabilities of 8 Packet Switched Networks, *Proceedings of Trends and Applications : Computer Networks,* June 1975, p. 3. Reprinted with permission of the IEEE.
n.a. indicates no information available.

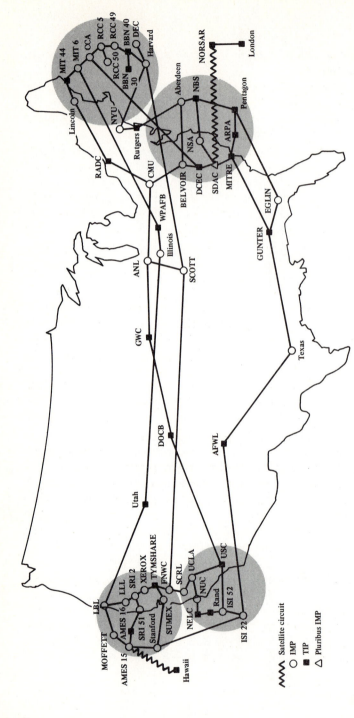

Figure 1-2 The ARPANET topology. (From R. J. Solomon, "Packet Networks," *Mini-Micro Systems*, March 1978, p. 52. Copyright 1978 by Cahners Publishing Company, division of Reed Publishing Corporation. Reprinted with permission.)

8

oped to estimate network performance, such as resource utilization, response time, and throughput.

A perspective is incomplete without an attempt to predict the future. Both the computing and communication communities are progressing toward a compatible and useful coexistence, leading to the emergence of hundreds of networks with thousands of terminals. It was projected that the number of terminals will grow from 250,000 in 1971 to about 4 million by 1980 [10, p. 271]. Development of in-house networks, such as the Ethernet* by the Xerox Corporation, has already started. It can be predicted that large and very large networks are also on the horizon. These networks will consist of 100 or more nodes that require several new techniques for their analysis. There will be a slow but growing trend toward the use of satellite links for networks spanning distant nodes. Existing approaches for message routing, topological design, flow control, and network management will have to be extended to apply to larger networks. Some efforts are already in progress to interconnect different computer networks. Recent developments in transmission technologies, such as in the field of optical fiber, promise to offer cheap and reliable transmission. The pace of transition to large networks will be determined directly by the rate at which the above problems are solved.

Technology is rapidly advancing toward cheaper processing. At the same time, communications costs are also being reduced, although at a rate less than that of the processing costs [11]. This is shown in Fig. 1-3. Such a trend points toward reduction in message size at the expense of additional processing. In other words, there will be more processing to permit smaller headers in transmitting messages. For example, consider the specification of a message route in the header. It may be achieved by including all the nodes (or node indexes) of the message route in the header. Alternatively, only the destination node is included in the header, and a routing table in each node determines the selected route. The latter approach will be attractive since it requires smaller headers at the expense of additional processing.

Several public data networks are currently being planned or are already operating. In the United States, the TELENET and TYMNET public networks are operating. In Canada, the DATAPAC network has been operating since June 1977. In Europe, the TRANSPAC network is operating in France, while several others are expected to operate soon. The uncontrolled proliferation of network offerings is

---

* Ethernet uses a coaxial cable to allow message transmissions in a user site.

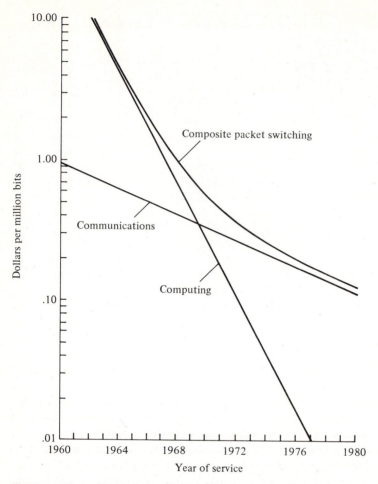

Figure 1-3 Projected costs of computing and communications. (From L. G. Roberts, "Data by the Packet," *IEEE Spectrum*, February 1974, p. 50. Reprinted with permission.)

expected to converge toward national and international standards, such as the CCITT (Consultative Committee for International Telegraph and Telephone) recommendations X.21 and X.25. At the same time, the public networks will advance toward commonalities and expansion of their services to include, for example, image processing, electronic mail, and database services. This trend is already evident from the adoption of CCITT recommendations by several of the above networks.

1-2 OBJECTIVES OF NETWORKS

Networks satisfy a broad range of purposes and meet various requirements. A major goal of ARPANET [3] is to permit resource sharing.
The Distributed Computing System [6, 7] is designed to provide reliable, low-cost facilities and easy addition of new processing services.
Some of the common objectives of computer communication networks are:

1. To provide sharing of (distant) resources such as information (databases) or processors (CPUs). Resource sharing is perhaps the most
   common objective for providing networks, within the constraints of
   cost and reliability of transmission links.
2. To provide interprocess communication, such as among users (or
   processes) and processors. Network users, located geographically
   apart, may converse in an interactive session through the network.
   In order to permit this, the network must provide (almost) error-
   free communication.
3. To improve reliability of networks through backup and redundancy. If one processor breaks down, another processor in the
   network can take its place. Similarly, if one link on a route fails,
   another route becomes available.
4. To provide distribution of processing functions. For example, a
   transaction is translated in one node, processed in another, and the
   response formatted in a third node. Distributed processing primarily implies taking processing out of a single, large computer
   and distributing it to where the raw information is generated or
   most of the transaction handling, calculations, or formatting is
   performed. Distributed processing is cost-effective since it provides
   offloading the relatively more expensive host processors and associated resources, and saves transmission costs.
5. To furnish centralized control for a geographically distributed
   system, such as inventory management in the manufacturing industry, managing prices and sales in the securities industry, and handling accounts in the finance industry. Defense networks may
   provide central control facilities for geographically distributed
   monitoring stations.
6. To provide centralized management and allocation of network resources: host processors, associated databases, transmission facilities, and the like.
7. To provide compatibility of dissimilar equipment and software.

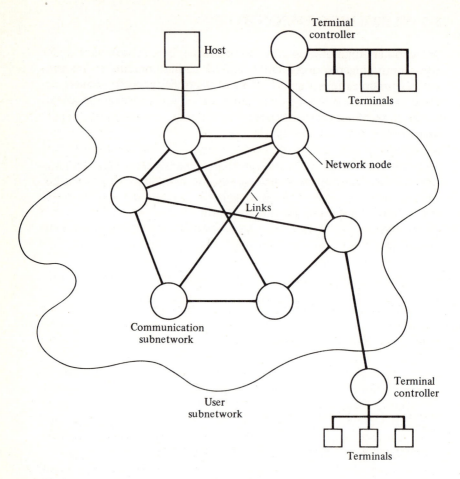

Figure 1-4 User subnetwork and communication subnetwork.

There is a growing trend toward compatibility, through standardization, for all types of communication hardware and software.
8. To provide network users with maximum performance at minimum cost. Network delay and throughput are the most commonly used measures of network performance.

Networks also provide an efficient means of transporting large volumes of data among remote locations. The concept of networks is also embedded in the various in-house communication systems and remote monitoring systems, such as those for manufacturing plants or defense-alert systems, respectively.

1-3 NETWORK COMPONENTS

A computer communication network consists of a collection of nodes with computing resources, and nodal-switching computers that provide communications through a set of transmission links. A user accesses the network through a terminal or a system console. Messages in the form of inquiries, transactions, file transmissions, and the like traverse the network through the switching nodes. In general, messages may be destined for another terminal user. Some messages may be sent to a processing node that provides computing resources and files. The transportation of messages to the receiving terminal or processing node is accomplished through a communication network. Thus, computer communication networks may be conveniently partitioned into two subnetworks, the user subnetwork and the communication subnetwork. This is shown in Fig. 1-4 and described below.

User Subnetwork

The *user subnetwork* provides the capability to access the network. As illustrated in Fig. 1-5, it consists of three types of components: host computers, terminal controllers, and terminals. Host computers pro-

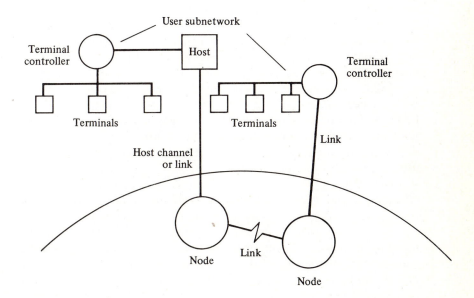

Figure 1-5 User subnetwork.

vide the databases and application programs to be accessed by various terminal users. The host computer is connected to a node of the communication subnetwork through a high-speed multiplexer channel or a communication link.

A terminal user generally accesses the network through a terminal controller. Terminal controllers may provide several controls for a group of terminals, thereby reducing the functions and the cost for the terminals. These controls may vary from managing the links to providing network protocol interfaces for each of the terminals. The terminal controller may be connected to a network node either directly or through a host processor. Alternatively, the function of terminal controller may be included in a network node. (For example, the IBM 3705 communications controller is a terminal controller as well as a network node for IBM's Systems Network Architecture.) In such cases, the terminal is connected directly to the network node.

Communication Subnetwork

A *communication subnetwork* is a collection of nodes at which reside the processes that communicate with each other through a set of links. An example of a communication subnetwork is illustrated in Fig. 1-6. It consists of network nodes, transmission links, and signal converter equipment.

The transmission links are the communication channels used to transmit data. The available circuit capacities for these links range approximately from 55 bits per second (bps) to 1.5 megabits per second (Mbps). In the last few years, satellite channels and radio communications have also been employed as transmission links. In certain cases, more than one link is used between a pair of adjacent nodes to provide greater bandwidth and improve reliability through redundancy. Signal converters provide the transformation between the digital signals acceptable to the network node and the analog signals used for transmission on the links.

The network node provides a dual role—an interface for the user subnetwork and a store-and-forward node for other network nodes. As a network interface node, it provides such functions as the receiving and delivering of messages, and the monitoring of message transmission status. The interface functions are tailored for the specific requirements of the intended user. As a store-and-forward node, it provides the switching functions, namely, the routing of messages in the network to appropriate destination nodes. It also cooperates with

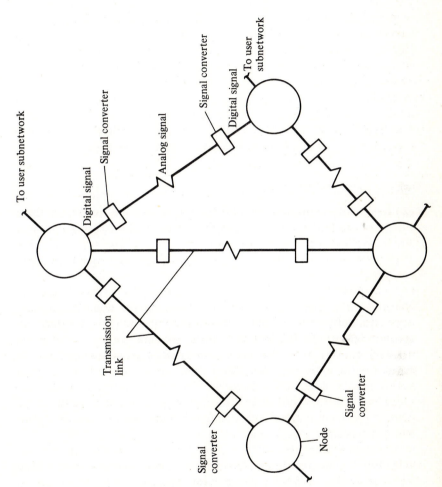

Figure 1-6 Communication subnetwork.

the remainder of the network in avoiding congestion and providing efficient use of network resources.

The software of a communication subnetwork node may consist of several components. First, it must observe the network protocols or rules that determine the contents and relative timings to exchange messages and control information with other nodes. Local software requirements of a network node include line management, message handling, and message buffer management. Additionally, it must provide appropriate interfaces for host processor(s), terminals, terminal concentrators, and message switching. The subject of network nodes is treated in Chap. 3.

1-4 MESSAGE TRANSPORT TECHNOLOGIES: CIRCUIT-SWITCHED, MESSAGE-SWITCHED, AND PACKET-SWITCHED NETWORKS

Networks may be conveniently classified by the technique employed in transporting messages between the nodes. We first introduce these classes of networks, and then describe their comparative advantages and disadvantages.

A *circuit-switched* network transmits a message by providing a complete path of transmission links from the message origination node to the destination node. This path is set up by a special signaling message sent by the origin node to the destination node. A response to this signaling message from the destination node informs the originating node to proceed with data transmission. The data is transmitted progressively over all the channels in the path with no intermediate store-and-forward delays. The entire fixed-delay path is allocated to this transmission, until the sender releases this path.

A *message-switched* network transmits a message among the nodes by moving the message through various transmission links and message buffers. A message is stored and then transmitted to the next node along the message path. A message transmission from a node does not start until a buffer at the next node on the route has been allocated for it. The path (or route) for message transmission may be fixed, or it may be determined dynamically as the message progresses toward its destination node. This class of networks is also called *store-and-forward* networks, since messages are stored in each node and then forwarded to the next node on its route. Due to the message storage in the intermediate nodes on a message route, some nodes may experience message queuing and congestion. An important attribute of a message-switched network is the wide variation in message delay through the network.

A *packet-switched* network differs from a message-switched network in that long messages are first decomposed into fixed-size segments called *packets*. These packets independently traverse the network until they reach the desired node, where they are reassembled into the corresponding message. Thus, many packets of the same message may be in transmission simultaneously, thereby providing an important advantage of packet switching: the pipelining effect. Packets belonging to a particular message are held in the memory buffers of a destination node until all the packets required to reassemble the entire message have arrived. Thus, besides the store-and-forward buffers, nodes in packet-switching networks (that allow packets to get out of order) also require reassembly buffers. In some cases, especially when all the packets of a message traverse the same physical path, out-of-sequence packets are discarded at the receiving node.

Comparison of Network Classes

Several studies have been undertaken to compare the above three classes of networks. As described below, studies have shown that packet-switched networks generally perform better than circuit-switched networks. An essential difference lies in the peculiar way network overloads are handled. An overloaded circuit-switched network delays a message transfer until a circuit becomes available. It works more efficiently if messages are blocked into large units. A packet-switched network segments the messages for transmission into packets, and queues the packets in each node. A circuit-switched network requires that all channels in a message transmission path are of the same speed. A setup signal may find it difficult to locate a complete path that is also available for use. However, circuit-switched networks provide a fast, efficient message transmission once the circuit has been allocated. Thus, circuit-switched networks may be more attractive for large-volume data transmissions among distant locations.

R. D. Rosner and B. Springer [1] analyzed a large network in which the traffic was equally divided between short messages and long messages. Under their stated assumption, packet-switched networks performed better than circuit-switched networks. K. Kümmerle and H. Rudin [2] have shown the crossover points for cost and performance among circuit-switched and packet-switched networks. In Table 1-3, we compare some of the properties of the three network classes.

Table 1-3 Comparison of the characteristics of circuit-switched, message-switched, and packet-switched networks

Description	Value code*	Circuit-switched	Message-switched	Packet-switched
1. Allow different speed links	+	No	Yes	Yes
2. Provide pipelining effect	+	No	No	Yes
3. Can change format/code during store-and-forward transmission process	+	No	Yes	Yes
4. Can adaptively select faster path for transmission as a function of network congestion	+	No†	Yes	Yes
5. Can transmit shorter messages first, due to fewer packets	+	No	No	Yes
6. Can provide error control	+	Some	Yes	Yes
7. Require buffering in the nodes	−	No	Yes	Yes
8. Possible queuing and congestion in the communication subnetwork	−	No†	Yes	Yes
9. Require routing and flow control procedures	−	No†	Yes	Yes
10. Require sequencing and numbering	−	No	Some	Yes
11. Require packetizing —segmentation and reassembly overhead	−	No	No	Yes
12. Applicability to time-dependent uses such as voice	+	Yes	(Under study)	

* Plus sign represents an advantage; minus sign, a disadvantage.
† Except when setting up message transmission path.

PROBLEMS

1-1 Write an essay on the requirements and areas of applications for networks. Identify those terminal applications that do not require a communication subnetwork.

1-2 Compare circuit-switching, packet-switching, and message-switching networks in the context of a hypothetical communication subnetwork you have been asked to design. The subnetwork will provide the function of message transportation between user premises for a cost based on the following factors: (*a*) transmission time, (*b*) reliability requirements of transmission, (*c*) connect time, and (*d*) extent of use of network links and nodes.

1-3 Describe at least six clear predictions for networks in the future. Support your claims by using specific examples or trends from the history of networks.

REFERENCES

1. R. D. Rosner and B. Springer, "Circuit and Packet Switching—A Cost and Performance Tradeoff Study," *Computer Networks*, Vol. 1, 1976, pp. 7–26.
2. K. Kümmerle and H. Rudin, "Packet and Circuit Switching: Cost/Performance Boundaries," *Computer Networks*, Vol. 2, 1978, pp. 3–17.
3. S. M. Ornstein, F. E. Heart, W. R. Crowther, H. K. Rising, S. B. Russell, and A. Michel, "The Terminal IMP for the ARPA Computer Network," *Proceedings of the Spring Joint Computer Conference*, May 1972, pp. 243–254.
4. L. G. Roberts and B. D. Wessler, "Computer Network Development to Achieve Resource Sharing," *Proceedings of the Spring Joint Computer Conference*, May 1970, pp. 543–549.
5. L. Kleinrock and F. Kamoun, "Hierarchical Routing for Large Network: Performance Evaluation and Optimization," *Computer Networks*, Vol. 1, 1977, pp. 155–174.
6. D. J. Farber and K. C. Larson, "The Structure of a Distributed Computing System—Software," *Proceedings of the Symposium on Computer-Communications Networks and Teletraffic*, Polytechnic Institute of Brooklyn, New York, April 1972, pp. 539–545.
7. D. J. Farber and K. C. Larson, "The System Architecture of the Distributed Computer System—The Communications System," *Proceedings of the Symposium on Computer-Communications Networks and Teletraffic*, Polytechnic Institute of Brooklyn, New York, April, 1972, pp. 21–27.
8. D. C. Wood, "A Survey of the Capabilities of 8 Packet Switching Networks," *Proceedings of Computer Networks*: Trends and Applications, June 1975, pp. 1–7.
9. D. J. Farber, "Networks: An Introduction," *Datamation*, April 1972, pp. 36–39.
10. L. Kleinrock, *Queueing Systems*, vol. II: *Computer Applications*, Wiley, New York, 1976.
11. L. G. Roberts, "Data by the Packet," *IEEE Spectrum*, February 1974, pp. 46–51.
12. R. J. Solomon, "Packet Networks," *Mini Micro Systems*, March 1978, pp. 48–53.

CHAPTER
TWO

TRANSMISSION LINKS AND PROCEDURES

CHAPTER OUTLINE

Transmission links, or channels, connect network nodes to provide physical connection for data communication. In this chapter, we describe the characteristics and analysis of problems associated with transmission links, along with the procedures to use them. The transmission technologies, including satellite links and optical fiber links, are described in Sec. 2-1. Section 2-2 presents various modes of transmission over a link such as the simplex, half-duplex, and full-duplex operation. Section 2-2 also includes a description of various polling algorithms, and approaches to estimate message delay in waiting for a poll. Link control protocols are addressed in Sec. 2-3. The related problem of assigning link capacities is deferred until Chap. 4, along with other topological design issues.

2-1 TRANSMISSION LINKS

Network nodes may be connected through terrestrial, satellite, or radio transmission links. This section provides a description of these technologies, along with various approaches to use them. The section concludes with an overview of some emerging transmission technologies, such as optical fiber.

Terrestrial Links

Switched and leased connections Terrestrial links are the ground wires that connect network nodes to terminals, hosts, or other network nodes, as shown in Fig. 2-1. The concept of switched and leased links is best explained by the telephone exchange system. When you talk to a friend, the telephone connection is provided through one or more exchanges. This connection is called *switched*, or *dialed*, and uses public lines. Alternatively, there could be a permanent connection among the two telephones; a *leased*, or *dedicated*, link.

Computer communication networks often employ leased (or private) links to interconnect network nodes. The link speeds are available in a wide range; from about 55 bps to AT&T's T1 service at 1.5 Mbps (or T2 at about 6.3 Mbps). Switched links are often used to connect network nodes to network users, such as host processors, terminals, or terminal controllers. A comparison of leased and switched links follows:

1. A leased link may be cost-effective if used for several hours in a day; a switched link is cheaper if used for shorter intervals. The

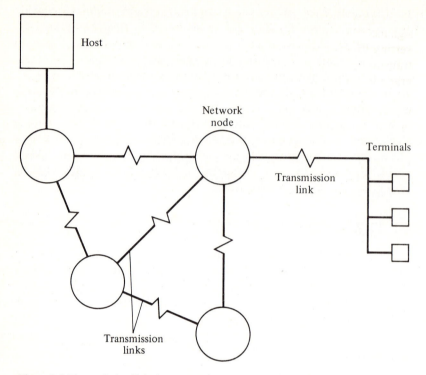

Figure 2-1 Transmission links in a network.

crossover point depends on the actual charges, which in turn are based on the distance involved.

2. A leased link requires less switching equipment and may be specially conditioned (to avoid distortion) to satisfy specific user requirements. The conditioning of a switched link depends on the specific circuits assigned at the time of connection establishment.

3. Leased links may be less expensive if the desired data rate does not vary significantly.

4. A switched link may be cheaper for low-use terminals, especially for long distances, and may offer a wide range of data rates.

Common carriers provide the transmission links and, optionally, the signal converters for communication networks. Common carrier services are regulated by the Federal Communications Commission (FCC).

Dataphone Digital Service Most data processing devices use digital signals. Thus, one can transmit signals in digital form without converting them to analog form. The Dataphone Digital Service* (DDS) transmits signals in digital form. Digital data transmission over voice-grade telephone links has existed since 1950s, but the quality of transmission links has limited its use for high-speed data transmission. The Bell System is offering a digital communication network service that is projected to connect 96 metropolitan areas. The DDS cities are organized in a three-level hierarchy. Level 1 consists of major cities that are interconnected. Each level 1 city may have one or more level 2 cities connected through it; each level 2 city, in turn, may provide connection for one or more level 3 cities.

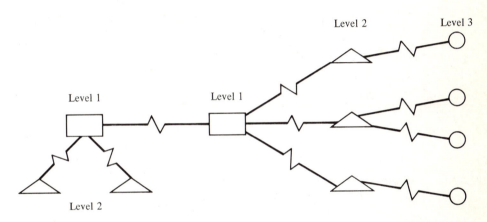

DDS provides private, point-to-point, and multipoint-digital links operating at 2.4, 4.8, 9.6, and 56 kbps. The customer's data processing system is connected by a four-wire full-duplex link to a local telephone central office. Thus, it provides use of existing digital facilities as well as savings of multiplexer cost through hierarchical clustering.

Figure 2-2 illustrates the options in using the Bell System's digital transmission. At the first level, the T1 link provides a short-haul cable-carrier at DS-1 (digital signal) rate of 1.544 Mbps. Because the T1 carrier requires amplifiers and repeaters about 1 mile apart, it is generally used for short-haul applications.

Based on requirements, DDS may expand and use higher levels as shown in Fig. 2-2. The next higher level is the long-haul carriers, such

* This description of DDS is primarily drawn from [17, pp. 167–171].

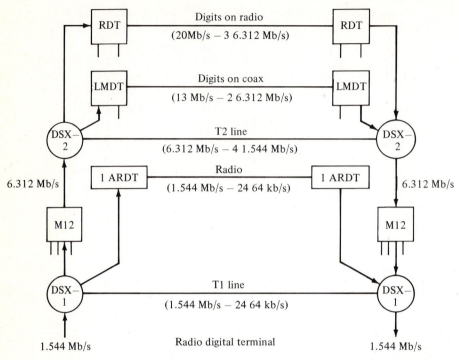

Figure 2-2 Bell System digital transmission hierarchy. (From D. R. McGlynn, *Distributed Processing and Data Communications*, Wiley, New York, 1978, p. 169. Reprinted with permission.)

as the 1A radio digital system (1A RDS) that operates at the same rate as the T1 carrier. The next higher level is the T2 link. Up to four DS-1 signals may be combined with the M12 multiplexer to form a DS-2 signal of 6.3 Mbps. Additional details on this hierarchy are given in [17, pp. 161–170].

Satellite Links

Satellites operate in geostationary orbits around the earth, thereby providing a means of communicating signals or messages between earth locations. Compared to terrestrial links, satellite channels may provide transmissions for long distances (between remote earth stations) and large capacities (about 1.5 Mbps). A received message is transponded to each of the earth stations within the shadow of the satellite, as shown in Fig. 2-3. As such, satellites provide a com-

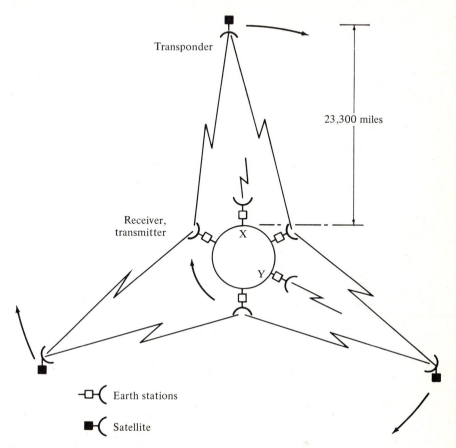

Transponder

23,300 miles

Receiver,
transmitter

X

Y

─□⊏ Earth stations

■⊏ Satellite

Figure 2-3 A synchronous satellite network.

pletely connected topology of the network. (For a given terrestrial N-node network, a completely connected topology would require $N(N-1)/2$ terrestrial links.) In other words, satellites offer insensitivity to distance as well as to connectivity. A satellite channel provides broad-band capacity, and requires an earth station to provide interface with the terrestrial network. Therefore, satellite links may be used to provide high-volume data transmission among distant terrestrial nodes.

The height of the satellite above the earth is important since it determines the duration for which an earth station may communicate. As shown in Fig. 2-3, a satellite is over an earth station for some time, depending on the satellite's relative speed. In order for a satellite to communicate permanently with one or more earth stations (within its line of sight), it must be over the equator, and it must orbit the earth in exactly 24 hours moving in the same direction as earth. Such satellites are called *synchronous satellites.* A synchronous satellite appears like a stationary article in space. Here, the earth station is not required to continuously look for and switch satellites. A synchronous satellite is over an earth station either always or never, depending on whether it is within the shadow of the satellite. The first commercial synchronous satellite, Early Bird, is located approximately 23,300 miles above the equator between Brazil and Africa over the Atlantic Ocean. It was launched from Cape Kennedy on April 6, 1965. The Early Bird satellite is traveling at 6900 miles per hour and its rotation time is 24 hours [14, pp. 349–351].

In certain cases, more than one satellite may be required to transmit messages between earth stations. Consider the satellite network shown in Fig. 2-3. In order to transmit a message from point X to point Y on earth, more than one satellite is required. The actual number of satellites required depends on the height of the satellites' orbit. INTELSAT III employs three satellites to provide communication among any two points on earth (except for some regions near the North and South Poles).* It employs earth stations that can transfer messages between adjacent satellites, as shown in Fig. 2-3.

A satellite acts as a pure transponder, repeating whatever messages it receives, by transmitting them back to earth stations. Every earth station in the shadow of the satellite can receive this transmission. Since the satellite is merely transponding, a situation can occur in which transmission from one earth station arrives at the same time that another transmission is being received and transponded. This "collision" may result in destruction of the two transmissions, and should be avoided. This problem is analyzed later in this section.

Satellite transmission technology has several other special characteristics. Satellite links impose a long propagation delay. The earth station has to sustain a high bit rate when receiving or transmitting with the satellite. Often, this bit rate is significantly higher than that for the terrestrial network.

Propagation delay Message transmissions using satellite links result in a propagation delay of hundreds of milliseconds (ms). The exact delay

* For more information on this, the reader is referred to [14, 19].

Table 2-1 Maximum propagation delay of a satellite channel

Distance (miles)	Approximate delay (ms)
7,000	100
10,000	140
20,000	250
22,300	270*
25,000	300

* Synchronous satellite.

Source: James Martin, *Telecommunications and the Computer*, Prentice-Hall, Englewood Cliffs, N. J., 1969, Fig. 20.6, p. 358. Adapted by permission.

depends on the height of the satellite's orbit. Table 2-1 gives an estimate of the one-way maximum propagation delay for various orbit heights.

A longer propagation delay results, in turn, in longer message transit time through the network. In Sec. 2-2, we describe hub polling as a possible approach to reduce the interval that a message in an earth station may have to wait for a poll. The above delay is generally acceptable for television or telegraph transmission. It is also acceptable for voice when transmission takes place over one satellite. However, this propagation delay may be significant for voice or other time-sensitive applications, when messages require transmission through more than one satellite.

The collision problem on satellite channels Consider the situation when transmission from an earth station arrives at the satellite at a given frequency just when the satellite is transponding a transmission from another station at the same frequency. The two transmissions interfere with each other, and both are destroyed. This phenomenon, called *collision*, results in the loss of messages that are in transmission. Collisions may be avoided if transmissions from each earth station are synchronized so that no two earth stations transmit at the same time. This solution, however, may be prohibitive due to the cost involved in synchronizing geographically-distant earth stations. In the following discussion, we describe two approaches: the pure ALOHA [1, 2] and the slotted ALOHA [2, 3]. Both techniques treat the problem for packets, but can be equally applicable to any fixed-size messages.

These techniques are also referred to as *multiple-access protocols* that determine which of several earth stations successfully transmits on the satellite channel.

Pure ALOHA The *pure ALOHA* approach applies independently to each transmitting earth station, without requiring any coordination with other stations. It is also called a *random-access* system. The approach relates average channel utilization to channel traffic by considering the message arrival rate and retransmission rate.

Let λ be the average rate of messages from each user, and let k be the number of active users. Then, the process of starting times of messages from k users has an average rate of occurence of $r = k\lambda$, where r is the average number of messages per unit time from the k active users. If t is the time for each message, the average channel utilization s is rt. Let R be the sum of the average number of messages and retransmissions per unit time from the k users. Then, channel traffic G is given by $G = Rt$. The channel traffic is the sum of messages (at the average rate of r) and their retransmissions.

Let us assume that the interarrival times of the point process defined by the start times of all messages and retransmissions are independent and exponential.* Then, the probability that there are no events (start of a message or a retransmission) in a time interval of T

$$= 1 - \text{probability that there is some event in } T$$

$$= 1 - (1 - e^{-RT})$$

$$= e^{-RT}$$

Now, the first message overlaps if there exists at least one other start point in t or less time before, or at least one other start point in t or less time after the start of the given message. Therefore, the probability that there is no event in time t is

$$= e^{-2Rt}$$

and the probability a message is retransmitted

$$= \text{probability that there is some event in time } t$$

$$= 1 - e^{-2Rt}$$

Therefore, the sum of message rate and retransmission rate per unit time,

---

* The exponential distribution is described in Sec. 8-1.

$$R = r + R\,(1 - e^{-2Rt})$$

or
$$Rt = rt + Rt(1 - e^{-2Rt})$$

$$= rt + Rt - Rt(e^{-2Rt})$$

or
$$rt = Rt(e^{-2R_t})$$

but
$$rt = s \text{ and } Rt = G$$

so

$$s = Ge^{-2G}$$

This expression gives the relationship between channel utilization s and total channel traffic including message retransmissions G.

Slotted ALOHA In case of the pure ALOHA described above, a user can initiate transmission at any time. The *slotted ALOHA* approach is based on fixed time slots for messages, in which one time slot is exactly equal to the transmission time of a message. Assuming that all messages are of fixed length, a central clock can synchronize all users to the beginning and end of message transmissions. Thus, if two messages conflict they will overlap completely, instead of partially. The time interval for each message is called a *slot*. In the following, we derive the normalized channel message rate using this approach.

Let n be the number of independent users. Then $G = \Sigma_{i=1}^{n}\, G_i$, where G_i is the probability that the ith user sends a message or message retransmission. G, as defined earlier, is the normalized channel traffic per slot.

Then, the probability that a message from the ith user will not be overlapped by a message from one of the other users is

$$\prod_{\substack{j=1 \\ j \neq i}}^{n} (1 - G_j)$$

Therefore, the probability that the ith user sends a message and it is not overlapped is

$$s_i = G_i \prod_{\substack{j=1 \\ j \neq i}}^{n} (1 - G_j)$$

Assuming all users are identical, then $s_i = s/n$ and $G_i = G/n$, where s is the channel utilization or normalized message rate. So,

$$s = \sum_{i=1}^{n} s_i$$

$$= \sum_{i=1}^{n} G_i \prod_{\substack{j=1 \\ j \neq i}}^{n} (1 - G_j)$$

$$= \sum_{i=1}^{n} \frac{G}{n} \left(1 - \frac{G}{n} \right)^{n-1}$$

$$= G \left(1 - \frac{G}{n} \right)^{n-1}$$

As n goes to infinity,

$$s = Ge^{-G}$$

The relationship of channel traffic G and channel utilization s is plotted for pure ALOHA and slotted ALOHA in Fig. 2-4. The maximum message rate for pure ALOHA and slotted ALOHA is $1/2e = .184$ and $1/e = .368$, respectively [2]. These values correspond to the message rate that can be sustained. Above these rates, the retransmission rate becomes unbounded; that is, the retransmission rate exceeds the arrival rate. Note that for pure ALOHA, this message rate is reached at channel utilization of .5; for slotted ALOHA, the channel utilization is as high as 1.

Frequency-division multiple access In this approach, the bandwidth of the satellite channel is divided into nonoverlapping subchannels. Each earth station is assigned a separate subchannel. Thus, each earth station uses a dedicated portion of the satellite channel at all times. The main advantage of this approach is that it requires no synchronization between the earth station.*

Time-division multiple access This technique permits each earth station to transmit to the satellite in nonoverlapping time slots. Each earth station is assigned a fixed slot of time that is mutually agreed upon (or known to) all the earth stations. Each earth station must also determine the satellite system time. Thus, earth stations are synchronized so that, at a given time, only one earth station is transmitting messages to the satellite. The total rate of transmission from an

---

* A good description of the various access methods for satellites is given in [27].

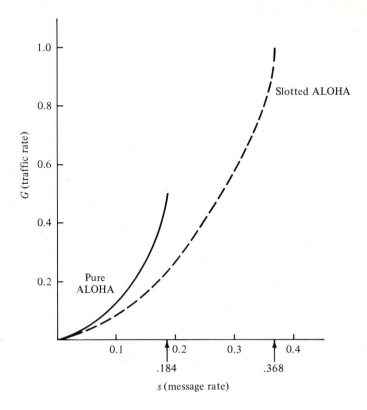

Figure 2-4 Traffic rate versus message rate for a pure ALOHA channel and a slotted ALOHA channel. (From N. Abramson, "Packet-Switching with Satellites," *Proceedings of the National Computer Conference*, 1973, p. 697, Fig. 1.)

earth station depends on the number of earth stations. This approach, as shown in Fig. 2-5, implies the added complexity of synchronizing all earth stations to the satellite system time. Its advantage is that, unlike frequency-division multiple access, there is a total connectivity between all the earth stations. Since each earth station receives transmission on a common channel, each earth station can communicate with every other earth station on the same channel.

Other multiple-access protocols Next, we briefly describe two techniques that were used in the early satellite protocols for ARPANET [5]. A satellite IMP (interface message processor) represents an earth station in ARPANET. A time slot of 30 ms was used, based on

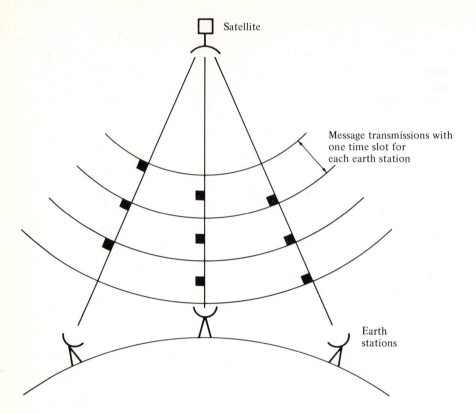

Figure 2-5 Time-division multiple access.

accommodating the maximum packet size and header fields. The time slots were grouped into routing frames, each containing 32 slots, or .96 s. In the beginning of each routing frame, every satellite IMP had one slot to send a packet. The remaining slots could be used by the particular multiple-access protocol.

First, in case of the fixed-time-division multiple access (F-TDMA) technique, each of the M earth stations was permanently assigned one slot in each frame of M slots. The assignment pattern was repeated in each frame. The value of M could be varied, thereby allowing the effect of different numbers of IMPs.

Next, in case of reservation-time-division multiple access (R-TDMA), the channel time was divided as shown in Fig. 2-6. Each routing frame was divided into reservation frames, and each such frame began with a group of reservation slots. Each satellite IMP had one reservation slot assigned in each reservation frame. The remainder of the reservation frame consisted of fixed-length data slots, grouped in data subframes. Each satellite IMP also had a fixed assignment of one data slot in each data subframe, as in F-TDMA. The number of slots in a data subframe was the same as the number of satellite IMPs. Each satellite IMP counted the number of packets that arrived since the last reservation frame was transmitted. It inserted this count in its reservation slot, announcing its need for data slots. Each satellite IMP monitored these reservation packets, and (at a globally agreed-upon time) added these values to a reservation table. When transmitting, a slot's owner transmitted if it had any outstanding reservations. If a slot owner had no outstanding reservations, another satellite IMP with outstanding reservations transmitted (on a round-robin basis). Further details of this approach are given in [5].

Finally, the reservation-upon-collisison technique [4] modifies the slotted ALOHA approach to allow for reservations on collisions.

Radio Links

Ground radio links may be used to connect several users together for access to some large computer network. The ALOHA system, shown in Fig. 2-7, employs radio links for communication between a computer and several consoles. An interface is required to provide radio communication between network nodes and the terrestrial network. The ALOHA system has been assigned two 100-kHz channels at 407.350 MHz and 413.475 MHz [1]. In November 1978, Xerox Corporation announced its plans for a domestic digital communication

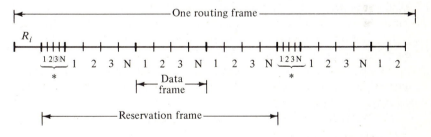

* Reservation slots

Figure 2-6 Reservation-time-division multiple access. (From R. Weissler, R. Binder, R. Bressler, R. Rettberg, and D. Walden, "Synchronization and Multiple Access Protocols in the Initial Satellite IMP," *Proceedings of the COMPCON*, 1978, p. 360.)

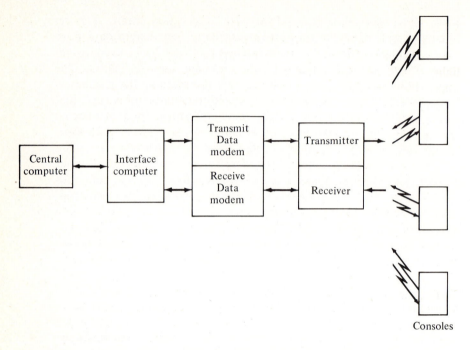

Consoles

Figure 2-7 The ALOHA system. (From N. Abramson, "The ALOHA System— Another Alternative for Computer Communications," *Proceedings of Fall Joint Computer Conference*, 1970, p. 282.)

network, XTEN, that will use radio links for local distribution and satellite links for distant city nodes, or earth stations [8].

Another radio network, the Bay Area Packet Radio Network [20], provides radio communication for directly connected host processors. This network is a collection of microprocessor-controlled digital radios. These units are called *packet radio units* and act as store-and-forward switches. The radio channel operates at 100 or 400 kilobits per second (kbps). The radios contend for the common radio channel using either pure ALOHA or carrier-sense multiple access techniques, described below.

Consider a collection of terminals, each of which transmits messages to a central station on the assigned radio channel. Any overlapped transmissions destroy the messages and require retransmissions. The pure and slotted ALOHA strategies, discussed in the preceding section, may be used to handle such collisions. We briefly describe two additional strategies from Kleinrock [13, p. 394].

First, let us estimate the ratio of propagation time to transmission time for radio links. Consider a 1000-bit message to be transmitted over a distance of 10 miles. The propagation time, using the speed of light, is .054 ms. Assuming that the radio channel operates at 100 kbps, the transmission time is 10 ms. Thus, we obtain the ratio of propagation time to transmission time as .054/10, or .005. Thus, a user can sense the channel and determine if it is idle. If the channel is busy, the user may try again after some interval. This approach is called *carrier-sense multiple-access (CSMA) method.*

Carrier-sense multiple-access method In the case of satellite channels, carrier-sense multiple access is not feasible since the propagation delay on satellite channels is much larger than the transmission delay. Thus, the information on channel availability applies to a message several transmissions old. For the above example of a 1000-bit message, the transmission delay is 10 ms. The propagation delay for synchronous satellite channels (Table 2-1) is approximately 270 ms. Thus, in the case of a satellite channel, about 27 messages have already been transmitted before it is determined whether the channel was available.

The CSMA approaches may be classified depending on the action taken by a terminal after sensing the channel. First, we describe the *nonpersistent* CSMA. In order to transmit a message, each terminal senses the channel and executes the following steps:

1. If the channel is idle, the terminal initiates its message transmission.
2. If the channel is busy, the terminal schedules transmission at a later time. At that time, the terminal senses the channel and repeats the algorithm.

A *persistent CSMA* approach allows a terminal to continuously sense the channel. If the channel is busy, the terminal continues to sense and wait for an idle condition. As soon as the channel is detected to be idle, the terminal transmits the message. If more than one terminal is waiting, a collision results. Therefore, this approach is modified for the idle condition. When a terminal finds the channel idle, it transmits with a probability, say, p. The terminal delays transmission (by one slot) with a probability $1 - p$. Thus, this approach is also termed *p-persistent CSMA*. It reduces collisions and improves throughput when an idle condition is reached.

Let us assume that a radio channel is noiseless and that all terminals are within line-of-sight (all terminals can "hear" each other).

Each packet is of constant length and requires P seconds for transmission. Let us also assume that there is an infinite number of users generating Poisson traffic. Let the average channel traffic due to these users be a total of G packets per P second. The average channel throughput is S packets per P seconds ($S \leq 1$). Each ready terminal has exactly one message waiting for transmission. The one-way maximum propagation delay, normalized over the transmission time P, is assumed to be 0.01 for all source-destination node pairs. Based on these assumptions, Kleinrock [13, pp. 397–400] provides throughput comparisons for pure ALOHA, slotted ALOHA, 1-persistent CSMA, and nonpersistent CSMA; the values are plotted in Fig. 2-8.

Optical Fiber

Besides terrestrial, satellite, and radio transmissions, optical fiber transmission is emerging as a viable technology that is currently being evaluated and implemented. In essence, optical fiber transmission replaces copper with an optical fiber. A given optical fiber transmits a signal-encoded beam of light from one end of the fiber to the other. It consists primarily of a highly refractive glass or plastic core that is covered by a cladding. The transmission of light is based on the principle of total internal reflection of light within the core. The cladding protects the fiber and prevents interference from other fibers in the same optical cable.

Bell Laboratories and Western Electric developed an experimental lightwave communication system in Atlanta, Georgia. The optical cable has 144 glass fibers. The transmission rate of digitized voice and data is 44.7 Mbps. There are 12 glass fibers packed in a flat ribbon, and 12 such ribbons are stacked and twisted along the length of the cable. The cable has an average loss of 6 db/km, and communication as far as 7 km is possible without regeneration of the light signal [17, pp. 189–190]. Another lightwave experiment involved interconnecting some buildings in Chicago, Illinois. The experiment demonstrated a system performance of more than 80 percent error-free days and an average of less than 1 error-second per day [21].

In January 1980, the Bell System filed an application with the FCC for a 611-mile lightwave transmission project scheduled to go into service in 1983. Intended initially for a Washington-Boston link, the cable will carry 144 fibers and pack about 80,000 simultaneous telephone conversations.

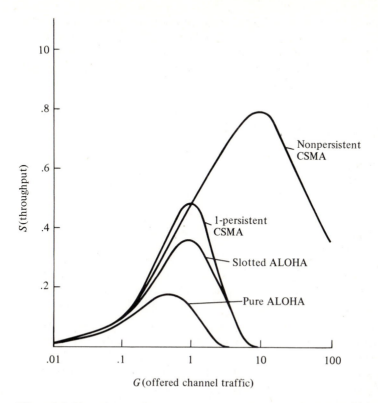

Figure 2-8 Throughput comparison of pure ALOHA, slotted ALOHA, 1-persistent CSMA, and non-persistent CSMA. (Values plotted from L. Kleinrock, *Queueing Systems*, vol. II: *Computer Applications*, Wiley, New York, 1976, p. 400. Reprinted by permission.)

An important advantage of fiber optic is its wide bandwidth. For example, a laser-driven fiber link has the potential of data transmission at speeds of up to 10^{14} bps. Thus, the optical fiber can be used for transmission when more than one link is needed for a desired bandwidth. Furthermore, due to its dielectric nature, optical fiber is immune to electromagnetic or radio interference. As a result, the bit error rate in fiber optic connections exceeds 10^{-9}, compared with an error rate of approximately 10^{-6} for metallic connections [6]. Other advantages of the optical fiber transmission are smaller physical size and weight, absence of spark or fire hazard, and a wide operating temperature range.

Besides the above factors, two important transmission properties of optical fiber are optical loss and signal distortion. Low optical loss means long repeater spans, and small dispersion implies large transmission bandwidths over long distances. Additional details on optical fiber transmission may be found in [6; 7; 17, pp. 187–190; and 21].

2-2 TRANSMISSION MODES

In this section, we describe the various ways in which transmission links are used to transport data between network nodes. First, we analyze the various modes of data transmission and the ways in which terminals or nodes may be interconnected. Then, we address various polling disciplines and include algorithms to estimate message delays due to polling.

Simultaneous Transmissions: Half Duplex and Full Duplex

Terminal equipment, signal converters (or modems), and transmission links may be designed to permit movement of data in either or both directions. A large number of communication links operate in *half-duplex mode*. In this mode, data is permitted to flow in either direction, but not simultaneously. At a given time, the transmission can take place only in one direction. In *duplex mode*, data may simultaneously flow in both directions. Sometimes, this mode of transmission is also referred as *full-duplex mode* or *two-way simultaneous transmission*. Full-duplex mode requires four wires, two for each direction of flow.*

Sometimes, a four-wire facility is also used for half-duplex mode. This four-wire facility always keeps two wires connected for each direction of transmission. Its advantage over the two-wire half duplex is the saving in modem turnaround time. This saving occurs whenever the direction of transmission has to be changed for a link in half-duplex mode. Finally, in simplex mode, movement of data can take place only in one given direction at all times.

---

* Additional wires may be used to transmit control signals. Sometimes, a two-wire facility can be used for full-duplex mode by using different frequencies or bandwidths for the two directions of message transmission.

| | Number of wires | | Transmission | Simultaneous |
	Two	Four	direction	transmission
Simplex	X		One	No
Half duplex	X		Both	No
Four-wire half duplex		X	Both	No
Full duplex or Duplex		X*	Both	Yes

* See footnote on p. 40.

The full-duplex mode offers maximum function and performance for a transmission link. In order to obtain a full-duplex operation, both the modems and the protocols controlling the transmission must provide full-duplex operation. The full-duplex operation also requires special considerations for buffer management. For example, simultaneous read and write operations also require simultaneous release and allocation of buffers in the message buffer pool.

Since bidirectional data transmission is simultaneous in full-duplex mode, one would expect that the utilization of a full-duplex link* is approximately half that of a half-duplex link. While there are some additional delays in duplex mode (such as waiting for acknowledgments), there is also some saving in link utilization, such as simultaneous transmission in both directions and absence of modem turnaround delays. We will now elaborate these points and identify the factors that affect link utilization.

Consider two terminals A and B connected by a link as shown in Fig. 2-9(a). We compare the total link time required to transmit n messages from terminal A to terminal B, and n messages from terminal B to terminal A. After transmission of, say, p messages, the receiving terminal must acknowledge before the sending terminal can transmit another p message. (The value of p depends on the transmission link protocols employed. In the case of synchronous data link control, described in Sec. 2-3, p cannot exceed 7.) Let TM_a and TM_b be the link time to transmit a message from terminal A and terminal B, respectively; TR, the time needed to change the direction of transmission in the modem (also called *turnaround time* and required only in half-duplex operation); and T_k, the link time to transmit an acknowledgment. For each acknowledgment, the direction of transmission on link may have to be changed twice—once to send the

* Link utilization is the fraction of time that the link is busy transmitting or receiving data or control (such as poll) messages.

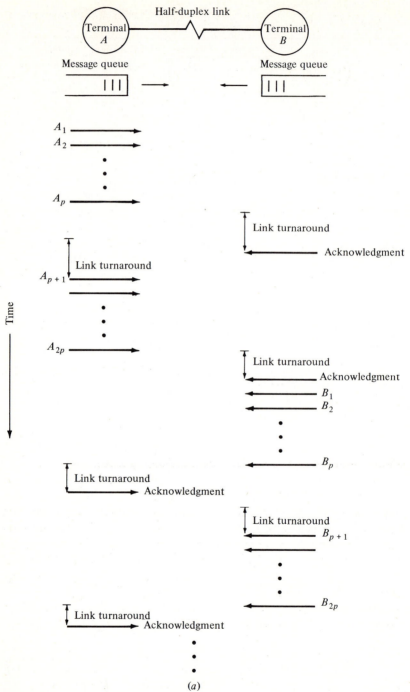

Figure 2-9(*a*) Half-duplex message exchange.

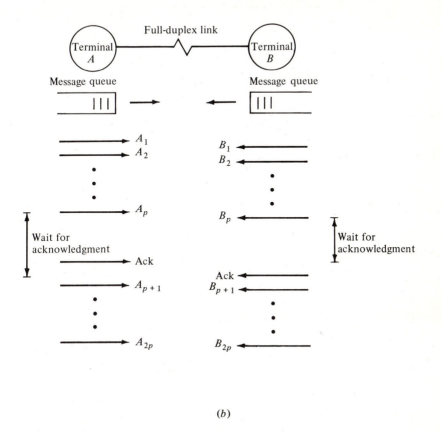

(*b*)

Figure 2-9(*b*) Full-duplex message exchange. (For simplicity, polling is not shown.)

acknowledgment and a second time to receive messages. Then, the link time in half-duplex mode to send *n* messages from terminal A to terminal B, and *n* messages from terminal B to terminal A, is

$$\text{THD} = n\,\text{TM}_a + \left\lceil \frac{n}{p} \right\rceil (\text{T}_k + 2\,\text{TR})$$

$$+ n\,\text{TM}_b + \left\lceil \frac{n}{p} \right\rceil (\text{T}_k + 2\,\text{TR})$$

where $\left\lceil \frac{n}{p} \right\rceil$ is the least integer value equal to or greater than n/p. (This is the total number of acknowledgments for *n* messages.)

Now, consider the case in which the link operates in full-duplex mode. Then, there is no modem turnaround time. Therefore, the link time in full-duplex mode to transmit n messages from terminal A to terminal B, and n messages from terminal B to terminal A, is

$$\text{TFD} = \left\lceil \frac{n}{p} \right\rceil (\max\,(p\text{TM}_a,\, p\text{TM}_b) + \text{T}_k)$$

The term $\max\,(p\text{TM}_a,\, p\text{TM}_b)$ provides the maximum time in either of the two directions of transmission to send p messages. After this duration, an acknowledgment may be sent. Note that terminal A may have transmitted its p messages before terminal B has sent its p messages. Then, A has to wait for an acknowledgment before proceeding to transmit additional messages; and this acknowledgment may only arrive after B has sent its p messages. For this duration, the link is not being used for transmission from A to B. Due to this difference, the time for a full-duplex link TFD may be more than half of the time for a half-duplex link THD. In fact, if we neglect turnaround time TR, and if each message in both directions is of the same size, only then is TFD half of THD. Even in packet-switched networks, this requirement is rarely satisfied, since the network control messages may be of a different size than the packet size. However, the performance of the above full-duplex connection may be improved by reducing the time spent by messages in terminal A in waiting for an acknowledgment from terminal B. This may be achieved by permitting the acknowledgment message to be transmitted at a higher priority than data messages. Alternatively, the acknowledgment could be encoded as a bit in the message header, and sent in any data message; this is known as *piggybacking*. Such changes prevent an acknowledgment from being delayed behind other messages.

Recall that a two-wire half-duplex line requires modem time to change the direction of transmission. This delay is introduced every time a given node changes from receive to transmit, or vice versa. Clearly, the link can be better utilized if messages are grouped together by withholding them at the sender. After a given number of messages have been collected, they are transmitted together to reduce the number of modem turnarounds. Furthermore, since messages are grouped together into single transmissions, it also reduces the total number of acknowledgment (messages) transmitted through the network. We hasten to point out that such an approach may impose additional delay for messages waiting to be transmitted, and may require additional buffers. As such, the above approach is desirable for batch transmissions, compared to such time-sensitive transmissions as voice or interactive applications.

Point-to-Point and Multipoint Link Controls: Polling

In order to transmit data between two nodes, the transmission link may be *dedicated* or *shared*. A dedicated, or point-to-point, link permits transmissions to take place between two nodes at any time. A shared, or multipoint, link connects several nodes together, but allows transmission between only one pair of nodes at a time. Often, one of the nodes (or stations) on the link is assigned, or may assume, the role of *primary* station. The remaining one or more nodes on the link are then called *secondary* stations. The primary station controls the operations on the link; transmission can take place only between the primary and one of the secondary stations at a given time.

Compared to a point-to-point link, a multipoint link control improves utilization of the link. It also imposes certain additional requirements, as described next. Each station is assigned an *address*, which enables a secondary station to identify messages destined for it. Transmission from the primary station to a secondary station takes place after the primary station sends a *select* message to the secondary station. Interference from other secondary stations is prevented by not permitting any other secondary station to initiate transmission. The basic exchange sequence of a multipoint operation is shown in Fig. 2-10. Transmission from a secondary station to a primary station can take place after the secondary station is allowed to do so by the primary station. The primary station sends a *poll message*, or *poll*, to the secondary station. This control message solicits data from a secondary station. The secondary station may respond negatively (no data to send) or send some data. (The terms selection and poll are, in fact, used in the link protocol called *binary synchronous communications*, which is described in Sec. 2-3.)

Polling prevents the interference that may result if more than one secondary station simultaneously initiates transmissions. Let us consider another form of control for a multipoint link. Here, any secondary station may interrupt the link for message transmission. If the link is already busy, the interrupt is queued. (In some cases, such as the satellite links, it causes collisions.) Whenever the link is free, this queue is scanned to serve another secondary station.*

Polling and hub polling Two types of polling algorithms are commonly used: *serial polling* and *hub polling*. In serial polling, the primary station maintains a list of all secondary stations. The primary station sends a poll to each secondary station, one at a time. (The

---

* It has also been described as a *contention network* [15, p. 158].

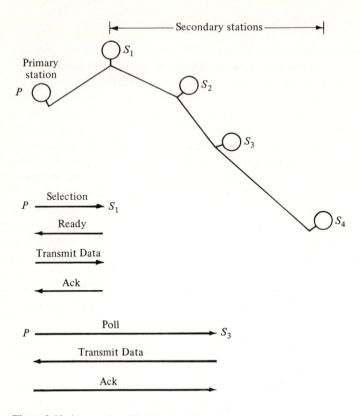

Figure 2-10 A general multipoint discipline.

primary station includes the address of the secondary station in the poll message.) If the polled secondary station has no data to send, it sends a negative response. If the station has data to send, it sends a positive response, followed by data. Next, the primary station sends a poll to another secondary station in the list. Several variations to this basic procedure may be developed and used.

The addressing between the primary station and a secondary station works as follows. The primary station includes, in the poll message, the address of the polled secondary station. Each secondary station, in essence, checks this address to determine whether the poll is destined for it. After receiving and processing a poll, a secondary station includes its address in the response message to the poll. This poll-response message may include data from the secondary station, or may indicate that the secondary station has no data to send. Because of direction of flow of the poll-response message, the message goes only to the primary station. The primary station identifies the secondary station that sent the message by checking the address included in the message.

A principal problem associated with polling is the overhead required in processing the nonproductive polls—polls for which a secondary station has no data to transmit. This overhead may be significant in certain cases. Consider a 56-kbps full-duplex link with a primary station P and two secondary stations S_1 and S_2, as shown in Fig. 2-11. As we will see in Sec. 2-3, a poll message may be assumed to consist of six characters. Then, on a 56-kbps link, it requires approximately 2 ms of link time to transmit a poll and its response. Assuming that both stations S_1 and S_2 have no data to send, the above calculation leads to approximately 500 nonproductive polls per second. Although no useful data transmission is taking place, considerable processing overhead may be imposed on both the primary and the secondary stations. Such overhead may be reduced by imposing a

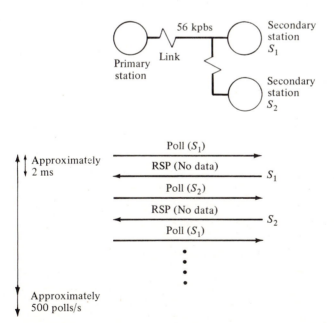

Figure 2-11 Poll exchange on a 56-kbps link between a primary station and two secondary stations, with no data to transmit.

fixed time delay between the successive polls generated at the primary station. However, due consideration should be given to its impact on the total message transmission delay through the network.

When secondary stations are located at long distances from the primary station, it is advantageous to send a common poll for all secondary stations. The poll is received by the first secondary station—station S_1 in Fig. 2-12. If station S_1 has no data to transmit, it sends a poll to the next station S_2, on behalf of the primary station. This process is repeated by station S_2, and so on, until a secondary station (if any) on the link is found that has data to send. Such a secondary station then sends data to the primary station, and the poll terminates. The primary station then resumes polling from this secondary station. (Alternatively, the secondary station sends the data, and then passes the poll to the next secondary station on behalf of the primary station.) The poll continues until the last secondary station S_n

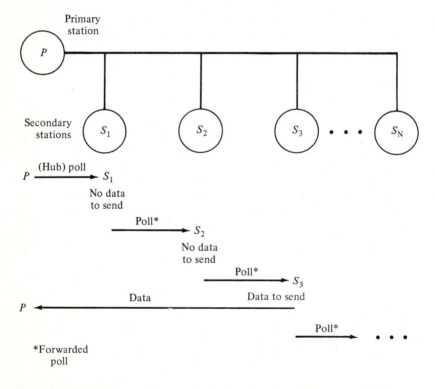

Figure 2-12 Hub polling.

has been polled. The secondary station S_n terminates the poll. This polling algorithm, called *hub* polling, reduces the link time of a poll and thus improves response time. This is true since a negative response from a secondary station, indicating no data to send, is also used as a poll for another secondary station. Hub polling is also useful when there is a long distance between primary and secondary stations. For example, in the case of satellite links, there may be a group of secondary stations clustered near a given earth station,* say, E. Then, using hub polling, a single poll message may be sent (from the earth station with primary capability) to E for all of the secondary stations. This scheme would significantly reduce use of the satellite link to transmit the polls; as well as improve the average poll delays for message transmission.

Poll time analysis In this section, we derive some estimates of delays due to polling. First, we compare the poll scan times for hub and serial polling, and then we estimate the message delay in a terminal waiting to be polled in serial polling. The term *poll scan time* is used here to represent the total time required to poll all secondary stations, assuming no secondary station has any data to transmit. Specifically, we obtain the time between successive polls of a given polled station using the multipoint configuration shown in Fig. 2-12.

Let n be the number of polled stations (terminals or concentrators); TS, the time required to process a received poll (and generate its response) by a secondary station engaged in serial polling; TH, the same as TS except that it applies to hub polling; TP, the time to initiate a poll in the primary station as well as to process a received response to the poll; and TL, the link time to propagate a hub or serial poll through all the stations (primary station P → station S_1 → station S_2 → ⋯ → station S_n). Then, the poll scan time for hub polling is the sum of times needed to generate a poll and process its response in the primary station, n times the duration required to process the poll in a secondary station, and the time needed to transmit the poll through all the secondary stations, or $\text{TP} + (n\text{TH}) + \text{TL}$.

For serial polling, a poll is created by the primary station and sent separately to each secondary station. For simplicity, let us assume that the distance between adjacent stations is equal. Then the time to send a poll to the first station and receive its response is the sum of (1) the processing time needed to generate the poll and process

---

* The term *earth station* refers to satellite transmission; primary and secondary stations refer to link transmission.

its response TP, (2) the link time required to transmit the poll assuming no link turnaround delay (TL/n), (3) the time needed to process the poll in the secondary station TS, and (4) the time required to transmit the response to the primary station (TL/n); or 2 TL/n + TS + TP.

For the second station, the above time is 2(2 TL/n) + TS + TP. The term 2 TL/n is multiplied by 2 to allow for the additional link time between the first and the second secondary station. Therefore, the total poll scan time for serial polling equals

$$\frac{2\ \text{TL}}{n}\ (1 + 2 + \cdots + n) + n\ (\text{TS} + \text{TP})$$

$$= n(\text{TS} + \text{TP}) + \frac{2\ \text{TL}}{n}\ \frac{n(n + 1)}{2}$$

$$= n(\text{TS} + \text{TP}) + \text{TL}\ (n + 1)$$

Based on above results and assumptions, hub polling is more desirable than serial polling when

$$(\text{TP} + n\text{TH} + \text{TL}) < n(\text{TS} + \text{TP}) + \text{TL}(n + 1)$$

or

$$n\text{TH} < n\text{TS} + (n - 1)\text{TP} + n\text{TL}$$

or

$$\text{TH} < \text{TS} + \text{TL} + \left(1 - \frac{1}{n}\right)\text{TP}$$

This observation applies only in the context of minimizing the poll scan time. Finally, we assumed that both serial and hub polling require the same processing time in the primary station, which is often not true. (In general, hub polling requires more processing in the primary station than serial polling).

We will now compare some properties of serial and hub polling.

1. Serial polling requires considerably more processing in the primary station than hub polling. The processing requirement may also depend on the link speed and frequency of polling.
2. Serial polling requires more link turnarounds than hub polling since, in serial polling, the direction of transmission is changed every time a station is polled.
3. Hub polling requires additional logic at each secondary station to generate a poll for the next station.
4. Without additional logic, hub polling does not permit selective polling of secondary stations. This situation may arise when some

terminals have considerably more traffic than others. Serial polling permits selective polling.

Next, we consider the duration that a terminal (or a secondary station) waits to be polled. This delay is the interval that a message is withheld in a secondary station until a poll is received. These estimates apply only to serial polling. (The reader may extend this analysis to hub polling.)

Assume that there are n secondary stations. Then, a particular secondary station may not have to wait to be polled, or may wait for as many as $n - 1$ stations to be polled. If no station has data to send, the mean waiting time to be polled is $t(n - 1)/2$, where t is the total time to poll (poll time) a secondary station. It is assumed that t is the average value. We can obtain some statistical measures for this delay. The variance* of this delay may be found by first obtaining the second moment. The second moment of waiting time is the weighted mean of the squares of possible polling times, or

$$\sum_{k=0}^{n-1} \frac{1}{n} (kt)^2$$

$$= \frac{t^2}{n} \frac{(n-1)n(2n-1)}{6} \qquad \text{using summation of series†}$$

$$= \frac{t^2}{6} (n-1)(2n-1)$$

Then, the variance of poll delay is

$$= \text{second moment} - (\text{mean})^2$$

$$= \frac{t^2}{6} (n-1)(2n-1) - \left(\frac{n-1}{2} t\right)^2$$

$$= \frac{n^2 - 1}{12} t^2$$

---

* See Chap. 8 for the concept of variance in probability theory.

† $\displaystyle\sum_{k=0}^{n} k = \frac{n(n+1)}{2}$

$\displaystyle\sum_{k=0}^{n} k^2 = \frac{n(n+1)(2n+1)}{6}$

More accurate results for the poll time and poll delay may also be derived [22, p. 618].

2-3 TRANSMISSION PROTOCOLS

Information, in the form of bits, can be transmitted over a link in either parallel or serial fashion. Serial transmission employs a single channel and successively transmits bits, one bit at a time. Parallel transmission frequently uses the same number of channels as the number of bits in a character. (An additional channel may be used to provide parity checking of transmitted bits.) In this case, the total character is transmitted simultaneously. In general, parallel transmission may transfer any number of bits at a time. Protocols to transmit data on transmission links are also classified as either *synchronous* or *asynchronous*, depending on whether the two ends are bit-synchronized for transmission. In the following section, we describe some commonly used link transmission protocols.*

Asynchronous Serial Transmission

In asynchronous serial transmission, data is transmitted one bit at a time, usually in groups of characters. In order to provide the receiver with information for the beginning and end of a character, each character is preceded by a *start* signal and followed by a *stop* signal. In general, the start signal is the same length, or time width, as an information unit. The stop signal is usually 1, $1\frac{1}{2}$, or 2 times the length of the information signal, as shown in Fig. 2-13. This transmission protocol is called *start-stop* and requires a single channel. Its main advantage is that the character is self-contained with all the information, and that the two ends of the link need not be synchronized. Its main disadvantage is the overhead for start and stop signals, and that of false recognition of start or stop signals due to noise on the channel. The asynchronous mode of operation is required for devices with keyboards that have no message buffers and operate on one character at a time. However, due to their improved performance, there is a noticeable trend toward synchronous rather than asynchronous transmission protocols.

* For further details, the reader is referred to [10, 11, and 12].

Synchronous Serial Transmission

Synchronous bit-serial transmission consists of a stream of bits transmitted on a single channel. Compared to the start-stop protocol, synchronous transmission uses synchronizing information on groups of characters, such as a message, instead of on each character. The receiving station operates in step with the transmitting station through the recognition of a specific bit pattern at the beginning of each transmission. Data is transmitted serially by providing control characters at the beginning and the end of a message. Thus, it requires specifying certain bit encodings to be used only for special characters, such as header, poll, start, and end of message. These special characters are also called *control characters*. The two ends of the link are synchronized, thereby avoiding the overhead for handling synchronizing information for each character. However, due to this approach, transmission error results in loss of a message, as compared to loss of a character in start-stop protocol. Two types of synchronous transmission protocols are described here: binary synchronous communications (BSC) and synchronous data link control (SDLC).

Binary Synchronous Communications

In binary synchronous communications (BSC), data is transferred as binary-coded characters made up of text and header characters. Also, data-link control characters are required to delimit various portions of the message and handle its transmission. A message transmission consists of one or more blocks of data. In general, each block of data is preceded by a Start of Text (STX) control character, and the end of the block is followed by an End of Text (ETX) control character. The

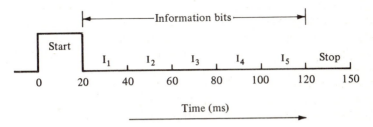

Figure 2-13 Example of a start-stop bit sequence for a 5-bit character. (From M. D. Bacon and G. M. Bull, *Data Transmission*, American Elsevier, New York, 1973, p. 60. Reprinted with permission from MacDonald & Janes Publishers, Limited, London.)

receiver acknowledges each block of data. The bit encodings for some of the control characters are shown in Table 2-2. We first provide a description of some commonly used control characters, followed by an example of their use.

1. SYN (Synchronous Idle). This control character establishes and maintains synchronization on the link. It is also used as a null character for the idle condition of the link.
2. SOH (Start of Header). This character identifies the beginning of the message header.
3. STX (Start of Text). STX indicates termination of a header and start of the text characters.
4. ETX (End of Text). ETX terminates a block of characters that started with STX or SOH. A *block* is an entity that is transmitted together without any intervening control characters.
5. ENQ (Enquiry). ENQ identifies the end of a poll or selection sequence.* It is also used to bid for the use of a point-to-point link, or to obtain a repeat transmission of the response to a message block if the original transmission was in error or not received.
6. EOT (End of Transmission). This character identifies termination of a transmission, consisting of one or more blocks. It is also used as a poll response when a secondary station has no data to transmit.
7. ETB (End of Transmission Block). ETB indicates end of a block of characters that started with SOH or STX.
8. ACK0|ACK1 (alternating affirmative acknowledgments) and NAK (negative acknowledgment). ACK0|ACK1 acknowledge that the previous block was received without error. NAK indicates that the block had an error.
9. BCC (Block Check Character). Each block of data is checked for transmission errors. An algorithm is executed for all bits in the data block, and the result is transmitted in the BCC character. The receiver executes the same algorithm and compares its result with the received BCC character, thereby determining if there was an error in transmission.

In Fig. 2-14, a sequence for multipoint binary synchronous operation is illustrated. The primary station polls a secondary station (address A), but the secondary station has no data to send. The pri-

---

* In a poll sequence, a primary station solicits a secondary station for any data to be transmitted from the secondary station to the primary station. In a selection sequence, a primary station sends data to a secondary station.

Table 2-2 Hexadecimal coding of binary synchronous communications control characters

	Code*	
	EBCDIC	ASCII
SYN	32	16
SOH	01	01
STX	02	02
ETX	03	03
ENQ	2D	05
ETB	26	17
NAK	3D	15
EOT	37	04

* The American Standard Code for Information Interchange (ASCII) uses 7 bits; the eighth bit is either set to 1, or used as a parity bit. The Extended Binary-Coded Decimal Interchange Code (EBCDIC) is an 8-bit code, using pairs of 4-bit hexadecimal digits.

Source: IBM Corporation, General Information—Binary Synchronous Communications, no. GA27-3004-2, 1970, pp. 8–11.

mary station then polls another secondary station (address B) and receives data. The transmission is completed after two blocks of data are received and acknowledged.

Synchronous Data Link Control

Synchronous data link control (SDLC) can provide full-duplex link operation. An important advantage of SDLC over BSC is that in the former the receiver can wait up to seven blocks before it has to send an acknowledgment. A message or a block, called an *information frame* or *I frame* in SDLC, has the format: flag byte (F), address byte (A), control byte (C), optional information field, frame check sequence field (FCS), and a flag byte (F). This is illustrated in Fig. 2-15. A poll message consists of six characters: F, A, C, FCS, F. We begin this section by describing these special characters, followed by an example of a full-duplex SDLC operation.

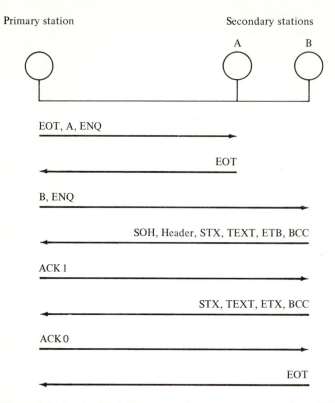

Figure 2-14 A simplified binary synchronous communications (BSC) multipoint sequence.

Flag character (F) This character has the unique bit format 0111 1110 and is used to separate information frames. The beginning flag character serves as the reference for the address and control characters. It also initiates checking of transmission errors. The ending flag character terminates the check for transmission errors. A series of contiguous flag characters may be transmitted to keep the link in an active state.

Bit stuffing Bit stuffing is the technique used to avoid occurrence of the flag bit pattern anywhere in the frame. The sending station examines the number of contiguous 1 bits being sent on the link. If the sending station detects five consecutive bits with a 1, it automatically inserts a 0, except if it is a flag character. Correspondingly, if the receiving station detects a bit stream for five consecutive 1 bits, it

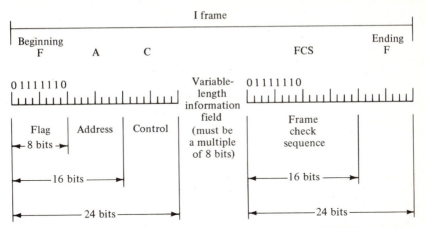

Figure 2-15 Format of an SDLC frame. (From IBM Corporation, "IBM Synchronous Data Link Control: General Information," GA27-3093-2, March 1979, Fig. 2-5, p. 2-4.)

checks the sixth bit. If the sixth bit is a 1, it often implies either a flag or an error. If the sixth bit is a 0, the bit is deleted. Thus, at no time can more than five consecutive 1s appear within an information frame. This applies to address, control, information, and frame check sequence fields.

Address character (A) The address character follows the beginning flag character in an information frame. In an information or control frame, a primary station is never identified. The secondary station is always identified; both for receive and transmit operations. Thus, the address character always has the address of a secondary station. An all 1s in the address character is often used as a broadcast or all-stations address. The setting of all 0s is reserved for null operations, such as testing. The remaining 254 values of the 8-bit character are available to identify secondary stations on an SDLC link.

Control character (C) The control character follows the address character, and provides the encoding of commands and responses to control a data link. The control character has three formats, as shown in Fig. 2-16. The information transfer format is used to transmit sequenced information frames. The supervisory format is used to convey ready or busy conditions, and the error due to out-of-sequence arrival of frames. This format is used for commands and responses, such as Receive Ready (RR) by the bit encoding (bits 0–3) 1000, and Receive

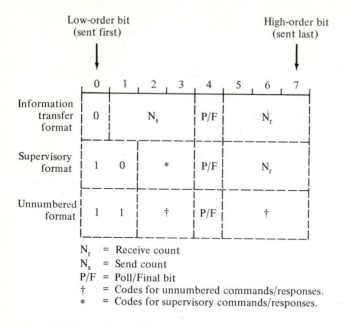

Low-order bit
(sent first)

High-order bit
(sent last)

N_r = Receive count
N_s = Send count
P/F = Poll/Final bit
† = Codes for unnumbered commands/responses.
* = Codes for supervisory commands/responses.

Figure 2-16 SDLC control character format. (Adapted from IBM Corporation, "IBM Synchronous Data Link Control: General Information," GA27-3093-2, March 1979, Figs. 2-8 and 3-1, pp. 2-8 and 3-3.)

Not Ready (RNR) by the bit encoding (bits 0–3) 1010. The unnumbered format is used to manage the link.

The N_r and N_s fields contain the receive and send counts of information frames. The P/F bit (for Poll/Final bit) provides the control to send or receive information frames. This bit is used as the *poll* bit by the primary station and the *final* bit by the secondary station. The primary station sets the P bit to 1 to poll a secondary station for data. The bit is set ot 0 if the primary station is only sending data. The secondary station sets the F bit to 1 only when it is sending the last frame.

Frame check sequence (FCS) The frame check sequence, also called *block check* (BC) or *cyclic redundancy check* (CRC), consists of 16 bits and immediately precedes the ending F character. This field permits checking for transmission errors in the frame. It is the result of a computation on the contents of address, control and information characters in the frame.

The above special characters are employed in controlling data transmission over an SDLC connection. Figure 2-17 illustrates a multipoint full-duplex SDLC exchange. It has a primary station A, and secondary stations B and C on a full-duplex link. For simplicity, the initialization sequence, flag characters, and FCS are not shown. Note that no N_s count is sent for a supervisory format, such as when sending Receive Ready (RR) command.

1. Primary station A polls secondary station C for data. The P/F bit is set to 1, and the N_r count is 0.
2. Secondary station C starts to send sequenced information frames to A.
3. At the same time, primary station A sends sequenced information frames to secondary station B.
4. Secondary station C sends three information frames. In the last frame, it sets the P/F bit to 1, indicating completion of sequence.
5. Having sent two frames to secondary station B, primary station A polls secondary station B for confirmation.
6. Primary station A confirms receipt of three frames from secondary

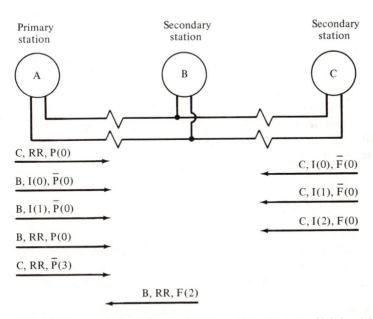

Figure 2-17 A multipoint full-duplex SDLC exchange. Format of labels—Address, Information/Control Frame (N_s), P/F setting (N_r); P/F setting: P (or F) = bit is set to 1 for Poll (or Final), $\bar{P}$ (or $\bar{F}$) = Bit is set to 0 for not Polled (or not Final).

station C. It turns off the P/F bit, since it does not intend to poll C for data.

7. Station B confirms the receipt of two frames from A.

The international standards community has also developed a high-level data link control (HDLC) protocol. HDLC has the same frame format as SDLC, namely, flag, address, control, information, FCS, and flag. The format of the flag byte is 0111 1110, which is the same as in SDLC. HDLC has a provision of extending the address field. By prior agreement, the address field is extended by a chain of address bytes. The first transmitted (least-significant) bit is set to 0 in all such bytes, except in the last address byte in which it is set to 1. Details on HDLC frame structure and protocols can be found in [24] and [25], respectively. Other references providing information on SDLC and HDLC are [12, app. D], and [18, sec. 11.5].

CCITT Recommendation X.21

The International Telegraph and Telephone Consultative Committee (CCITT) has established interface standards for use in connecting terminals and networks. The CCITT recommendation X.21 specifies a general-purpose interface for synchronous operation on public data networks.* This recommendation was adopted in 1972, and revised in 1976.

In order to describe the X.21 interface, we first define some terms that are illustrated in Fig. 2-18. The Data Terminal Equipment (DTE) can be any type of user facility, ranging from a large computer system to a very simple terminal. The Data Circuit-Terminating Equipment (DCE) terminates the access link from the network, and provides interface from the network to the DTE. A *calling DTE* is a DTE that originates a call to establish a connection; a *called DTE* is the DTE that is the destination of the call. The DTE-DCE interface may be provided at three levels. The X.21 interface applies to the first level, which is also served by other interface standards, such as the EIA RS-232C and RS-366. X.21 connections require 15 pin connectors; the RS-232C/RS-366 require about 25. As currently defined, the X.21 interface is character-oriented. It uses IA 5, the International Alphabet Number 5, which is essentially the same as ASCII in the United States. (CCITT recommendation X.25, which serves some of the higher levels of DTE-DCE interface is described in Chap. 5.)

---

* The CCITT recommendation X.21 is described in [9; 18, pp. 600–607; and 23].

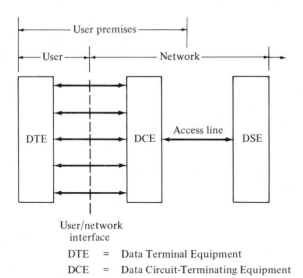

DTE = Data Terminal Equipment
DCE = Data Circuit-Terminating Equipment
DSE = Data-Switching Exchange

Figure 2-18 X.21 connection. (From R. J. Cypser, *Communications Architecture for Distributed Systems*, Addison-Wesley, Reading, Mass., 1978, Fig. 17.1, p. 594. Reprinted with permission.)

There are three time phases that may exist between the DTE and DCE.

1. The *idle or quiescent* phase is the interval when the interface is inactive. It is similar to the "on-hook" condition in a telephone network.
2. The *control* phase is the time period for Call Establishment and Call Clearing. *Call Establishment* refers to the exchange of control signals that establish communication between a calling DTE and a called DTE. *Call Clearing* refers to the exchange of control signals that leads to discontinuing the connection.
3. The *data transfer* phase pertains to the duration when the connection is established and data may be transferred.

An important aspect of the X.21 interface is that it permits any bit sequence to be transferred during the data transfer phase. The X.21 interface requires the use of five interchange circuits, as shown in Fig. 2-19. The T (transmit) and R (receive) circuits are provided for transmit and receive side of data transmission. A third circuit, S (signal

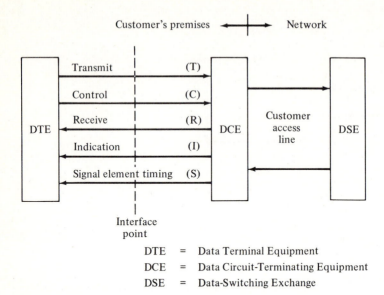

DTE = Data Terminal Equipment
DCE = Data Circuit-Terminating Equipment
DSE = Data-Switching Exchange

Figure 2-19 X.21 interchange circuits. (From H. C. Folts, "Status Report on New Standards for DTE/DCE Interface Protocols," *IEEE Computer*, vol. 12, no. 9, September 1979, p. 16.)

element timing), provides the bit timing so that synchronous bit transmission is obtained. Circuit C (control) is used by the DTE to indicate the conventional on-hook/off-hook condition. Finally, circuit I (indication) is used to indicate the start of the data transfer phase.

A sample sequence for a connection using X.21 is shown in Fig. 2-20. For simplicity, the settings of the circuits are not shown; instead, the symbolic names for the X.21 states are included, as indicated by the interchange circuits. We have also excluded any indications for the timing limits of various events. To begin with, both DTEs are in Ready states. The calling DTE initiates the call by indicating the Call Request state. The DCE responds by indicating the Proceed to Select state. The calling DTE provides the identification of the called DTE through selection signals. The DCE uses this identification and signals Incoming Call to the called DTE. One or more Call Progress Signals (described below) may be sent by the DCE to the calling DTE. When the called DTE signals Call Accepted, the DCE optionally provides the identification of the called DTE to the calling DTE. DCE presents DCE Waiting and Connection in Progress. This establishes the call and is followed by the exchange of data. The calling DTE can request

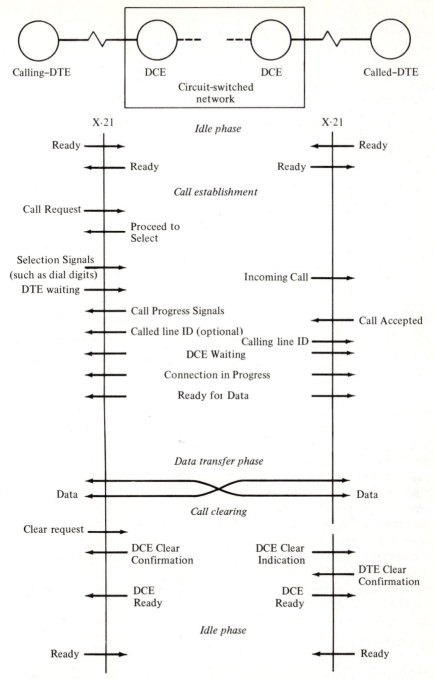

Figure 2-20 A sample exchange sequence using X.21. (Circuit settings and relative timings are not shown.)

call clearing by signaling Clear Request. The DCE signals Clear Confirmation to the calling DTE, and Clear Indication to the called DTE. The call is cleared and the connection is discontinued when the called DTE signals Clear Confirmation. Network resources are returned to an idle pool.

Call Progress Signals are provided by the DCE to inform the DTE of the network condition and the result of the call. The Call Progress Signal include codes that, for example, inform the calling DTE to try again if the called DTE had been busy or indicate if the called DTE is out of order. Such signals may also indicate that the network is temporarily congested; thus, the calling DTE should wait for a certain time before reattempting the call. The X.21 interface protocol is being implemented by Norway, Sweden, Finland, and Denmark in their Nordic Public Data Network (described in the App. A), and by Japan and West Germany [23].

X.21 bis When new data networks, such as the Nordic Public Data Network, come into operation, some terminals may not be ready for operation on X.21. Instead, such terminals may be operating on the synchronous V-series (V.24 or RS-232C) interface. The facility to attach such terminals to X.21 networks is called *X.21 bis*. Although it appears that the X.21 bis requires no change to the existing DTEs that use the RS-232C interface, the X.21 bis user may not get all the X.21 advantages, such as the Call Progress Signals.

SUMMARY

This chapter describes the characteristics and analyzes the behavior of transmission links in computer communication networks. Four types of transmission links have been presented: terrestrial, satellite, radio, and optical fiber. There is considerable interest in each type of link, depending on network topology and requirements. Some results for estimating the effects of polling have been developed. Finally, three types of link-level protocols—BSC, SDLC, and X.21—have been described in detail.

PROBLEMS

2-1 Describe the relative advantages and disadvantages of (*a*) terrestrial links, (*b*) satellite links, (*c*) radio links, and (*d*) optical fiber transmission.

2-2 Derive the ratio of channel utilization to channel traffic for pure ALOHA, assuming that the distribution is binomial and not Poisson. (You may need to review Chap. 8 for this problem.)

2-3 Repeat prob. 2-2 for slotted ALOHA.

2-4 Suppose the message (or acknowledgment) transmission time is r times the modem turnaround time m. An acknowledgment must be received after p messages are transmitted.

(*a*) Derive the ratio of time required to transmit $k/2$ messages from each end for half-duplex and full-duplex operation.

(*b*) Suppose that k is greater than p, r is .5 for messages from the primary station to the secondary station, and the size of messages sent from the primary station to the secondary station is half of that sent from the secondary station to the primary station. Derive the ratio of transmitting k messages from the primary station to the secondary station, and k messages from the secondary station to the primary station, for half-duplex and full-duplex mode.

2-5 Assume that a poll and its response take 6 characters. The link operates in half-duplex mode at 9600 bps. The modem turnaround time is 8.5 ms.

(*a*) How many polls per second will occur if there is no data to send ?

(*b*) Assuming there are 8 secondary stations, estimate the average delay it takes to send a data message (100 characters) from a secondary station to the primary station. Calculate the above for serial polling.

2-6 In Sec. 2-2, we compared poll scan times for serial and hub polling. One result of the comparison showed the conditions in which hub polling is better than serial polling. However, it assumed that the time spent in the primary station is the same for both polling schemes. Derive the above results assuming that the time spent in primary station for hub polling is twice that for serial polling, and that the link time (TL) is the same as the time needed to process a serial poll in a secondary station (TS).

2-7 Compare poll scan times for hub polling and serial polling for these two cases:

(*a*) The use of TL for transmission time (of a poll or response) is an approximation. If there is a fixed modem synchronization time TM and propagation delay TD between any two secondary stations, then derive the poll scan time using these two delays, and not the TL approximation.

(*b*) Derive the poll scan time, in terms of other delays, for which the scan times of hub polling and serial polling are the same.

2-8 (*a*) Compare the advantages and disadvantages of BSC and SDLC protocols.

(*b*) Describe a sample SDLC exchange sequence for half-duplex operation.

2-9 (*a*) If p is the probability that a character has an error during transmission through the network, then the probability that a message is transmitted with some error is $1 - (1 - p)^S$, where S is the message size. Prove it. (Refer to Chap. 8 for a description of the concepts in probability theory.)

(*b*) Suppose that a data block of 1 million characters will be sent over a network link. Find the optimal message size so that the number of characters retransmitted is minimum if the probability that a character is in error is (*a*) 10^{-8}, (*b*) 10^{-5}, (*c*) .001.

REFERENCES

1. N. Abramson, "The ALOHA SYSTEM—Another Alternative for Computer Communications," *Fall Joint Computer Conference*, 1970, pp. 281–285.

2. N. Abramson, "Packet Switching with Satellites," *Proceedings of the National Computer Conference*, 1973, pp. 695–702.

3. L. Kleinrock and S. S. Lam, "Packet-Switching in a Slotted Satellite Channel," *Proceedings of the National Computer Conference*, 1973, pp. 703–710.

4. F. Borgonovo and L. Fratta, "A New Technique for Satellite Broadcast Channel Communication," *Proceedings of the Fifth Data Communications Symposium*, Snowbird, Utah, September 1977, pp. 2-1–2-4.

5. R. Weissler, R. Binder, R. Bressler, R. Rettberg, and D. Walden, "Synchronization and Multiple Access Protocols in the Initial Satellite IMP," *COMPCON*, 1978, pp. 356–362.

6. R. C. McCaskill, "Fiber Optics: The Connection of the Future," *Data Communications*, January 1979, pp. 67–73.

7. Tingye Li, "The Future of Optical Fibres for Data Communications," *Proceedings of the Fifth Data Communications Symposium*, Snowbird, Utah, September 1977, pp. 5-1–5-6.

8. "Xerox Plans to Offer Network Combining Satellite, Radio Links," *Computerworld*, November 20, 1978, p. 1.

9. The International Telephone and Telegraph Consultative Committee, "Interface between Data Terminal Equipment (DTE) and Data Circuit-Terminating Equipment (DCE) for synchronous Operation on Public Data Networks," CCITT draft recommendation X.21, draft revision 4, April 1979.

10. M. D. Bacon and G. M. Bull, *Data Transmission*, American Elsevier, New York, 1973.

11. IBM Corporation, "General Information—Binary Synchronous Communications," no. GA27-3004-2, October 1970.

12. IBM Corporation, "IBM Synchronous Data Link Control—General Information," no. GA 27-3093-2, March 1979.

13. L. Kleinrock, *Queueing Systems*, vol. II: *Computer Applications*. Wiley, New York, 1976.

14. J. Martin, *Telecommunications and the Computer*, Prentice-Hall, Englewood Cliffs, N. J., 1969.

15. J. Martin, *Teleprocessing Network Organization*, Prentice-Hall, Englewood Cliffs, N. J., 1970.

16. Dixon R. Doll, *Data Communications: Facilities, Networks and Systems Design*, Wiley, New York, 1978.

17. D. R. McGlynn, *Distributed Processing and Data Communications*, Wiley, New York, 1978.

18. R. J. Cypser, *Communications Architecture for Distributed Systems*, Addison-Wesley, Reading, Mass., 1978.

19. J. Martin, *Communication Satellite Systems*, Prentice-Hall, Englewood Cliffs, N. J., 1978.

20. J. F. Shoch and L. Stewart, "Interconnecting Local Networks via the Packet Radio Network," *Proceedings of the Sixth Data Communications Symposium*, November 1979, pp. 153–158.

21. S. Personick, "Optical Fiber Communications," tutorial sponsored by the National Telecommunications Conference, Washington, D.C., November 1979.

22. J. Martin, *Systems Analysis for Data Transmission*. Prentice-Hall, Englewood Cliffs, N. J., 1972.

23. H. C. Folts, "Status Report on New Standards for DTE/DCE Interface Protocols," *IEEE Computer*, vol. 12, no. 9, September 1979, pp. 12–19.

24. International Organization for Standardization, "Data Communication—High-Level Data Link Control Procedures—Frame Structure," reference no. ISO-3309-1979(E).

25. International Organization for Standardization, "Data Communication—High-Level Data Link Control Procedures—Elements of Procedures," reference no. ISO-4335-1979(E).

26. V. Ahuja and A. S. Barclay, "Compatibility of Systems Network Architecture and the CCITT X.21 Interface," *Proceedings of the National Telecommunications Conference* Washington, D.C., November 1979, pp. 3.41–3.47.

27. C. Retnadhas, "Satellite Multiple Access Protocols," *IEEE Communications* magazine, vol. 18, no. 5, September 1980, pp. 16–24.

CHAPTER
THREE

DESIGN AND ANALYSIS OF
NETWORK NODES

CHAPTER OUTLINE

The term *network node* has a variety of meanings and implies several interpretations. Network nodes are used to describe front-end processors, network controllers, communication processors, concentrators, and the like. A careful study reveals that these terms represent the corresponding aspects of services provided by network nodes. For example, a concentrator provides the message switching and network interface for terminals, and a front-end processor provides functions to primarily offload the host. This chapter addresses the problem of designing and analyzing the components of a network node. Section 3-1 discusses the functional requirements of a network node. Sections 3-2, 3-3, and 3-4 provide a brief description of the hardware and the software of a network node; it also includes approaches to estimate processor capacity, memory size, and the rate of message retransmissions resulting from buffer depletion.

3-1 NODE DESIGN

Network nodes encompass nearly all the functions needed to operate and control the network, and to provide communication between network users. Thus, the requirements for a network node may range from handling link errors to managing network topology. The different types of requirements for a network node may be grouped into three categories, as illustrated in Fig. 3-1.

First, the source/destination functions pertain to providing an interface to the network user (equipment), such as terminals, terminal controllers, and host processors. These functions also include the management of end-to-end message transmission between a source node and a destination node. Such functions may be visualized by assuming that there is a logical communication channel between the two end nodes that are communicating, such as nodes S and D in Fig. 3-1. Then, the interface of this channel to the network users and the management of this channel to provide error-free transmissions are the subject of this class of functions.

The second class of functions, store-and-forward functions, provide the services for message transmission through a network node. A given node, such as node T in Fig. 3-1, receives a message, stores it, and then forwards it to the next node on the route. These functions include message routing, message acknowledgments between adjacent nodes, and flow control mechanisms to protect node resources from

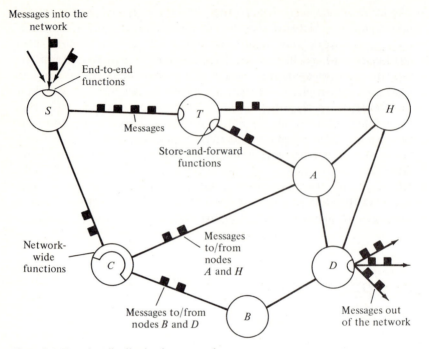

Messages into the
network

End-to-end
functions

Messages

Store-and-forward
functions

Network-
wide
functions

Messages
to/from
nodes
A and H

Messages to/from
nodes B and D

Messages out
of the network

Figure 3-1 Function distribution in a network.

being exhausted. (For networks that do not employ store-and-forward message transmission, these functions may be included in the source/destination functions.)

The third class of functions, network-wide functions, pertain to the management and maintenance of the network, and the measurement of its behavior. These functions include preventing network-wide congestion, maintaining topological awareness, bringing up or taking down network nodes or links, and measuring network performance.

Source/Destination Functions

These functions provide the protocols* required between the source node and the destination node, in order to permit communication between network users. Here, we also address the protocols that are required to interface with the network users' equipment.

---

* *Protocols* are often described as a set of rules designed to permit two or more network components to exchange useful information. This topic is treated in greater detail in Chap. 5.

End-to-end protocols The network node must provide for an end-to-end exchange so that a source node can transmit messages and a destination node can receive them. Specifically, it should provide for the situation in which the destination node has no buffers and, therefore, it may not permit the source node to transmit messages for it. The destination node may do so by withholding permission for the source node to send messages, as long as its buffers are not available. The permission may also be used to acknowledge messages received by the destination node. This exchange is illustrated in Fig. 3-2. Destination node D sends permission to source node S for a predefined number (say, k) of messages. Node D may not send permission to node S until D has sufficient buffers to receive k messages. This permission may also be used by node D to request a change in the number of messages being transmitted, that is, an increase or decrease in the value of k. Furthermore, this permission may also be used to acknowledge the previously received k messages.

Network interface The network node should provide interface protocols for terminals or host processors. For communication with termin-

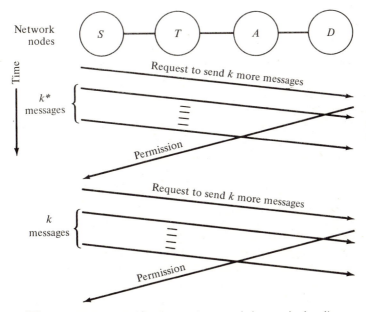

*These messages are sent in response to a permission received earlier.

Figure 3-2 End-to-end flow control.

als, a link protocol such as synchronous data link control (described in Sec. 2-3) may be employed. The channel protocols for interface to a host processor may be significantly different than those for terminals. The network interface may also provide for formatting and code conversion of messages (or transactions), facsimile, or other services for network users.

Segmenting and reassembly Messages may sometimes be divided into smaller data units, or packets, before transmission. As pointed out in Sec. 1-4, these packets may sometimes traverse the network independently, until they reach the destination node.* This requires segmenting messages into packets at the source node, and then reassembling the packets into messages at the destination node. Furthermore, the packet header must provide some information, such as a message number, to identify packets that belong to the same message. An important consideration for segmentation is the establishment of a packet size. Compared to variable-size packets, fixed-size packets provide several advantages:

1. For a network with fixed-size packets, the buffer unit size is fixed throughout the network. Often, a single buffer unit is used to store a packet in a network node.
2. With fixed-size packets, it is simpler to prevent congestion at a destination node, since the destination node may accurately estimate the amount of buffers needed to receive messages.
3. Fixed-size packets imply simpler buffer-management algorithms, and their use may result in lower programming costs.

The primary disadvantage of a fixed packet size is the loss due to unused buffer space when the message size slightly exceeds an integral multiple of the packet size. For example, consider a message size of 250 characters to be transmitted in a network with packet size of 120 characters. This message requires three packets, but in the network buffer(s) for the third packet only 10 of 120 bytes are used. Due to increasingly cheaper memories, such additional storage may become insignificant from a cost viewpoint. However, it would still imply additional transmission overhead on the network links. A smaller (fixed) packet size may also alleviate this problem, at the expense of

---

* Comparative studies for circuit switching and packet switching are described in [1, 2].

more packets in the network for the same message size, resulting in transmission and management of additional packets in the network.

Sequence numbers *Sequence numbering* is a mechanism used by a source node to provide message identification for use by other nodes, particularly the destination node. The source node includes a number, usually an integer, in the message (or packet) header. This number often starts with 0 or 1. (In principle, the number may begin at any integral value.) Everytime a new message is sent, this number is incremented by 1 and inserted in the header. When the maximum permitted value (described later) is reached, the number is reset to a predefined value and the above procedure is repeated. Any loss of data in the network is easily detected by checking the sequence numbers at the destination node. The destination node may send a signal, such as a control message, to the source node requesting retransmission of the lost message. Thus, a certain degree of data transmission integrity is obtained using sequence numbers.

Sequence numbers may also be used to ensure ordering of the messages. Due to alternate routing, network load variations, packetizing, and the like, messages may get out of sequence as they arrive at the destination node. Unless these messages are reordered to the same sequence as they entered the network, lockups or other erroneous conditions may result. This problem is illustrated in Fig. 3-3. Because of out-of-sequence arrival and processing at the destination node, terminals A and B are "hung." Terminal A assumes it is not in session with B, but terminal B assumes it is. This condition may continue until some action is taken to reset the (hang) condition of terminal A. We hasten to point out that the requirement for sequenced arrivals do not apply to the datagram service, in which each message unit is independent of the message units ahead of or following it. Furthermore, the above example uses certain types of control messages, and may not necessarily apply to all types of messages.

Finally, sequence numbers may also be used to discard duplicate messages, such as those generated to provide reliable message transmission through error-prone routes—for example, flooding technique in routing, which is described in Sec. 7-3.

Establishment of sequence numbers requires resolution of several design problems. We will use the term *sequence number space* to represent the sequence of consecutive integers within the minimum and the maximum values of permissible sequence numbers. The sequence number space must be larger than the maximum number of messages

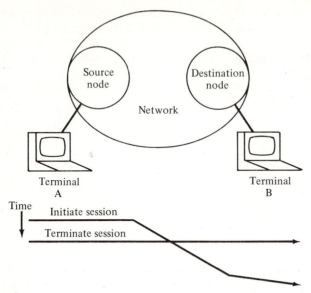

Figure 3-3 A lockup condition resulting from out-of sequence transmission and delivery.

that may be simultaneously in transmission between the two given end nodes. (See probs. 3-1 and 3-2.) However, a large sequence number space implies a large number of bits (in the message or packet header) to carry the sequence numbers. This problem is especially significant for satellite channels because of their large capacity and long propagation delay. Consider a 1.2 Mbps satellite channel. The propagation delay to the satellite and back is, say, .3 s. Then, neglecting the processing time at the receiver, the sequence numbers must permit a total of at least $1.2 \times .3 \times 2$Mb, or .72Mb, in transmission on the channel. (The estimate is multiplied by 2 to include messages, for both send and receive sides, between terminals.) Thus, for a packet size of 250 bytes, the sequence number space must be at least 360, or 9 bits in the header. (The maximum sequence number space size available with k bits in the header is 2^k.)

Finally, special considerations are required for providing rollover of sequence numbers, that is, the resetting of the sequence number to the minimum permitted value after reaching the maximum permitted value. Assume that sequence numbers may vary from 0 to $2^8 - 1$, or 255. After reaching 255, the sender assigns the number 0 to the next message. The receiver must now consider a message with a sequence number of 230 to be ahead of one with a sequence number of 0, assuming that the former message was sent before the latter. But what about a message with a sequence number of 120 ? Was this message sent before or after the message with sequence number 0 ? In order to resolve this problem, the destination node should include special logic or protocols to handle this condition. One possible solution is not to send messages after reaching sequence number 255, until the destination node has acknowledged receipt of each message up to and including sequence number 255. In particular, the previous message with a given sequence number should be acknowledged before another message with the same sequence number can be sent. However, exchange of these acknowledgments implies that no transmission of data messages is taking place on the link for a certain duration.

In the above estimates, we excluded messages that were in the message queue awaiting transmission. This is shown in Fig. 3-4, and is explained by this example.

Example Suppose that there is a full-duplex 56,000-bps link between two nodes. The maximum propagation delay through the link is 1 s, the packet size is fixed at 100 characters, and there are 50 messages/s transmitted on the link on each side. What is the required sequence number space size for this link?

The total number of unacknowledged messages in transmission (or waiting for transmission) is the sum of messages in the queues at the two ends and those in transmission on the link.* Using Fig. 3-4, this number is $q_1 + L_1 + q_2 + L_2$. Let us suppose that queues are served by the link in such a way that the message arrivals in the queue are coming at random with Poisson distribution, and that the link spends an amount of time on each message that is exponentially distributed.† Then, the probability that the value of q_1 exceeds k is p, where

$$k = \frac{\log p}{\log R} - 1 \quad k \geq 0$$

and $\quad R$ = average link utilization

$$= \frac{50 \times 100}{7000 \times 2} \quad \text{Divide by 2, since it is a full-duplex link.}$$

$$= .36$$

---

* We have assumed here that the sequence number is assigned before a message is placed in the queue for transmission. Alternatively, the message may be assigned a sequence number just before transmission, in which case queuing delay should not be considered.

† This system is also called an M/M/1 system, as explained in Chap. 8.

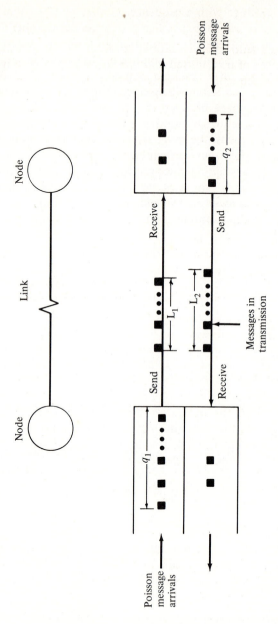

Figure 3-4 Message queues for transmission between adjacent nodes.

In order to obtain the value of k, we must assume some value for the probability that there is no sequence number available for assignment. (This situation, as discussed earlier, arises when the number of transmitted and unacknowledged messages is the same as the sequence number space size.) If we choose that this probability p should not exceed .001 (also called $100 - .001 = 99.9$th percentile), the value of k using the above expression is 6. Therefore, the desired sequence number space is given by $L_1 + L_2 + 2k$, or 112, where the value of both L_1 and L_2 is given to be 50. Note that, in this example, we assumed that there is only one hop between the two end nodes. This assumption is not always true. If there is a message route using h links, where each link is considered similar to the above example, the required sequence number space is approximately $112h$. Here, we have made a simplifying assumption that each link and its associated message traffic is operating independently as an M/M/1 system.

Creation and deletion of headers The message header for source/ destination functions is created in the source node, used in each node on the route, and deleted in the destination node. This header may include the following information:

Network address of the source and destination nodes
Flow control information, such as permissions to send additional
    messages, or flags for changing the rate of flow
Packet size, if the packets are permitted to be of more than one size
Message (or packet) sequence number
Message routing information
Several flag bits, such as to identify whether it is a control or data
    message, segmented (split into smaller-size message units) or not,
    fixed length or variable length, and the like
Message priority

Message headers may also be created, and deleted, to communicate information between adjacent nodes. Examples are the data link header, such as synchronous data link control described in Sec. 2-3, and control information, such as routing table updates.

Store-and-Forward Functions

Store-and-forward functions encompass the requirements for a transit or an intermediate node. A *transit node* is a node in a message route other than the source or destination node. For the network shown in Fig. 3-5(a), and for the messages from node A to node B, the nodes T_1 through T_6 are the transit nodes. In general, a given network node may be a source or a destination node for some messages and a transit node for other messages. However, certain nodes, such as node T_1, may simply be included in a network for use as a transit node. The functions of a transit node are described below.

Routing Perhaps the most significant function of a transit node is to forward received messages to an adjacent node, for progressing toward the destination node. *Routing* is defined as the process of determining the transmission path of a message through the network to reach its destination node. Consider the network shown in Fig. 3-5(a). Messages entering node A that are destined for node B are sent to transit node T_1. Node T_1 determines if the messages should be routed to node T_2 or T_3. This determination is the essence of the routing mechanism. Routing may be accomplished through message headers or routing tables. In the case of message headers, the address of each node in the message route may be included in the header. Then, a transit node, such as node T_1 in the above example, simply checks the header to determine the next node to forward the message. This approach involves overhead in transmitting the additional bits in the header over the links, but savings in routing table storage and some node processing.

In the routing tables approach, the determination of the next node on the route depends on rules established a priori. The routing may be *static*, such that messages for a given source-destination pair always follow a predefined fixed path through the network. The node processor uses the routing tables, such as the one for node T_2 shown in Fig. 3-5(b) for the network in Fig. 3-5(a), to determine the adjacent node for forwarding a given message. Alternatively, routing may be *dynamic*, in which a message path through the transit nodes is determined as the message progresses toward the destination node. This decision may be based on factors such as network loads, link capacities, and estimated delays to reach the destination node. The minimum expected delay (to reach a destination node) approach is used in ARPANET (see Chap. 7). In this approach, each node routes a received message to that adjacent node through which the message may reach the destination node in minimum expected time. In either case, the source node and the destination node cooperate in establishing the message path. We present the topic of network routing in greater detail in Chap. 7.

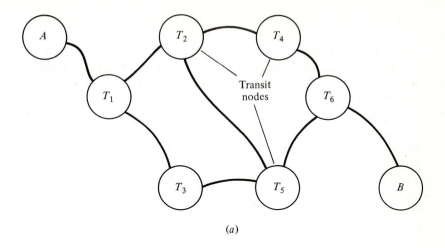

(a)

Destination node ⟶

		B		T_3	T_4	T_5	
A	T_4			T_5	T_4	T_5	
T_3	T_4			—	T_4	T_5	
T_4	T_5			T_1	—	T_5	
T_5	T_4			T_1	T_4	—	

Source node

(b)

Figure 3-5(a) Source node, transit node, and destination node for a message flow. (b) Routing Table for node T2, with partially complete entries. Each entry in the table identifies the adjacent node to forward the message. [Note: a routing table may be based simply on the destination node, thereby eliminating the need to include the source node. In that case, the routing table reduces to a vector (or an array), resulting in fewer routes than those provided by the above table.]

Local flow control and lockups The subject of flow control and dead-locks is treated in detail in Chap. 6, but is introduced here in the context of a transit node.

Each network node must protect its resources. When each message buffer in a node has been allocated and no free buffer exists, the node is said to be *congested*. The phenomenon of *store-and-forward lockups* may result under such conditions. Consider a set of two or more connected nodes that have all their buffers allocated to messages, and thus have no available message buffers. Assume that each message in these nodes is to be forwarded to a node within this set. Then, no movement of messages can take place, and this part of the network is in a store-and-forward lockup, as shown in Fig. 3-6. For simplicity, each node is assumed to have two message buffers. This phenomenon has been investigated by several authors [3, 4, and 7].

The mechanism to prevent congestion and store-and-forward lockups for a transit node is called *local flow control*. A simple approach to provide local flow control is to establish a threshold for the number of occupied buffers, out of the buffer pool in each node. Whenever the threshold is reached, that node may inform (through some control messages) each of its adjacent nodes to cease all message transmissions to it. The threshold should be established so that extreme situations can be avoided. If the threshold is set very high (say,

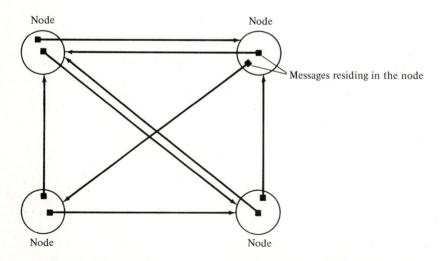

Figure 3-6 Lockup condition in a set of interconnected nodes. A message at the trailing edge of an arrow is waiting for a buffer in the node at the leading edge of the arrow.

98 percent), the above situation may result in a *near-deadlock* condition. In this condition, it may be too late to prevent complete depletion of the free buffers in the node. On the other hand, a very low threshold (say, 50 percent) may result in unnecessary rejection of message transmissions to the nodes, thus leading to longer message delays and to additional processing of control messages.

Error control *Error control* pertains to detection of and recovery from errors during message transmission. Error control for message transmission may be performed as follows. A transit node detects and identifies transmission errors in messages from its adjacent nodes. Using the frame check sequence characters described in Sec. 2-3, a node may determine if the message transmission was successful. Otherwise, a negative acknowledgment is sent for that message. Upon receiving a negative acknowledgment, the sender retransmits the same message. Besides frame check sequence, a transit node may employ other techniques, such as checking the end-to-end sequence numbers, to provide error control.

Network-Wide Functions

Network-wide functions pertain to the behavior of the network, such as its performance measurement and configuration management. These functions may be centralized in a single node of the network. In this case, a control node performs all these functions with minimal involvement from other nodes. Alternatively, each node may individually perform most of the functions and periodically update the control node, if required. The above two approaches are often called *centralized network management* and *decentralized network management*, respectively.

Network flow control The network must be globally protected from congestion; that is, it must avoid excessive demand on its resources, such as message buffers. Messages that cannot be delivered within an expected time should not be permitted to enter the network. Network flow control prevents congestion by managing message traffic that either is within the network or is entering the network.

Topological awareness and modification A network may be represented as a graph $G = (X, A)$, where X is the set of nodes and A is the set of arcs that join the nodes in X. The term *network topology* implies defining sets X and A of the network graph G. In other words, it defines the locations of the nodes and establishes the connections to be made between them. Network topology is used to determine message routes and to implement network flow control. Network topology may change over time as a result of the addition or deletion of nodes or links. Some nodes or links may temporarily fail, or the network operator may take down some nodes or links for short periods to perform testing or maintenance.

In networks with centralized route assignments, the topological information is maintained in a central node. The central node periodically sends a test message to each node and receives the status of that node. Furthermore, any change in topology is communicated immediately to the central node as follows. Suppose that node H fails in the network of Fig. 3-1. Each adjacent node (T, A, and D) then sends a control message to central node C. This node processes the control messages and sends updates for the routing tables in nodes T, A, and D, so that an alternate path may be used for routes that were previously directed through node H. A corresponding action brings up or adds a node or link to the network. The primary advantage of the centralized route assignment scheme lies in the ease with which network topology and total traffic can be managed. The disadvantages include the overhead for transmitting control messages to the central node for notification of topological changes, and the delay in updating routing tables resulting from these changes.

Topological information may also be distributed in each node. In this case, each node remembers the status, or existence, of each attached link and adjacent node. Message routing is determined by each node depending on its adjacent nodes and attached links. Distributed schemes, such as this, are attractive for those networks in which frequent topological changes are anticipated. They minimize the overhead for the special control messages (required in the centralized scheme) that broadcast topological changes, and their updates are timely. However, distributed schemes do not provide a convenient means of collecting network-wide information, such as total network traffic.

Network performance measurement and monitoring Network performance may be measured periodically to record its behavior. A central node may receive control messages at fixed time intervals from each node. The control message(s) may contain information on the performance of the node in which the message originated and on its associated transmission links. The parameters of general interest are the message transit time through the network and the throughput of the network. The throughput may be considered as the number of messages or characters per unit of time through the network. Other performance measures of interest may be buffer utilization, message queuing statistics, node processor utilization, and link utilization statistics.

In addition to measuring performance, some functions may be included to monitor network components. For example, the existence of a *near-deadlock* condition (described earlier) may be detected. At times, certain links may encounter consistent transmission errors, resulting in an above-average frequency of retransmissions. The network operator may take remedial action, such as discarding messages in a congested node or taking down the error-prone link. Extensive monitoring of network behavior has been provided for the ARPA-NET [5, 10]. Finally, the network nodes should permit a broad range of on-line testing of links, routes, and nodes.

3-2 NODE ARCHITECTURE AND ANALYSIS

The architecture of a network node defines its logical components, their characteristics, and interfaces. As shown in Fig. 3-7, a network node consists of a software system, a memory for the software system (including a set of message buffers), one or more central processors, and associated peripheral or interface hardware. The software consists

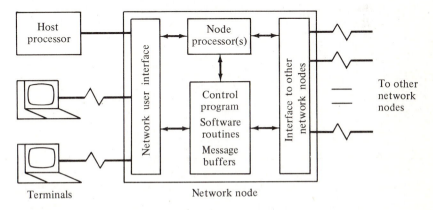

Figure 3-7 Components of a network node.

of a control program for the node, and possibly some software routines for transaction processing. The message buffers provide storage for queuing messages through the node. The node processors execute instructions under the supervision of the control program. The interface hardware of a given node permits communication between the node and network users, as well as other nodes, through transmission links.

Software

A communication network is operated, controlled, and managed through control programs that reside in various components of the network. The host processor may contain application programs, databases, files, and communication-access methods. A communication access method, such as IBM's Virtual Telecommunications Access Method or TeleCommunications Access Method, is a set of software routines used by a host operating system to interface with telecommunication equipment. The communication-access method may be viewed as the host interface for network nodes, terminals, or terminal equipment. The software routines for a network node provide the functions described earlier and shown in Fig. 3-8. We summarize these functions here from the network software viewpoint. (The processing hierarchy for these functions is described in Sec. 3-3.)

Error-handling routines. Handle errors in software, memory, or processor(s).

Link-handling routines. Provide link controls such as acknowledgments, polling, and link errors, and assemble the bits from the links into characters or segmenting characters into bits for transmission on the links. (This function is also called *serializing* and *deserializing*.)

Message handling routines. Store and move messages through the node, message routing, and flow control.

Network protocol routines. Handle end-to-end protocols, sequence numbers, transit node protocols, flow control, and user interface protocols to access the network.

Queue management routines. Handle message queues for links or host processors. These routines also manage the task queues to process messages within the node.

Buffer-management routines. Manage the pool of available (free) and allocated buffers for messages. In a given node, these buffers are used for message or packet switching, and for assembling packets

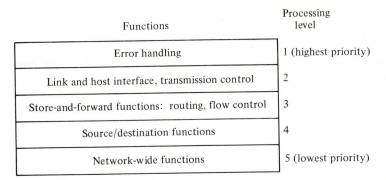

Figure 3-8 Network node software structure and corresponding processing hierarchy.

into messages destined for the node in which the buffers reside (if packet switching is used).

User exits. Permit user exits for special processing, such as data or code conversion, formatting, transaction handling, and report generation.

Support programs. Initial node activation (generally called *initial program load*, or IPL). Provide maintenance routines such as dump, test routines, operator interface, and other network-wide functions.

The IBM 3705 communications controller may be viewed as a network node for IBM's Systems Network Architecture.* An overview of the structure of IBM 3705 communications controller is included at the end of this chapter.

Interface Hardware

The interface hardware of a network node provides connection to the network users, such as terminals and host processors, and to other nodes in the network. The interface for the host processor cooperates with the host access method in executing channel protocols. The link protocols are executed through the link interface. In general, a separate interface may be needed for each type of link protocol, such as start/stop, binary synchronous, or synchronous data link control (described in Sec. 2-3), due to the unique characteristics of the protocols, such as the acknowledgment scheme, idle characters, and block check characters. Several functions described as software routines may be

* SNA is described in Chap. 5.

included in the form of microcode in the interface hardware. Finally, separate microprocessors may be employed to perform individual functions.

The interface hardware includes the attachment facilities and the appropriate modem interfaces for adjacent terminals, nodes, or host processors. It may also include *interface buffers*, which provide intermediate buffering between links and message buffers. As shown in Fig. 3-9, these buffers are used in assembling characters for the bits received from or transmitted to the link. In the following section, we analyze the problems associated with overflow on these buffers.

Message retransmission caused by overflow on intermediate buffers Link-handling routines may be part of the control program or may be microcoded separately in the link interface hardware. As described earlier, these routines accumulate the received bits from the links into a character, and then transfer the character to the message buffer. Link-handling routines also determine whether a received character is a control character (such as a poll or an acknowledgment character) or a data character, perform block checking, and store the

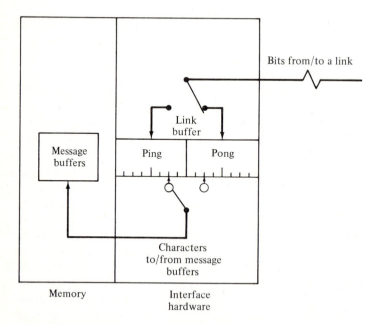

Figure 3-9 Data movement between transmission links and message buffers.

characters accordingly. The above functions are executed for the receive side. (A corresponding action takes place for the transmit side.) Any delay in this processing may result in an overflow of the interface buffer, thereby requiring retransmission of the received message. Thus, the result of such an error is similar to a link-transmission error. Hence, in general, such retransmissions may be satisfactory if the rate of buffer overflow does not exceed the transmission error rate on the link. This phenomenon is analyzed for the receive operation by using the example of a communication link scanner that operates on a character basis.

Figure 3-9 shows the operation of a communication scanner that transfers a character at a time to the message buffer in the node. The link-handling hardware receives the bits and saves them in 1 of the 2 link character spaces of the link buffer. (There is one such 2-character buffer for the receive side of each link.) Once 8 bits from the link have been received in a character buffer, say, PING, the next 8 bits from the link are saved in the other character buffer, or PONG. The completed character (in PING buffer) is transferred into the message buffer, while, at the same time, the link interface hardware is filling the other (PONG) character buffer. Thus, the PING buffer must be emptied within 8 bit times of its associated link. Otherwise, the new bits arriving from the link cannot be saved anywhere, resulting in the bits being discarded and eventual retransmission of the message. Since the link interface hardware accumulates and then moves a character at a time, it is called a *character-level scanner*. So, the request to move the character must be handled by the node processor within one character time of the link. But there may be several links attached to the node that are bringing characters to be processed. Thus, to avoid overflow of link buffers, the node processor should be able to service all such requests in one character time of a given link.

Let τ be one character time of the highest-speed link receiving characters, later referred to as *critical time*. If link speeds are different, critical time is the character time of the highest-speed link receiving characters. Also, let PR be the processor time required to service one request, that is the same as executing link-handling routines to check and move a character into the message buffer from the link buffer. Then, the maximum number of serviceable requests within a given critical time is simply FLOOR(τ/PR) or, say, r. The FLOOR function provides the highest integer that is less than its argument. If there are N links with identical link speed, and the probability that a given link is receiving characters is p, then the probability of overflow α of a link buffer can be derived by adding all the probabilities for r or more lines being active at the same time. Then, using the binomial distribution,*

$$\alpha = \sum_{k=r}^{N} \binom{N}{k} p^k (1 - p)^{N-k} \tag{3-1}$$

For large N, we can use the Poisson or normal approximation. If S is the average message size in characters, the probability that a given message is retransmitted is

$$1 - (1 - \alpha)^S \tag{3-2}$$

assuming that the message traffic is independent at each character time. Often, all links on a node do not operate at the same speed. Let there be m link groups, such that the link speed, message size, and message rate within each link group is the same. For each link group i, we compute the probability of overrun. If LS_i is the speed in characters per second for each link in this group, a request for any link in the group must be serviced in one character time, or

$$CT_i = \frac{1}{LS_i} \tag{3-3}$$

The probability that there are b service requests from the jth link affecting service for the ith link group, or $p(i, b, j)$, is determined as follows. In order to obtain b interrupts, the jth link group should only have $b/\text{CIEL}(LS_j/LS_i)$ links active. The function CIEL assigns the next higher integer value to its argument, if the argument does not have an integral value. So, let $y = b/\text{CIEL}(LS_j/LS_i)$. Then

$$p(i, b, j) = \binom{N_j}{y} p_j^y (1 - p_j)^{N_j - y} \tag{3-4}$$

where N_j is the number of links in the jth link group, p_j is the probability that a given link in jth group is active, and $y = 1$ to N_j.

For each link group j, and the value of y ranging from 1 to N_j (number of links in link group j), we obtain the probability that the jth link group has b requests, or $p(i, b, j)$. (Recall that these probabilities are only with respect to a specific link group, the ith group). For each value of b, the processing time required is, say, T'. Let D_j be the resulting density function (or the values of p versus T') for link group j. But there may be several such link groups. In order to obtain the total effect of these link groups, we must combine these probabilities

* Described in Chap. 8.

into a single probability function, or "convolve" these probability density functions. Thus, we convolve the density functions for all link groups in the network node to obtain a composite density function. Let P denote the final probability function for all link groups, and T the corresponding processing time requirements. Then, the probability of a character overflow on the ith link group is given by

$$\alpha_i = \sum_{T(z) > CT_i - t_i} P(z) \tag{3-5}$$

where $P(z)$ is the probability corresponding to the processing time $T(z)$, such that $T(z)$ is more than the difference of CT_i (critical time for a link in the ith link group) and the time to process one service request (t_i).

In other words, the probability for overflow of a character is the sum of all probabilities (given by P in the convolved distribution) for which the required processing times (T in the convolved distribution) exceeds the available time ($CT_i - t_i$). Then the probability of re-transmission of a message on the ith link group is given by

$$1 - (1 - \alpha_i)^{S_i} \tag{3-6}$$

Note that in computing the density functions, we should consider $N_i - 1$ links for the ith link group in eq. (3-4). This is true since we are considering the overflow probability for a given link (that cannot have any more character arrivals) in that link group. Processing for this given link in the ith link group may be interrupted by other ($N_i - 1$) links in the ith link group. In the above analysis, we also assumed that no other process may interrupt the processing of received characters. This is a simplifying assumption that may not be always true. (For example, a higher priority process, such as error handling, may interfere with servicing requests for character transfers.) Such interference may be accounted for by reducing the value of available processor time CT_i by a time interval equal to the higher priority processing expected to occur in time CT_i.

Example Let us consider a specific link configuration for a node. There are six half-duplex links operating at 9600 bps, and six half-duplex links operating at 4800 bps. The message size is 100 characters, and each of the 12 links transmits 4 messages/s. There is a 2-character link buffer for each link, as shown in Fig. 3-9. What is the probability of overflow on a link buffer assuming it takes 100 μs of the node processor to service a request?

Link time for 1 character on 9600-bps link

$$= (1/1200) \text{ s}$$

$$= 833 \ \mu\text{s}$$

$$= CT_i$$

We estimate the probability of overflow on a 9600-bps link. Let us assume (the worst case) that a given link had a service request and that it is the last link serviced in the 833-μs interval. Therefore, the time available for other service requests is

$$833 - 100 = 733 \ \mu\text{s} \tag{3-7}$$

Thus, if there are more than seven other service requests in the 833-μs interval, then an overflow will occur. The probability for seven or more service requests is estimated as follows.

Now, the probability that a 9600-bps link is busy is

$$= \frac{\text{Number of messages per second} \times \text{message size}}{\text{Link speed}}$$

$$= \frac{4 \times 100}{1200} = .33$$

Then, the probability density function for the number of service requests from the remaining five 9600-bps links (note that the sixth link has already indicated a service request, and we are estimating its link buffer overflow) is given by the binomial distribution

$$\binom{5}{k} \times .33^k \times (1 - .33)^{5-k}$$

where k is the number of service requests. The values are tabulated below:

Number of service requests	Probability
0	.13
1	.33
2	.33
3	.16
4	.04
5	.01

In order to include the effect of all links on the given 9600-bps link, we must also consider links that operate at 4800 bps. The probability that a 4800-bps link is busy is

$$\frac{4 \times 100}{600} = .67$$

Then, the probability density function for service requests from these links is given by

$$\binom{6}{k} \times .67^k \times (1 - .67)^{6-k}$$

These values are tabulated below:

Number of requests from 4800 bps links (k)	Number of requests considered for 9600 bps links	Probability
0	0	0
1	1	.02
2	1	.08
3	2	.22
4	2	.33
5	3	.26
6	3	.09

The middle column gives the effective number of service requests from the 4800-bps links, to be considered for the 9600-bps links. (This is due to the fact that characters may arrive on 4800-bps link every 1666 μs, compared to 833 μs on the 9600-bps links.) By convolving the density functions for 9600-bps and 4800-bps links, we obtain the composite function for the node configuration. This provides the buffer overflow probability for a 9600-bps link, as tabulated below:

Number of requests	Probability
0	0
1	.013
2	.1045
3	.26
4	.313
5	.2075
6	.079
7	.0195
8	.0035

But we already established in eq. (3-7) that a buffer overflow will occur only if the number of service requests exceeds seven. Therefore, in the above example, there is at most a .0035 probability that a 9600-bps link will have a link buffer overflow. Then, the probability that a message on the link is to be retransmitted is

$$\leq 1 - (1 - .0035)^{100} \qquad \text{or} \qquad \leq .296$$

Transmit processing may also result in *underruns* (no character available to be transmitted) due to the delay in bringing a character from a message buffer into the link buffer. In binary synchronous protocols (Sec. 2-3), SYN characters are used to fill these underruns.

The frequency of retransmission may be reduced by permitting larger link buffers. This would simply permit more requests to be serviced, thus reducing the probability of overflow. For example, in the above analysis, we may provide storage for 4 characters for each of the link buffers. This will increase the value of available service time for a request, or CT_i in eq. (3-3), to $3/LS_i$, allowing the fourth buffer for transferring a character to the message buffers. Now, the number of character arrivals in a given link group will also increase correspondingly. But it will result in a reduction in the probability of message retransmission. We leave it as an exercise for the reader to verify this statement (prob. 3-5).

Besides extending the link buffers, the link-handling routines may be partially microcoded in the link interface hardware. In this case, all character processing may be completed by the link interface hardware, except for the insertion of the character into the message buffer. The character may be moved into the message buffer by requiring a single memory access. However, an interrupt of the control program by the link interface hardware is required at the beginning and end of each message.

3-3 NODE PROCESSOR

The network *node processor* executes the software routines and manages the communication links. The node processor may be interrupt-driven based on a priority structure. Several tasks, such as line character handling, should be given a higher priority than routing or testing. A possible priority structure is shown in Fig. 3-8. The highest priority is assigned to error-handling routines. The link-handling routines process requests to service the links, such as handling the receipt or transmission of characters on the links. These tasks should be assigned the next-highest priority so that there is minimal interference from other processes leading to message retransmissions, as discussed in the preceding section. The message routing and local flow control (store-and-forward functions) are proposed at the next level. All source/destination functions should be executed at the next priority. Thus, the message traffic, such as that associated with a transit node (such as node T in Fig. 3-1), is processed at a higher priority than the end-to-end processing. Network-wide functions, such as performance measurements, network monitoring, and the like, may wait in deference to the above functions. (An exception is the network-wide function of global flow control, which should be given a higher priority.) The underlying principle here is to minimize queues for time-dependent processes, such as receiving or transmitting data on the links. An alternate approach is to assign one or more microprocessors to each of the above levels. This approach may offer added capacity, but involves overhead for coordinating the different processors.

An important performance aspect of node architecture is the processor overhead required to change interrupt levels. This change permits a higher priority task to take over the processor and, at the end of this task, returns the processor to the next (lower) priority. The resulting processing overhead may be significant because of the high frequency of changing processing levels in the node processor. Each interrupt level may be identified by a set of user registers and an instruction address register. Upon changing an interrupt level, the register values may be saved, and retrieved later when the processor returns to its previous level. The saving and retrieving of registers should be performed efficiently, thereby reducing overhead. Alternatively, a separate set of registers may be provided for each interrupt level.

It may be desirable to permit (network) user-specified priority. The user may desire that some of the terminals (and therefore, the links) be serviced at a higher priority than other terminals. Even from a performance viewpoint, a higher-speed link should, in general, be processed at a higher priority than a lower-speed link. This may be implemented by assigning the processing for high-priority links to higher-priority processing levels.

The instruction set for a network node should be optimized for character, buffer, and address handling. For example, the processor may be designed to provide fast Move Character and Store/Load

Character instruction at the expense of slow Divide and Multiply instructions. Perhaps the most frequently executed instructions are Load and Store, resulting from data movement through the node. The next most frequent instructions may be for buffer or message handling, such as Branch, Compare, and Add.

Processor Capacity Estimation

The required capacity of a node processor may be estimated in terms of the number of instructions it executes each second. We use the following notation: N is the number of transmission links attached to the node (for simplicity, we assume that each link has identical characteristics, described below); LS, the link speed in characters per second; SI, the average size in characters for incoming messages to the node; SX, the average size in characters for outgoing messages from the node; SC, the average control message size in characters, such as a poll; RI, the incoming message rate per second per link; RX, the outgoing message rate per second per link; RC, the control message rate per second per link; PI, the number of instructions required to process an inbound message; PX, the number of instructions required to process an outbound message; PC, the number of instructions required to process a control message, such as a poll or acknowledgment; and T', the capacity of the node processor in instructions per second.

Let us digress temporarily and discuss the above parameters. First, we assume that each type of instruction requires an equal amount of processing time. (Otherwise, we should work with some other unit, such as the total number of processor cycles required.) Second, the number of instructions PI and PX are assumed to be fixed, but may actually depend on several parameters, such as the size of the respective messages. A long message may require several message buffers and thus more processing to handle those buffers.

The poll rate RC may be derived from link speed, message rate, and message size. Assuming that the link is polled whenever it is not receiving or transmitting messages, the poll rate may be estimated by dividing the time on the link (in terms of characters) when there is no receive or send traffic, by the time for a poll. So,

$$RC = \frac{LS - (RI \times SI) - (RX \times SX)}{SC}$$

Then, the average processor capacity required is simply

$$N[(PI \times RI) + (PX \times RX) + (PC \times RC)]$$

instructions per second.

Next, we address the estimation of excess processing demand on the node processor. The processing of asynchronously arriving messages may result in an excessive instantaneous demand on the node processor. Since the processor can service only at a fixed rate, some message processing may be delayed. Excessive delay in processing may result in poor performance, such as a longer transit time through the network. If sustained for long, this delay may lead to long message queues and a depletion of available memory buffers. We describe an approach to estimate the probability distribution of processing demand for a given network node. The measure we derive should give an estimate of that instantaneous demand on the processor which must be deferred.*

We illustrate this measure with an example.

Example Assume that a node processor has 100 cycles available in 1 s. There are two half-duplex links being serviced; each is active 40 percent of the time and requires 30 cycles/s. Then, the average utilization of the processor is $30 + 30 = 60$ percent. Now, consider the interval when both links are active. Assuming that the activity on the two links is mutually independent, the probability that both links are active is $.4 \times .4 = .16$, or a time interval equivalent to 16 processor cycles in each second. But, during this interval, each link demands $16 \times 30/40 = 12$ cycles. Thus, the two links require 24 cycles during which interval only 16 cycles are available. Therefore, we conclude that there is a 16 percent probability that processor demand will reach 24/16, or 150 percent.

The processing demand measure is derived for a set of links that have identical characteristics, such as link speed and message rate. A given link may be in one of exactly four possible states:

1. Receive state (receiving characters into the network node).
2. Transmit state (transmitting characters from the network node).
3. Control state (sending or receiving a poll, or acknowledging a message transmission).
4. Idle state (performing none of the above functions).

---

* This work was developed by V. Ahuja and Frank E. Herin. Mr. Herin is currently at the IBM Commercial Branch Office, Atlanta, Georgia.

We make a simplifying assumption that, in a given state, the processing demand for the link is that required to process characters associated with that state. The probability that a link is in the receive state is $SI \times RI/LS$. The processing required in the receive state for the link is $PI \times RI$ instructions per second. Thus, we obtain the probability density function for the processing demand for a link as follows:

State	Probability	Processing demand
Receive	$SI \times RI/LS$	$PI \times RI/T'$
Transmit	$SX \times RX/LS$	$PX \times RX/T'$
Control	$SC \times RC/LS$	$PC \times RC/T'$
Idle	$1 -$ sum of above probabilities	0

Now, this is the discrete density function for a single link. The density function for two links $P_x(z)$ is obtained by convolving the two density functions, as follows:

$$P_{x1+x2}(z) = \int_0^z P_{x1}(z_1)P_{x2}(z - z_1) \, dz, \, z_1 \leq z$$

The process may be repeated for several links. Then, the distribution function for processing demand is simply

$$\text{Prob}(x > u) = \int_u^\infty P_x(z) \, dz$$

for the probability that the processing demand exceeds u.

Example There are four 4800-bps half-duplex links attached to a node processor. Each link is receiving and transmitting one 100-character message/s, and is polling at the fixed rate of 6 polls/s. Assume that it takes 2000 instructions to process a received or a transmitted message, and 80 instructions to process a poll. If the processor can execute 50,000 instructions/s, then what is the probability that processing demand will exceed the processor capacity?

Using the above approach, and considering the processing demand as the random variable, we obtain the probability for the time that the link is busy providing a given function. For example, for the receive state, the processing demand is 2000/50,000, or .04. The probability for the random variable (the processing demand) to attain this value is the fraction of the time the link is in receive state, or $100/600 = .16$. We assume that each poll takes 12 characters on the link. The probability density function for the processing demand is tabulated below.

Link operation	Processing demand	Probability
Receive	.04	.16
Transmit	.04	.16
Polling	.01	.12
Idle	0	$1 - .44$

In order to obtain the processing demand for four links, we convolve the above function four times. The resulting processing demand function is plotted in Fig. 3-10. Thus, in this case, processing demand does not exceed capacity (1.0 in Fig. 3-10).

Now, let us assume that the message size is 10 characters and that

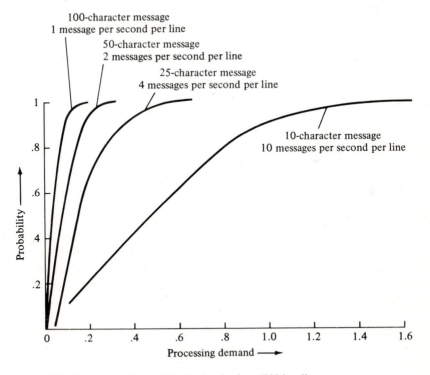

Figure 3-10 Processing demand distribution for four 4800-bps lines.

each link receives and transmits 10 messages/s. Total processing demand, using the above procedure, is also shown in Fig. 3-10. Here, the probability that the processing demand exceeds capacity is (1 − probability for processing demand of 1) or .09. The processing demand is also plotted for two 50-character messages/s and four 25-character messages/s. Note that in each case the links are nearly equally loaded for receive, transmit, and poll operations. The difference in processing demand exists since processing is fixed on a message basis, not on a character basis.

The computational cost of such an approach increases rapidly with the number of links. This is true because of the large number of entries in the discrete function resulting at the end of each convolution step. But the central limit theorem helps here. By this theorem, if there are n identically distributed random variables $X_i, \ldots, X_n$, then the distribution of the sum $S_n = X_1 + \cdots + X_n$, for large n, may be given by

$$P(S_n \leq x) \approx \Phi\left[\frac{(x - E(S_n))}{\sqrt{V(S_n)}}\right]$$

where Φ is the standard normal distribution, $E(S_n)$ is the mean of S_n, and $V(S_n)$ is the variance of S_n. Assuming that events on all links are independent and the corresponding random variables are identically distributed, the mean and variance of S_n is simply the sum of means and variances of the random variables $X_1, \ldots, X_n$. Hoel, Port, and Stone [12, p. 186] quote numerical studies indicating that, in typical practical applications, $n = 25$ is sufficiently large for the above approximation to be useful.

3-4 NODE MEMORY

The memory for network nodes should permit fast access by the processor and the interface hardware so as to permit timely operations on the links and host channels. If direct memory access is provided, the interface hardware may save or retrieve data, for links or host channels, from the memory without assistance from the node processor. If several microprocessors are used, such as one or more for each of the levels in Fig. 3-8, the memory may permit access to several processors at the same time. The problems of contention on the memory and simultaneous write operations may be resolved by such techniques as queuing the requests and permitting memory access

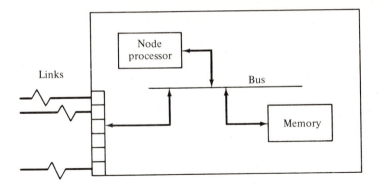

Figure 3-11 Memory structure of a network node.

only to a single processor at a time. Figure 3-11 illustrates a simple memory structure of a network node.

Network nodes may also employ *cache* memory, in which more than one memory levels is available, with each level offering a different memory access time. Level 1 (or cache) offers a faster speed, say S', for each memory access than level 2, which has access speed S''. (The memory access speed is the time required to perform a read or write operation for a fixed-length data, such as 1, 2, or 4 bytes, on the memory.) Thus, the commonly accessed software routines are copied from level 2 into level 1. One of the common schemes to use the cache is described next. Every memory access begins with the cache memory. If there is a miss (the desired data is not in cache), then the level 2 memory is accessed. This implies that the address translation algorithm should first map memory access into the cache, and only a miss is to be forwarded to the level 2 memory. In addition, a mechanism is required to continually update the cache from level 2 memory, in order to minimize the number of accesses that are forwarded to level 2.

In the following discussion, we obtain some simple measures that estimate performance improvement attributed to cache memories over other memories.*

For cache memories, assume that the probability a memory access is required in level 1 is p, which depends, on the size of the cache as well as on other factors. Any memory access that is finally resolved in level 2 must have been checked first for the cache memory, thereby requiring $S' + S''$ access time. If there is a total of R memory

* The reader is referred to [9] for details on cache memories.

accesses per unit time (this time unit being the same as that for S' and S''), the total access time for cache memory is

$$pRS' + (1 - p) R (S' + S'')$$

Next, the total access time for the memory without cache is simply RS, where S is the access speed for the memory without cache. Let F be the improvement factor of cache memory compared to that without cache; that is, F is the ratio of total access time for memory without cache to that with cache. We may estimate the value of F as follows. Let $S' = kS''$. Then,

$$RS = F(pRS' + (1 - p) R (S' + S''))$$

$$= FpkRS'' + (FR - FRp) S'' (1 + k)$$

$$= FpkRS'' + FRS'' + FRS''k - FRpS'' - FRpS''k$$

After some simplification, we obtain

$$F = \frac{S}{S''(1 + k - p)} \tag{3-8}$$

Next, we derive the average time spent in a single memory access, including the waiting time, considering the memory as an M/M/1 system.* The average service time for cache memory is simply the total access time (derived above) divided by R, or $S''(1 + k - p)$. The average service time for memory without cache is S. (But these time estimates do not include waiting times.) The average utilization of memory without cache is RS. For the memory with cache, it is given by

$$RS''(1 + k - p)$$

Now, the mean time spent by a customer in an M/M/1 system is given by the average service time, which is S and $S''(1 + k - p)$, for non-cache and cache memories, respectively, multiplied by average memory utilization, and divided by 1 minus the average memory utilization. Thus, the total time, including the waiting time, for an access is $RS^2/1 - RS$ for the memory without cache, and

$$\frac{R(S''(1 + k - p))^2}{1 - RS''(1 + k - p)} \tag{3-9}$$

for the memory using cache.

---

* In an M/M/1 system, the arrivals come at random with a Poisson distribution, and the service time is exponentially distributed. See Chap. 8 for details.

Memory Size Estimation

The total memory size required for a network node is the sum of the requirements for (1) the control program, (2) the transaction processing routines, and (3) the message buffers. The first two depend on the software design of the individual communication processor. In this section, we address the problem of estimating the amount of message buffers. The first approach is based on the M/M/1 system (exponential arrival and single exponential server) and draws heavily from [11]; the second approach derives from [6].

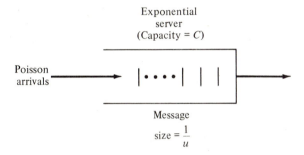

Beginning with the first approach,* let λ be the average message arrival rate, $1/u$ the average message size, and C the capacity of the outbound link. We find the probability $p_n(t)$ that there are n messages present in the buffer at time t. Then, the state p_n can be reached from the states p_{n-1}, p_n, or p_{n+1}, in time dt as follows.

As $dt \rightarrow 0$, no more than one message may arrive or depart. Thus, the probability that the buffer is in state p_n at time $t + dt$ is the sum of (1) $p_n(t)$ times the probability that there is no arrival $(1 - \lambda \, dt)$ and no departure $(1 - uC\lambda \, dt)$, or one arrival $(\lambda \, dt)$ and one departure $(uC \, dt)$; (2) if the buffer is in state p_{n+1} at time t, then $p_{n+1}(t)$ times the probability for no arrival and one departure; and (3) if buffer is in state p_{n-1} at time t, then $p_{n-1}(t)$ times the probability for one arrival and no departure. So,

$$p_n(t + dt) = p_n(t)[(1 - uC \, dt)(1 - \lambda \, dt) + uC \, dt \, \lambda \, dt]$$
$$+ p_{n+1}(t)[uC \, dt \, (1 - \lambda \, dt)]$$
$$+ p_{n-1}(t)[\lambda \, dt \, (1 - uC \, dt)] \tag{3-10}$$

* Mischa Schwartz, *Computer-Communication Network Design and Analysis*, Prentice-Hall, Englewood Cliffs, N.J., 1977, pp. 156–157. Adapted by permission.

Assuming that the probabilities for various states are continuous, the steady-state solution of the eq. (3-10) is

$$p_n(t + dt) = p_n(t)[1 - \lambda\, dt - uC\, dt + 2\, uC\, dt\, \lambda\, dt]$$
$$+ p_{n+1}(t)[uC\, dt - uC\, dt\, \lambda\, dt]$$
$$+ p_{n-1}(t)[\lambda\, dt - \lambda\, dt\, uC\, dt]$$

or $\quad p_n(t + dt) - p_n(t) + p_n(t)[\lambda\, dt + uC\, dt - 2\, uC\, dt\, \lambda\, dt]$

$$= p_{n+1}(t)[uC\, dt - uC\, dt\, \lambda\, dt]$$
$$+ p_{n-1}(t)[\lambda\, dt - \lambda\, dt\, uC\, dt]$$

As $dt \to 0$, $t + dt \to t$ and terms with $dt \times dt$ may be neglected; thus,

$$p_n(t)[\lambda\, dt + uC\, dt] = p_{n+1}(t)[uC\, dt] + p_{n-1}(t)[\lambda\, dt]$$

Canceling dt throughout the expressions,

$$p_n(t)[\lambda + uC] = p_{n+1}(t)[uC] + p_{n-1}(t)[\lambda]$$

or for steady state

$$p_n[\lambda + uC] = p_{n+1}[uC] + \lambda\, p_{n-1} \qquad (3\text{-}11)$$

For $n = 0$, there will be no terms using p_{n-1} in eq. (3-10) and there is no departure in state p_0; therefore,

$$p_0(t + dt) = p_0(t)[(1 - \lambda\, dt) + uC\, dt\, \lambda\, dt]$$
$$+ p_1(t)[uC\, dt(1 - \lambda\, dt)]$$

Its steady-state solution is

$$\lambda\, p_0 = uC\, p_1$$

So $\qquad p_1 = \dfrac{\lambda\, p_0}{uC}$

$$= \rho\, p_0 \qquad (3\text{-}12)$$

where $\qquad \rho = \dfrac{\lambda}{uC}$

$$= \text{server utilization}$$

or the traffic intensity, which is the ratio of the offered load λ, and the capacity uC.

Using eq. (3-11),

$$p_1[\lambda + uC] = p_2[uC] + \lambda\, p_0$$

$$p_2 = p_1[1 + \rho] - p_0\,\rho \qquad \text{using } \rho = \lambda/uC$$

$$= \rho^2\, p_0 \qquad\qquad \text{using } p_1 = \rho\, p_0$$

or

$$p_n = \rho^n\, p_0$$

Assuming the buffer size is N, we know that

$$\sum_{n=0}^{N} p_n = 1$$

$$= p_0 \sum_{n=0}^{N} \rho^n$$

$$= p_0\, \frac{1 - \rho^{N+1}}{1 - \rho}$$

using the sum of a geometric progression. Therefore,

$$p_0 = \frac{1 - \rho}{1 - \rho^{N+1}}$$

or

$$p_n = \rho^n\, \frac{1 - \rho}{1 - \rho^{N+1}} \tag{3-13}$$

Now, new messages are rejected if there are already N messages in the node. But the probability that there are N messages is the same as when the buffer is in state p_N. Therefore,

$$p_N = p_0\, \rho^N$$

$$= \frac{(1 - \rho)\rho^N}{1 - \rho^{N+1}}$$

$$= \text{probability of overflow (or } p_{of}).$$

Figure 3-12 relates the buffer size—in characters, equal to N/u—average message size $1/u$, and traffic intensity ρ. It assumes that the probability of overflow is 1 in 10^6.

The second approach is due to Chu [6; 11, pp. 155–159] and is based on enumerating specific expressions for buffer occupancy and solving them. For the following analysis, let N be the number of characters in the buffers, t the service time during which at most 1

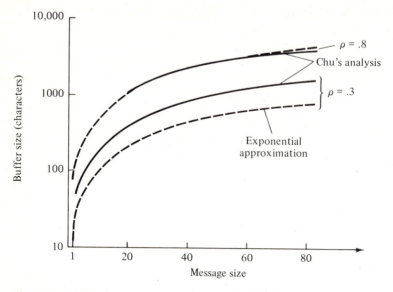

Figure 3-12 Buffer size versus message length, $P_{of} = 10^{-6}$. (From W. W. Chu, "Buffer Behavior for Batch Poisson Arrivals and Single Constant Output," *IEEE Transactions on Communication Technology*, COM-18, no. 5, October 1970, pp. 613–618. Adapted by permission.)

character is released by the buffer, Π_k the probability of k characters arriving in t seconds, and p_n the probability that n characters are present in the buffer.

We assume that the system has reached an equilibrium state. The state of the buffers is represented by p_n, with n varying from 0 to N. The set of equilibrium equations that relate the various states of the buffer is derived as follows. First, the probability p_0 is based on the events that (1) there was 1 character in the previous interval and no character arrived but the character served left ($\Pi_0 p_1$), or (2) there is no character in the buffer and none arrived ($\Pi_0 p_0$). Therefore,

$$p_0 = \Pi_0 p_1 + \Pi_0 p_0$$

Next we derive the probability p_1 for 1 character present in the buffer. This is the sum of three conditional probabilities:

1. Two characters were present; 1 character left, and none arrived: $\Pi_0 p_2$.
2. One character was present and left, and 1 character arrived: $\Pi_1 p_1$.

3. There is no character in the buffer; thus, no character left the buffer but 1 character arrived: $\Pi_1 p_0$.

So,

$$p_1 = \Pi_0 p_2 + \Pi_1 p_1 + \Pi_1 p_0$$

Thus, the set of probabilities is given by

$$p_0 = \Pi_0 p_1 + \Pi_0 p_0$$

$$p_1 = \Pi_0 p_2 + \Pi_1 p_1 + \Pi_1 p_0$$

$$p_2 = \Pi_0 p_3 + \Pi_1 p_2 + \Pi_2 p_1 + \Pi_2 p_0$$

$$\bullet$$
$$\bullet$$
$$\bullet$$

$$p_n = \Pi_0 p_{n+1} + \sum_{i=1}^{n} \Pi_{n-i+1} p_i + \Pi_n p_0$$

$$\bullet$$
$$\bullet$$
$$\bullet$$

$$p_N = p_N \sum_{i=1}^{\infty} \Pi_i + p_{N-1} \sum_{i=2}^{\infty} \Pi_i + \cdots$$

$$+ p_2 \sum_{i=N-1}^{\infty} \Pi_i + (p_1 + p_0) \sum_{i=N}^{\infty} \Pi_i$$

$$= p_N (1 - \Pi_0) + p_{N-1}(1 - \Pi_0 - \Pi_1) + \cdots$$

$$p_{i>N} = 0, \qquad \sum_{i=0}^{N} p_i = 1. \tag{3-14}$$

One can derive the Π_i's from the message input statistics. Then, the values for p_i's can be found by solving the above equations recursively on a computer. Let us now relate the values for p_i's to the probability of overflow. Let λ be the average arrivals per unit time, or the Poisson parameter* (based on the Poisson arrivals), α the characters per second leaving the buffer, and $1/\mu$ the average message size in charac-

---

* Described in Chap. 8.

ters (as before). Then, the average number of characters arriving is λ/μ. If P_{of} is the probability of overflow, then the average number of characters that are blocked is $\lambda P_{of}/\mu$. Thus, the average number of characters that leave the node are

$$(1 - P_{of})\lambda/\mu$$

The average number of characters that leave in time t is:

$$\alpha t = (1 - P_{of})\frac{\lambda t}{u} \tag{3-15}$$

Now by definition, 1 character may leave in t seconds. However, this occurs only if there is at least 1 character in the buffer, or $1 -$ (the probability that there are no characters). Thus, the probability that a character leaves is $1 - p_0$. Then, the average number of characters that leave in t seconds is the number of characters (which is 1) times $1 - p_0$ or $1(1 - p_0) = 1 - p_0$. But this is also αt. Thus,

$$\alpha t = 1 - p_0 \tag{3-16}$$

The solution of eq. (3-14) gives the value of p_0. The value of t is determined by the node and link speed. Thus, eq. (3-16) gives the value of α, and then eq. (3-15) gives the value of P_{of}.

Figure 3-12 relates N with $1/u$ for two values of ρ. For example, assume that there are 12 messages per second leaving a node, and each is 30 characters long (including the header characters). If the link speed is 9600 bps (or 1200 char/s), $\rho = 12 \times 30/1200$, or .3. For this value of ρ and an average message size of 30 characters, Chu's analysis leads to the value of N as approximately 800. Thus, 800 characters are needed in the buffer to limit the probability of overflow to less than 10^{-6} (less than 1 overflow in 10^{-6}).

3-5 IBM 3705 COMMUNICATIONS CONTROLLER

Before concluding this chapter, we review the design of a network node that operates as an end node, as well as a transit node, within IBM's Systems Network Architecture. The essential purpose of the IBM 3705 communications controller is to transmit data received from a host processor or an IBM 3705 to other host processors, terminals, cluster controllers, or other IBM 3705s; to receive data from the host processors, terminals, clusters controllers, or other IBM 3705s; and to send this data to the host or an IBM 3705. Figure 3-13

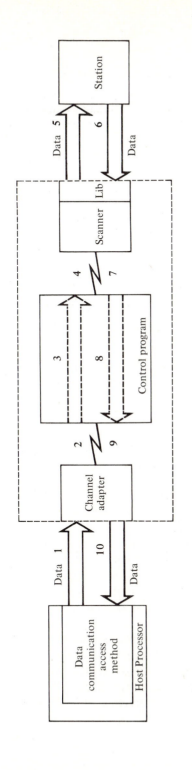

Host Processor to Station

1 Host processor sends data to the controller.

2 Channel adapter notifies control program as data arrives.

3 Control program processes data, prepares it for the station.

4 Control program activates the communication scanner when data is ready to be sent to the station.

5 Data is transmitted across the communication line to the station

Station to Host Processor

6 Station sends data to the controller.

7 Communication scanner notifies the control program as data arrives.

8 Control program processes data, prepares it for host processor.

9 Control program activates the channel adapter when data is ready to be sent to host processor.

10 Channel transfers data to host processor.

KEY

⟹ Data flow outside the controller

⇢ Data flow through the control program

⚡ Control program/hardware communication in the controller

Figure 3-13 IBM 3705 communications controller data flow. (From "IBM 3704 and 3705 Communications Controller: Principles of Operation," GC30-3004-6, October 1979, Fig. 1-9, p. 1-13.)

illustrates the functional components of the IBM 3705. The channel adapter is the interface hardware that receives (or transmits) data from (or to) a host processor. A line scanner and a line interface board (LIB) are used to interface with terminals or other communication controllers. This interface hardware provides assembly of bits into characters. The central control unit operates under the control of the network control program, which resides in the memory.

The IBM 3705 communications controller has two types of registers—general and external. The external registers are used to store information that is exchanged between the control program and the hardware circuits. The control program uses input or output instructions to load or store data in the external registers. There are thirty-two 16-bit general-purpose registers available. The central control unit provides five interrupt-driven processing levels in the IBM 3705. The thirty-two registers are divided into four groups of eight registers each. The first group is shared by levels 1 and 2. Each of the levels 3, 4, and 5 are assigned a group of eight registers. Only one group of registers—the group associated with the active program level—is active at a time. The functions performed at the various levels are shown in the table on the opposite page.

SUMMARY

An efficient design of network nodes is an important step toward development of a viable network. This chapter started with a discussion of the various functions inherent in a network node. Three classes of functions were included: end-to-end or source/destination functions, store-and-forward functions, and network-wide functions. Then, in Secs. 3.2, 3.3, and 3.4, four components of a network node were discussed: software, interface hardware, node processor, and memory. We also addressed the approaches for designing and analyzing the behavior of each of these components.

In Chap. 2, we presented the topic of transmission links. With this background information on the two basic network components, transmission links and network nodes, we proceeded to discuss techniques for putting these components together into a network. Thus, the next chapter treats the subject of establishing interconnection of nodes through the transmission links, or the *topological design* of a network.

Level 5	Level 4	Level 3	Level 2	Level 1
Interpretation of commands, from the host	Buffer management	Timer functions	Buffer or character service for communication links (assemble or segment bits from the links to characters or message buffers)	Machine check (hardware error) handling
Control of polling and addressing	Queue management	Channel adapter management		Program check (software error) handling
Data-handling functions	Task dispatching	Transit node functions		IPL (initial program load) procedures
	Supervisory services			

PROBLEMS

3-1 (*a*) Consider a network that must establish the sequence number space for a route using four nodes; *A*, *B*, *C*, and *D*. Fixed-size packets (100 characters each) at the rate of 30 packets/s must be sent from node *A* to node *D*, through nodes *B* and *C*. Each link operates at 56 kbps, with a propagation delay of 100 ms. Find the minimum size of the sequence number space for this route.

(*b*) Assume that the header (which includes the sequence number) is not included in the packet size of 100 characters. Derive an expression for the number of bits (for sequence numbers) as a function of message size, number of nodes, link speed, propagation delay, and node processing time.

3-2 Describe a scheme to use dual sequence numbering, send and receive, with and without separate message acknowledgments.

3-3 Derive the probability density function for processing demand on a network node with *k* link groups, with each group having identical characteristics.

3-4 (*a*) Derive the probability of message retransmission for a character-level link scanner and 10 links, each operating at 56 kbps, requiring 20 μs to service each request to move the character; each link either receives or transmits three messages of 400 characters/s.

(*b*) Derive the probability of message retransmission for the character-level scanner described in 3-4(*a*), but assume 30 links and Poisson arrivals for the number of service requests to move the characters.

3-5 Derive an expression for the probability of message retransmission for a link scanner that has a *k*-character buffer for each of the links. See eqs. (3-1) to (3-6).

3-6 (*a*) Derive eqs. (3-8) and (3-9) in terms of S' instead of S''.

(*b*) Discuss your results in terms of the factors that affect the improvement factor for the cache memory.

3-7 Derive the performance improvement factor, as derived in eq. (3-9), for a three-level memory. Develop a generalized result for a memory with an arbitrary number of memory access levels.

3-8 Equation (3-12) provides the steady-state solution for buffers with one message. Derive it in detail.

3-9 Derive the results shown in eq. (3-13), assuming that the number of message buffers is infinite.

REFERENCES

1. R. D. Rosner and B. Springer, "Circuit and Packet Switching—A Cost and Performance Tradeoff Study," *Computer Networks*, vol. 1, 1976, pp. 7–26.
2. K. Kümmerle and H. Rudin, "Packet and Circuit Switching: Cost/Performance Boundaries," *Computer Networks*, vol. 2, 1978, pp. 3–17.
3. R. E. Kahn and W. R. Crowther, "Flow Control in a Resource-Sharing Computer Network," *IEEE Transactions on Communications*, vol. COM-20, no. 3, June 1972, pp. 539–546.
4. D. W. Davies, "The Control of Congestion in Packet-Switching Networks," *IEEE Transactions on Communications*, vol. COM-20, no. 3, June 1972, pp. 546–550.

5. L. Kleinrock and W. E. Naylor, "On Measured Behavior of the ARPA Network," National Computer Conference, *AFIPS Conference Proceedings*, vol. 43, 1974, pp. 767–780.
6. W. W. Chu, "Buffer Behavior for Batch Poisson Arrivals and Single Constant Output," *IEEE Transactions on Communication Technology*, vol. COM-18, no. 5, October 1970, pp. 613–618.
7. V. Ahuja, "On Congestion Problems in Communication Networks," *Proceedings of Trends and Applications: Distributed Processing*, Gaithersburg, Md., May 1978, pp. 40–46.
8. IBM Corporation, "IBM 3704 and 3705 Communications Controllers: Principles of Operation," no. GC30-3004-6, October 1979.
9. H. S. Stone (ed.), *Introduction to Computer Architecture*, Science Research Associates, Chicago, 1975.
10. L. Kleinrock, *Queueing Systems*, vol. II: *Computer Applications*, Wiley, New York, 1976.
11. M. Schwartz, *Computer-Communication Network: Design and Analysis*, Prentice-Hall, Englewood Cliffs, N. J., 1977.
12. P. G. Hoel, S. C. Port, and C. J. Stone, *Introduction to Probability Theory*, Houghton Mifflin, Boston, 1971.

FOUR

TOPOLOGICAL DESIGN

CHAPTER OUTLINE

In the preceding two chapters, we presented the characteristics and behavior of transmission links and network nodes. This chapter addresses the approaches to interconnect the nodes and links, namely, the topological design of the network.

The topological design of a network assigns the links and link capacities for connecting the network nodes. This is a critical phase of network synthesis, partly because the routing, flow control, and other behavioral design algorithms rest largely on the given network topology. The topological design has also several performance and economic implications. The node locations, link connections, and link speeds directly determine the transit time through the network. For reliability or security considerations, some networks may be required to provide more than one distinct path for each node pair, thereby resulting in a minimum degree of connectivity between the nodes. (For example, requirements for the ARPANET topology specified at least two disjoint paths for each pair of nodes [1]). Transmission links, such as terrestrial and satellite, are available at discrete speeds and costs. Thus, the topological design algorithms must select links and discrete link capacities within several constraints, such as connectivity, message-transmission delay, cost, and network traffic. Perhaps the most difficult aspect of topological design is to permit possible future expansion of the network. Such expansion may require increased link capabilities or additional links or nodes. ARPANET experienced a remarkable growth: from 4 nodes to 40 within about 3 years [1].

A network topology may be developed in three parts, as shown for the network in Fig. 4-1. First, the terminals are divided into groups, with one terminal location in each group to serve as a terminal concentrator. Next, the connectivity within each terminal group is established as a multipoint link connection. Finally, links and link capacities between terminal concentrators are established. Thus, the three distinct phases of topological design are:

1. Dividing terminals into groups, and then selecting a terminal concentrator location (or network node) within each group.
2. Assigning links for multipoint connections between each terminal concentrator and its neighboring terminals.
3. Assigning links and link capacities to connect the terminal concentrators.

These steps may also be viewed as partitioning the network into two levels of nodes, and establishing connectivity at each level. The

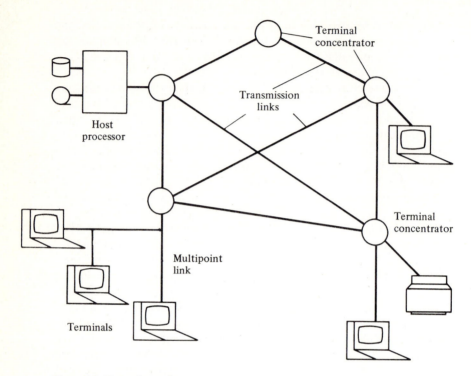

Figure 4-1 Network topology.

lower level corresponds to all terminal locations, while the higher level represents the terminal concentrators. For networks with a very large number of nodes (say, more than 100), it may be desirable to extend the above approach to a hierarchy of more than two levels. The hierarchical levels are established based on the terminal locations and terminal processing capacity. Figure 4-2 shows one possible hierarchical linkage between the nodes. Within the hierarchy, levels 1 to n are assigned such that all level i terminals are connected to terminals of levels $i - 1$, i, or $i + 1$. Furthermore, out of each group of terminals at level i, only one terminal is connected to a terminal at level $i + 1$.*

A topological design algorithm usually consists of two parts: the first part initializes the topology, and the second part iteratively im-

---

* This hierarchical structuring concept is used in several other aspects of network design, such as the Dataphone Digital Service (Sec. 2-1) and hierarchical adaptive routing (Sec. 7-4).

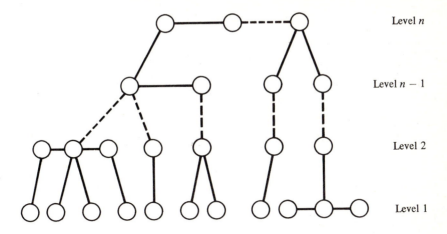

Figure 4-2 Hierarchical linkages between nodes.

proves it. Specifically, such an algorithm begins by obtaining a feasible network topology. Then, as shown in Fig. 4-3, counters are established to track the given optimization function, such as network delays, link costs, or link capacities. The third step attempts to optimize the network topology. The counters established earlier are examined for improvement as well as for feasibility. The optimization step is repeated until further improvement is not feasible; the resulting network design is the output of the algorithm.

With the above introduction in mind, we now proceed to describe some algorithms and approaches for the three phases of topological design.

4-1 SELECTING TERMINAL-CONCENTRATOR LOCATIONS

Given a collection of terminal locations, what are the optimal locations for terminal concentrators? The concentrator selection depends on the number of terminals to be attached to it, the amount of traffic generated at each terminal, and the link and concentrator capacity. This problem, along with that of connecting terminals and concentrators, has been addressed by Dysart and Georganas [5]. Here, we describe their algorithm, which selects terminal concentrator

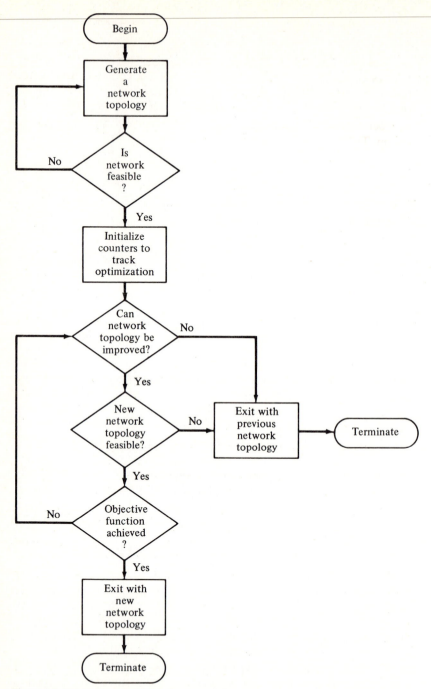

Figure 4-3 General topological design approach.

120

locations based on distances between the nodes. This algorithm constitutes the first part of the Dysart-Georganas algorithm that determines the candidates for concentrator sites. Let N be the total number of terminal locations, and k be a design parameter that specifies the number of nearest terminals to be considered for each terminal location. The steps of the heuristic algorithm are:

1. List each of the N terminals in the network and its k nearest neighbors.
2. For each terminal determine its frequency of occurrence in the terminal-neighbor list, obtained in step 1.
3. Each terminal will have one of the frequencies p, $p = 1, \ldots, F$, where F is the maximum frequency of occurrence. Partition all the nodes into lists $S(p)$, $p = 1, \ldots, F$, where the list $S(p)$ includes the nodes with frequency p.
4. Obtain the weighted mean plus 1, KM, as

$$KM = \left(\sum_{p=1}^{F} \frac{p \; x(p)}{N} \right) + 1$$

where $x(p)$ is the number of terminals in list $S(p)$. Note that

$$\sum_{p=1}^{F} x(p) = N$$

5. The initial concentrator location list is obtained by the terminal locations in the list $S(F)$. Further additions are provided by including the terminals from the lists $S(p)$, $KM < p < F$.

This algorithm selects those terminals for concentrators that are close to other terminals. The remaining terminals are connected to the selected concentrators.* Figure 4-4 illustrates the application of the algorithm for a set of 10 terminals with parameter k set to 3.

Two variations of the selected list of concentrators are possible. First, it is possible that the chosen concentrators are close to each other, requiring removal or change of one or more of them from the list. Second, it is likely that some concentrator is overloaded, thereby requiring some terminals to be disconnected from that con-

---

* In this section, we have described only part of the Dysart-Georganas algorithm. In [5], Dysart and Georganas continue the algorithm to partition the network and check the capacity constraints.

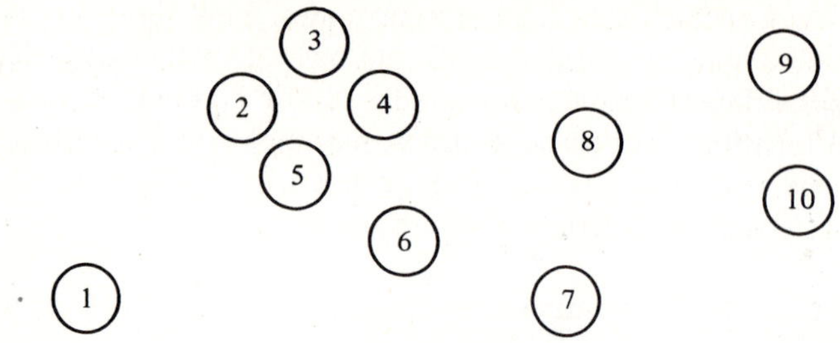

Terminal location	List of the terminal and its K-nearest neighbors	Frequency of occurance
1	1, 2, 5, 6	1
2	2, 3, 4, 5	5
3	3, 2, 4, 5	3
4	4, 3, 2, 5	6
5	5, 2, 4, 6	6
6	6, 5, 4, 7	5
7	7, 6, 8, 10	5
8	8, 7, 4, 6	4
9	9, 8, 7, 10	2
10	10, 7, 8, 9	3

S_i: Ordered list of terminal locations, where i is the frequency of occurrence

$$S_1 = (1)$$
$$S_2 = (9)$$
$$S_3 = (3, 10)$$
$$S_4 = (8)$$
$$S_5 = (2, 6, 7)$$
$$S_6 = (4, 5)$$

KM = weighted mean + 1

$$= \frac{1 + 2 + 6 + 4 + 15 + 12}{10} + 1$$

$$= 5$$

|

Concentrator location list $= \left\{ 2, 4, 5, 6, 7 \right\}$ with $k = 3$

Figure 4-4 Concentrator selection for a network with 10 terminals.

centrator. The terminal to be dropped must be the one that incurs minimum additional cost in changing connection to another concentrator. Let C be the set of concentrators, and C_j be the overloaded concentrator. For each terminal t_i on concentrator C_j, obtain the value

$$D_i = [\min(d_{ik})] - d_{ij}$$
$$C_k \neq C_j$$

where C_k is in C, d_{ij} and d_{ik} are the costs to connect terminal t_i to concentrator C_j and C_k, respectively, and $\min(d_{ik})$ is the minimum value of d_{ik} for all k. Then, drop terminal t_i from concentrator C_j, for which the value of d_{ik} is minimum. Include terminal t_i in concentrator C_k, if the addition of this terminal does not overload the concentrator C_k. (Otherwise, try the concentrator next in cost D_i.) By selecting the location for the minimum value of d_{ik}, the increase in cost to remove a terminal from concentrator C_j is minimized.

The selection of terminal concentrators is the first step in the process of network topological design, followed by that of establishing a multipoint link between each of the selected terminal concentrators and their neighboring terminals.

4-2 MULTIPOINT CONNECTIONS BETWEEN A TERMINAL CONCENTRATOR AND NEIGHBORING TERMINALS

This section addresses the problems of attaching a terminal concentrator to its adjacent terminal nodes. Such problems often involve a multipoint connection between the concentrator and the terminals. The problem of designing multipoint teleprocessing networks is stated as follows: Given the terminal and terminal concentrator locations, within the constraint of a specified limit of maximum message traffic (load) permitted on the multipoint link, determine the multipoint layout that minimizes the cost.

Several authors have addressed the above problem, and have developed algorithms for multipoint connections. We begin by describing the *minimum spanning tree*, that is, a graph with a minimum number of links that connects each node of the network. (There is a path from each node to every other node.) The spanning tree algorithms often do not account for the link capacity constraints. Chandy and Russell [9] have described a minimum-cost algorithm, which we will present later in this section. Heuristic algorithms have also been developed that reduce computation costs, but produce suboptimal results. Chou and Kershenbaum [14] show that many heuristic algorithms may be considered special cases of a generalized algorithm. We conclude this section with a description of the Chou-Kershenbaum algorithm.

Minimum Spanning Tree

A network may be treated as a graph $G = (X, A)$, where X is the set of nodes and A the set of links joining the nodes in X. A spanning tree for G is a graph $G' = (X, A')$, such that (1) each link in A' is also in A, (2) A' has no circuits (no path through G' initiates and terminates at the same node), and (3) for each node x in X, there is at least one link in A' that is connected to node x. Thus, given a network, a spanning tree ensures that each network node may communicate with another. Clearly, the desirable solution is to obtain a spanning tree with a minimum total length of links.

Given the set of nodes and the distances between them, in terms of the lengths of the links, the following algorithm (Kruskal [15]*) determines a spanning tree with minimum total length of the links.

1. Index the links in increasing order by lengths, so that the length of link a_i is less than or equal to the length of link a_j, whenever $i < j$.
2. Start by selecting link a_1 for the spanning tree, and then add link a_2 if a_2 does not form a circuit.†
3. Continue to consider links of successively higher indices, selecting a link whenever it does not form a circuit with the previously selected links, and rejecting it otherwise.

We use the configuration in Fig. 4-5 to illustrate this algorithm. It has one terminal concentrator and four terminal locations. Each link is labeled with the link index, as described in step 1 of the algorithm. Following step 2, we select links (1), (2), (3), and (4). Link (5) will form a circuit between nodes 2 and 4, so it is not included. Finally, link (6) is added to connect to node 5. All six nodes are now connected. The minimum spanning tree is shown in Fig. 4-6. The total link length is 16.

---

* A proof of the Kruskal algorithm appears in [15].
† The problem of checking the existence of circuits in graphs is addressed in [11, 12, 13].

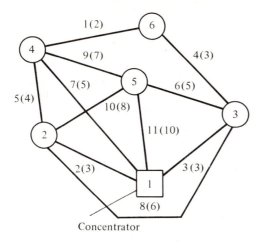

Links are labeled with indices:
link lengths are in parenthesis

Node	1	2	3	4	5	6
1		3	3	5	10	
2	3		6	4	8	
3	3	6			5	3
4	5	4			7	2
5	10	8	5	7		
6			3	2		

Table of link lengths between nodes (using above figure)

Figure 4-5 A configuration of a terminal concentrator and five terminals.

The preceding minimum spanning tree approach, although straightforward and efficient, does not satisfy constraints, such as those for link capacity. Thus, it is called the *unconstrained* solution. Algorithms for a constrained solution include a check for the link capacity, which, in turn, is related to message transmission delay through the network. For simplicity, these algorithms assume that all links in the multipoint connection have the same capacity. (Another

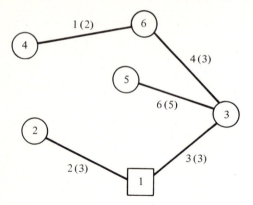

Figure 4-6 Minimum spanning tree for network shown in Fig. 4-5.

relevant and difficult problem is to minimize the total link capacity of the network). We first describe an optimal algorithm by Chandy and Russell [9] that assumes the same capacity for all links in the network.

Chandy-Russell Algorithm

The Chandy-Russell algorithm begins with the unconstrained minimum spanning tree. If the unconstrained solution is feasible in the constrained solution, then it is also optimal and the algorithm terminates. Otherwise, the cost for the unconstrained solution is a lower bound on the cost of a feasible solution to the constrained problem. In this case, the algorithm partitions the set of all solutions into subsets. At each step, the partitions are refined and a lower bound on the cost is determined for each subset. The subset with the lowest bound is checked for a feasible solution. The algorithm terminates if a feasible subset with a cost equal to the lowest bound is found. Otherwise, this subset is further partitioned by considering a link that was previously neither included nor excluded, and the above process is repeated. We follow the Chandy-Russell description* by using the sample configuration used in their paper [9] and shown in Figs. 4-7 and 4-8, along with the input loads M_i in terms of messages per time unit. The link lengths, or costs, are shown in the matrix of Fig. 4-8.

The first step in the Chandy-Russell algorithm is to obtain an unconstrained solution using a minimum spanning tree algorithm. A

---

* Adapted by permission from the IEEE and Prof. K. M. Chandy.

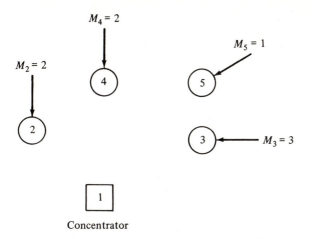

Figure 4-7 Input loads (M_i) for a configuration with a terminal concentrator and four terminals.

Node	1	2	3	4	5
1	—	3	3	5	10
2	3	—	6	4	8
3	3	6	—	3	5
4	5	4	3	—	7
5	10	8	5	7	—

Figure 4-8 Cost matrix C (C_{ij} = cost of connecting terminals i and j).

minimum spanning tree is shown at the top of page 128, and its total cost is $C_{21} + C_{43} + C_{53} + C_{31} = 14$ units, where C_{ij} is the cost of link connecting terminals i and j. Next, we impose the constraint that no link may transmit messages at a rate higher than, say, 5 messages per time unit. Then, the total message traffic on the link between terminals 3 and 1 exceeds its capacity, as shown below. Thus, the unconstrained minimum spanning tree solution is not feasible.

This part of the Chandy-Russell algorithm partitions the set of possible connections into subsets, and checks for a lower bound based on the minimum spanning tree. Chandy and Russell have shown that if the unconstrained solution has terminals connected directly to the

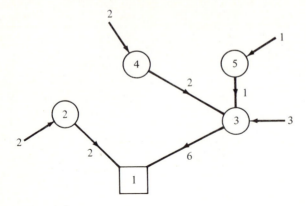

central node, then there exists an optimal solution to the constrained problem that includes these links. Therefore, we define two subsets A and B as follows:

A = Includes links 2–1 and 3–1
B = Does not allow at least one of the
two links (2–1, 3–1). (This subset is the
complement of subset A.)

Since subset A includes links that connect terminals directly to the control node, subset A contains the desired solution. Therefore, subset B is eliminated from further consideration. The algorithm expands the configuration one link at a time and considers all possible options. The link to be added is a *free link*, that is, a link that has not been included or "not allowed" in a subset. Thus, subset A is further partitioned by including, for example, link 4–3 in one partition and not allowing it in the other. Thus, the new subsets are:

AA = 2–1, 3–1, 4–3   links not allowed: none
AB = 2–1, 3–1   links not allowed: 4–3

Considering AA first, links 2–1, 3–1, and 4–3 are included. The minimum spanning tree may be obtained directly, as follows. Traffic flow on link 3–1 attributed to terminals 3 and 4 is 5 messages. Therefore, terminal 5 cannot be connected through terminals 3 and 4, since it will increase traffic on link 3–1. Alternatively, we may select link 5–2 or 5–1. Since the cost of these links is 8 and 10, respectively, we select link 5–2 as shown below. Thus, the total cost is $C_{21} + C_{43} + C_{31} + C_{52} = 17$ units.

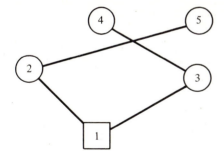

Now consider the subset AB. Since links 2–1 and 3–1 will be included, assign $C_{21} = C_{31} = 0$. Also, since links 3–4 and 4–3 will not be included, set $C_{34} = C_{43} = \infty$. These cost changes are temporarily included in the cost matrix to obtain a lower bound. Using the new cost matrix, the minimum cost spanning tree is obtained, as shown below. It is easily verified that this solution is also feasible, since the flow on each link is less than the maximum permissible flow.

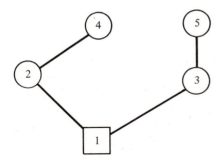

The lower bound for subset AB is thus the cost of this tree using the original cost matrix, or $C_{21} + C_{31} + C_{42} + C_{53} = 15$. Then, the least lower bound for AB is 15. Since the lower bound for subset AA is 17, we choose 15 as the least lower bound for the subsets AA and AB. Thus, an optimal solution may be obtained if there is a feasible solution with a cost equal to 15. Since the above solution in subset AB is also feasible, the algorithm selects the solution in subset AB and terminates. If the solution in subset AB was not feasible, the next step would involve partitioning the subset AB.

Thus, the algorithm selects a subset, partitions it, and checks for a feasible solution with lower bound. Starting with subsets A and B, we selected subset A, and partitioned it into AA and AB. The solution for subset AB had the lower cost and is also feasible, resulting in the selection of the solution in subset AB. Thus, the algorithm is:

1. Partition the set of all solutions into two subsets. One subset includes all links of the unconstrained solution that are directly connected to the concentrator site. The other subset excludes them.
2. Suppose the ith partition is being processed. The subsets are $S_i(1)$, $S_i(2)$, ..., $S_i(p)$, and the corresponding lower bounds on the cost are $L_i(1)$, ..., $L_i(p)$. Let $L_i(j)$ be the least value in $L_i(k)$, $k = 1$ to p.
3. Check subset $S_i(j)$ for a feasible solution. If a feasible solution exists, it is also the optimal solution, since it has the lowest lower bound $L_i(j)$, and the algorithm terminates. If not, proceed to step 4.
4. Relabel set j to set k. Partition $S_i(k)$ into $S_{i+1}(k)$ and $S_{i+1}(k+1)$. This partition is obtained by including a previously free link in $S_i(k)$ to form the subset $S_{i+1}(k)$, and by excluding that link in $S_i(k)$ to create the subset $S_{i+1}(k+1)$. Compute new lower bounds for solutions in subsets $L_{i+1}(k)$ and $L_{i+1}(k+1)$, and proceed to step 2.

Heuristic Algorithms

An optimal algorithm is computationally quite expensive. One can, therefore, consider heuristic algorithms that are computationally efficient but provide solutions close to the best possible. Chandy and Russell have shown that solutions from certain heuristic algorithms are in general within 5 or 10 percent of the optimal solutions for network configurations that they examined. The heuristic algorithm by Esau and Williams [8] begins by connecting each terminal to the concentrator location, and then reconnects those terminals to their neighboring location that provides the greatest cost benefit. The Kruskal algorithm [15] connects the least-cost links, one link at a time. We first describe the above algorithms and then conclude the section with a description of the Chou-Kershenbaum unified algorithm that encompasses heuristic algorithms. Several other topological algorithms have been published, and [6, 7] describe some algorithms not presented here. For the following heuristic algorithms, we use the network configuration shown in Fig. 4-9. Here, the capacity of each link is limited to 10 messages/s.

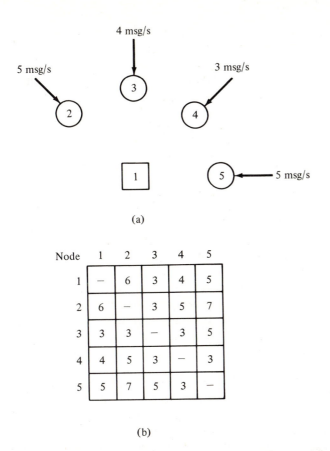

(a)

(b)

Figure 4-9 A network configuration with message traffic to each node and distances (or cost) between nodes.

Esau-Williams Algorithm

The Esau-Williams algorithm first connects all terminal points to the concentrator node. It then attempts to insert those links between terminals (and remove their connection to the concentrator) that maximize the cost reduction.

1. Calculate the tradeoff parameters $d_{ij} = C_{ij} - C_{i1}$, for all i, j, where 1 is the concentrator location. For the sample configuration of Fig. 4-9, the values are:

$$d_{23} = C_{23} - C_{21} = -3$$
$$d_{32} = C_{32} - C_{31} = 0$$
$$d_{24} = C_{24} - C_{21} = -1$$
$$d_{42} = C_{42} - C_{41} = 1$$
$$d_{25} = C_{25} - C_{21} = 1$$
$$d_{52} = C_{52} - C_{51} = 2$$
$$d_{34} = C_{34} - C_{31} = 0$$
$$d_{43} = C_{43} - C_{41} = -1$$
$$d_{35} = C_{35} - C_{31} = 2$$
$$d_{53} = C_{53} - C_{51} = 0$$
$$d_{45} = C_{45} - C_{41} = -1$$
$$d_{54} = C_{54} - C_{51} = -2$$

Thus, the algorithm first finds the cost difference in connecting each node i to 1 (the concentrator), compared to connecting it to another node.

2. Parameters with a value greater than 0 are excluded from consideration, since it is cheaper to connect the terminal location in question to the concentrator node than to the other node. Select the locations i, j corresponding to the minimum value of d_{ij}.

In the above example, $d_{23} = -3$ is minimum, so locations 2 and 3 are considered as follows.

3. Check whether the constraints are satisfied by the connection between locations i and j (message traffic going from node i to node j). Proceed to step 4 if the constraints are satisfied. Otherwise, set d_{ij} to infinity, and return to step 2 to select again.

The flow through link 2–3 would be 5, which is less than 10, and the constraint is satisfied.

4. Add link $i - j$ and remove link $i - 1$. Also, label node i with the label of node j to show that the two are connected. (Note that terminal location i is connected to the concentrator through terminal j, instead of directly.) Reevaluate the constraints and the parameters. Then, go back to step 1.

In the above example, connecting location 2 to location 3, instead of to the concentrator, results in a total traffic of 9 messages per unit time for link 3–1. Since this message traffic is less than 10, the constraint is satisfied.

In case of the sample configuration of Fig. 4-9, the next link to be considered is 5–4, since $d_{54} = -2$. The message traffic on link 5–4 would be 5, and on link 4–1 would be 8, which is less than 10. Next, links 4–3 and 2–4 would result in violating the message constraint of 10 on the links. The resulting configuration is shown below. The total cost is $C_{31} + C_{23} + C_{14} + C_{45} = 3 + 3 + 4 + 3 = 13$ units.

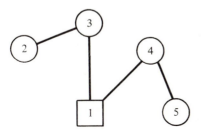

Kruskal Algorithm

This algorithm selects the least-cost links one at a time, checks the constraints, and repeats this procedure until all locations have been connected. It employs the Kruskal algorithm [15] in selecting links and includes a test to check the constraints.

Consider the sample configuration shown in Fig. 4-9. The table of links versus link cost for that configuration is given below.

Link	Cost
1–3	3
2–3	3
3–4	3
4–5	3
1–4	4
1–5	5
2–4	5
3–5	5
1–2	6
2–5	7

We proceed by selecting link 1–3. Next, link 2–3 is added. Link 3–4 cannot be added, since it would violate the message constraint on link 1–3. Next, links 4–5 and 4–1 are added. Thus, it leads to the same configuration as that with Esau-Williams algorithm. [To observe the difference in results from Esau-Williams and Kruskal algorithms, apply these algorithms to the configuration shown in Figs. 4-7 and 4-8 (Problem 4-6).]

Generalized Heuristic Algorithm

Kershenbaum and Chou [14] have shown that the preceding heuristic algorithm and others referenced in their paper are special cases of a generalized heuristic algorithm. The Kershenbaum-Chou algorithm uses a weighting factor w for each terminal location. Specific heuristic algorithms are obtained depending on the definition of w. Considerations in selecting rules to assign values for w are discussed following the description of the generalized algorithm. Let w_i be the weighting factor associated with terminal i, and C_{ij} be the link cost in connecting terminals i and j. Based on [14], the generalized heuristic algorithm may be summarized as follows:

1. Initialize w_i, for $i = 1$ to N, where N is the number of terminal locations. Initialize the constraints.
   Evaluate $d_{ij} = C_{ij} - w_i$, for all i, j when C_{ij} exists and no constraints are violated with the connection $i - j$.
2. Determine $d_{i'j'} = \min (d_{ij})$, for all i and j, such that $i \neq j$. If $d_{i'j'} = $ infinity, terminate the algorithm. Otherwise, go to step 3.
3. Evaluate the constraints under connection $i' - j'$. If any constraint is violated, then set $d_{i'j'}$ to infinity, and go to step 2. Otherwise, proceed to step 4.
4. Add link $i' - j'$, and relabel one of the terminals i' or j' to correspond to the other. Reevaluate the constraints, obtain new values for w_i ($i = 1$ to N) and d_{ij} (for all i such that w_i has changed), and return to step 2.

The weight associated with a given terminal (say, i) may be based on several considerations. It may be a function of the cost of connecting terminal i to the concentrator, or C_{i1}. It may also depend on the cost C_{i2} of connecting location i to its second nearest-feasible neighbor that does not violate any constraints. Kershenbaum and Chou have found a useful rule: $w_i = a[b \, C_{i1} + (1 - b) \, C_{i2}]$, where a and b are constraints such that $a \geq 0$ and $0 \leq b \leq 1$; C_{i1} and C_{i2} are described above. If a is set to 0, it yields the Kruskal algorithm. If a and b are both set to 1, it gives the Esau-Williams algorithm.

The above heuristic algorithm is of the order of complexity N^2. The $O[N^2]$ is required for the case every time a node is linked, d_{ij} values have to be updated or examined, thus requiring $N(N - 1)$ or potentially $O[N^2]$ updates. For networks with several nodes and large distances, there is no need to examine node pairs that are far apart. Let K be the number of nearest neighbors that are considered for connection to each node. Then, the complexity of the above algorithm is

$$A\,(N^2) + BKN + CKN \log_2 K$$

where A, B, and C are constants. If the w rules do not require updates for every terminal, the term $A\,(N^2)$ may disappear. Then, the computational complexity reduces to $BKN + CKN \log_2 K$ operations.

4-3 LINK AND LINK CAPACITY ASSIGNMENT BETWEEN NETWORK NODES

In the beginning of this chapter, we outlined the three phases of the network topological design process. The first two phases, described in Secs. 4-1 and 4-2, respectively, consist of selecting terminal concentrator locations, and establishing a multipoint teleprocessing network layout for a concentrator and its neighboring terminals. In this section, the problem of interconnecting terminal concentrators is addressed. Here, we will use the generic term *network node* to represent the terminal concentrators.

Given a set of node locations, the problem of interconnecting the network nodes consists of three interrelated subproblems. First, the nodes should be connected under certain constraints, such as minimum cost or delay. Second, the link capacity should be assigned, perhaps based on the discrete set of capacities available. Finally, the message traffic or flows should be assigned based on link capacities. We describe the algorithms that provide optimal or near-optimal (heuristic) topology. In the first algorithm, the cut saturation algorithm by Gerla, Frank, Chou, and Eckl [4], the link assignment problem is addressed. This algorithm is followed by a result and an algorithm for assigning link capacities.

Cut Saturation Algorithm

The cut saturation algorithm is based on an iterative procedure of assigning flows and modifying the topology. Given the link assignments, link capacities, and traffic requirements, a flow assignment algorithm is employed to assign optimal or near-optimal flows. The topology is changed to reduce the cost while satisfying throughput constraints. The goal is to achieve a desired throughput with least cost. The algorithm is described assuming the same capacity for all links.

The cut saturation algorithm consists of executing a combination of five basic steps in each iteration.

1. *Routing.* This step is performed after each network modification to generate new optimal link flows. One such algorithm, the flow deviation method, is described in Chap. 6.
2. *Saturated cutset determination.* Given the flow assignments, the links are ordered according to their utilization and removed successively. The minimal set of the links that disconnects the network is called the *saturated cutset.*
3. *Add-only step.* This step adds the least cost link that joins the two subnetworks, say, K_1 and K_2, on either side of the cutset. The objective in adding the link is to improve the throughput by diverting the traffic from the cutset. Thus any link considered must connect some node pair (x, y), where node x is in the subnetwork K_1 and node y is in the subnetwork K_2. A useful approach in establishing the link is to connect the "centers of traffic" of the two subnetworks. This may be accomplished through a heuristic choice, such as for large networks, selecting those nodes for connection that are at least two links away from the nodes adjacent to the cutset. In Fig. 4-10, links connecting a node from the set {1, 2, 3, 4, 5, 6} to a node from the set {13, 14, 15} are considered. If this is not possible because of small subnetwork size, nodes adjacent to the cutset nodes are also considered.
4. *Delete-only step.* At each iteration of this step, a link is removed based on its utilization and cost, thus resulting in a reduction of throughput and cost. One approach, described in [4], removes the most expensive and underutilized link. Thus, the link that maximizes the quantity

$$E_i = D_i \frac{C_i - f_i}{C_i}$$

is removed, where D_i is the cost, C_i the capacity, and f_i the flow on link i; $(C_i - f_i)/C_i$ is the normalized excess capacity of the link.
5. *Perturbation step.* Given a configuration that provides a desired throughput TH, this step attempts to reduce cost while satisfying the throughput requirements. In any exchange algorithm, the throughput is allowed to vary within specified limits, say $TH(\text{min})$ and $TH(\text{max})$, that may be within 5 percent of the desired throughput. Each iteration begins with the routing step, followed by the

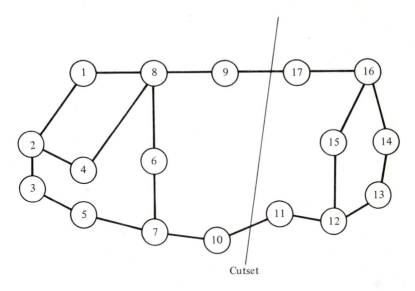

Figure 4-10 Node selection for add-only step.

cutset determination step. The routing step provides a new value of TH. The add-only and delete-only steps are executed one at a time, respectively, depending on whether the throughput is below or above the desired limits. The add-only step adds a link, and the delete-only step deletes a link at a time. Iterations with the value of TH falling within TH(min) and TH(max) are permitted as long as they reduce the cost.

Gerla et al. observe in [4] that the best starting topology seems to be a two-connected network, in which there are at least two disjoint paths for any two nodes to communicate. They compared the cut saturation algorithm with the branch exchange technique, or BXC [2, 20], for networks with 10, 26, and 40 nodes. In no case was a BXC solution better than the cut saturation solution, and each BXC solution required more computation time than the comparable cut saturation solution. The comparison for a 26-node network is shown in Fig. 4-11. The computational complexity C of the cut saturation algorithm for sufficiently large networks is found to depend on the square of number of links M or $C = \delta(M^2)$, where δ depends on the code and desired accuracy. The value of δ, using per iteration time on a CDC 6600, were obtained by Gerla et al. and are tabulated as follows:

Number of nodes	Links	TR*	TT	δ
10	20	.5	.3	.002
26	30	1.2	.7	.0021
	39	1.8	.8	.0016
40	54	3.2	1.2	.0015
	61	4.7	1.5	.0017

* TR = running time for the routing step in seconds.
TT = running time for the cutset step in seconds.
Source: M. Gerla, H. Frank, W. Chou, and J. Eckl, "A Cut Saturation Algorithm for Topological Design of Packet Switched Communication Networks," *Proceedings of the IEEE National Telecommunications Conference,* San Diego, December 1974, pp. 1074–1085, table 1 and page 1078.

These values demonstrate that the value of δ does not fluctuate significantly by the number of nodes or links, thereby supporting the validity of the computational complexity expression $C = \delta(M^2)$.

Capacity Assignment

Given a network topology, the link capacities are assigned depending on the cost and network traffic. In the cut saturation algorithm, note that link capacities were assumed to be the same for all links. The goal here in assigning link capacities is to minimize the message delay T through the network within a total cost constraint D. The message delay through the network may be estimated by

$$T = \sum_{i=1}^{M} \frac{\lambda_i}{\gamma} \frac{1}{uC_i - \lambda_i} \tag{4-1}*$$

where M = number of links
λ_i = average message rate on the ith link per second
C_i = capacity of the ith link in bits per second
$1/u$ = average message size in bits
γ = total external traffic entering the network per second

We present a result derived in [16, pp. 329–331]† to obtain the theoretical properties of optimal capacity assignment. It assumes that

* This expression is derived in Chap. 8.
† Adapted with permission from John Wiley & Sons, Inc.

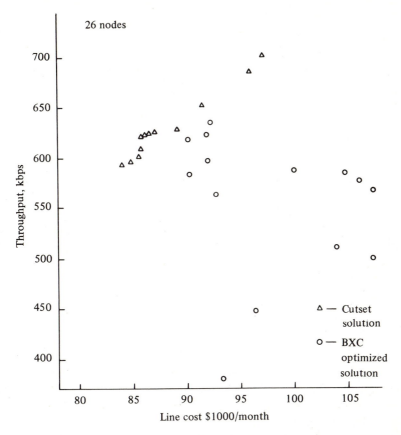

Figure 4-11 Comparison of cut saturation versus BXC solution for a 26-node network. (From M. Gerla, H. Frank, W. Chou, and J. Eckl, "A Cut Saturation Algorithm for Topological Design of Packet Switched Communication Networks," *Proceedings of IEEE National Telecommunications Conference*, San Diego, December 1974, p. 1083.)

capacities are available in continuous sizes, and that link cost is a linear function of link capacity; that is, $d_i(C_i) = d_i C_i$, where d_i is the cost for each unit of capacity built into the ith link. To minimize the value of T, we first form the lagrangian as

$$G = T + \beta\left(\sum_{i=1}^{M} d_i C_i - D\right)$$

where β is the lagrangian multiplier and D is the total link cost. We wish to determine the minimum value of G with respect to the capacity assigments $\{C_i\}$. Thus, the set of M equations, $(\partial G/\partial C_i) = 0$, $i = 1$, ..., M, must be satisfied. This yields

$$0 = -\frac{\lambda_i}{\gamma}\frac{u}{(uC_i - \lambda_i)^2} + \beta d_i$$

or

$$C_i = \frac{\lambda_i}{u} + \frac{1}{\sqrt{B\gamma u}}\sqrt{\frac{\lambda_i}{d_i}} \qquad i = 1, 2, \ldots, M \qquad (4\text{-}2)$$

Multiplying by d_i and summing on i,

$$\sum_{i=1}^{M} d_i C_i = \sum_{i=1}^{M} \frac{\lambda_i d_i}{u} + \frac{1}{\sqrt{B\gamma u}}\sum_{i=1}^{M}\sqrt{\lambda_i d_i}$$

But since the left-hand side is simply D,

$$\frac{1}{\sqrt{B\gamma u}} = \frac{D - \displaystyle\sum_{i=1}^{M}\frac{\lambda_i d_i}{u}}{\displaystyle\sum_{i=1}^{M}\sqrt{\lambda_i d_i}}$$

Let the excess dollar

$$D_e = D - \sum_{i=1}^{M}\frac{\lambda_i d_i}{u}$$

Then, solving for C_i from eq. 4-2, the optimal solution is

$$C_i = \frac{\lambda_i}{u} + \left(\frac{D_e}{d_i}\right)\frac{\sqrt{\lambda_i d_i}}{\displaystyle\sum_{i=1}^{M}\sqrt{\lambda_i d_i}} \qquad i = 1, 2, \ldots, M$$

Note that the above solution distributes the excess money D_e, normalized over the link cost factor d_i, and weighted over by $\sqrt{\lambda_i d_i}$.

The above result provides optimal capacity assignment, but assumes that link capacities are available in continuous size. It also assumes that link costs increase linearly with capacities. In reality, link capacities are available at discrete values (like a step function), and link costs depend on such factors as tariffs and distances. These considerations lead us to examine some heuristic techniques. We describe a heuristic algorithm that assigns link capacities, using discrete capacities and cost functions.

Discrete Link Capacity Assignment

The following heuristic algorithm, by Maruyama and Tang [3], minimizes total link cost for the network while satisfying the delay constraints for each class of messages on each path in the network. A *path* is defined by a sequence of links through the network that forms a message route. The algorithm employs a set of subalgorithms that are used to increase or decrease the capacity of the links offering maximum reduction in delay (or cost). The algorithm attempts to increase link capacity if a delay constraint is not satisfied, and to decrease link capacity to reduce cost. For estimating the delays T on network paths, one may use eq. (4-1). The subalgorithms are described below.

1. SETLOW. Assign the minimum required capacity to each link. This is the total traffic on the link in terms of, say, bits per second. If, for any link, there is no available capacity to satisfy the minimum capacity requirement, no feasible solution exists. Otherwise, check the delay T_{ik} on path i and message class k, for all i and k. If T_{ik} is less than the delay constraint (referred to as B_{ik}) for all i and k, this minimum capacity assignment is the desired solution.
2. SETHIGH. Assign the maximum available capacity to each link. If some delay constraints are not satisfied by these capacities, there is no feasible solution.
3. ADDFAST. Repeat the following steps until the delay T_{ik} is less than or equal to the constraint B_{ik}, for all i and k.
   (a) Find path P_{io} for the message class k_o such that

$$\frac{T_{ioko}}{B_{ioko}} = \max_{i,\,k} \left\{ \frac{T_{ik}}{B_{ik}} \right\}$$

That is, find the path and message class (for increasing link capacity) that is likely to yield maximum reduction in message delays.
   (b) Find link L_{jo} on path P_{io} for which

$$\frac{t_{joko} - t_{joko}^+}{D_{jo}^+ - D_{jo}} = \max_{L_j \in P_{io}} \left\{ \frac{t_{jko} - t_{jko}^+}{D_j^+ - D_j} \right\}$$

where t_{jk} is the average delay on link L_j with capacity C_j for message class k, D_j is the cost of link L_j with capacity C_j, D_j^+ is the cost of link L_j with capacity C_j^+ on the jth link, and t_{jk}^+ is the average delay on link L_j with capacity C_j^+ for message class k. The term C_j^+ represents the next highest capacity for link L_j.

This step determines the link on the path selected in step (a) such that the ratio of reduction in message delay to increase in cost is maximum.

(c) Assign the next highest capacity C_j^+ to link L_{jo}.

4. DROPFAST This step reduces the link capacity so that the ratio of increase in network delay and decrease in cost is minimum. Repeat the following steps until just before $T_{ik} > B_{ik}$ holds for some i and k.

(a) Find path P_{io} for class k_o such that

$$\frac{T_{ioko}}{B_{ioko}} = \min_{i,\,k} \left\{ \frac{T_{ik}}{B_{ik}} \right\}$$

(b) Find link L_{jo} on path P_{io} such that

$$\frac{t_{joko}^- - t_{joko}}{D_{jo} - D_{jo}^-} = \min_{L_j \in P_{io}} \left\{ \frac{t_{jko}^- - t_{jko}}{D_j - D_j^-} \right\}$$

where t_{jk}^- and D_j^- are, respectively, the network delay t_{jk} and link cost D_j for the next lowest capacity C_j^- on link L_{jo}.

(c) Assign the capacity C_j^- to link L_{jo}.

5. ADD This step increases link capacities for links in which the ratio of reduction in network delay and increase in link cost is maximum. Repeat this step until the bound $T_{ik} \le B_{ik}$ is satisfied for all i and k.

For each link L_j, compute its "figure of merit" F_j, defined as

$$F_j = \frac{\sum\limits_{i,\,k} \{[T_{ik} - \max(T_{ik}^+, B_{ik})]/B_{ik} \mid T_{ik} > B_{ik}, \text{ and } L_j \in P_i\}}{D_j^+ - D_j}$$

Find the link L_{jo} with maximum value of F_j, and assign capacity C_j^+ to link L_{jo}.

6. DROP This step decreases link capacities until the delay constraint is satisfied. It selects the links for which the ratio of increase in network delay and decrease in link cost is minimum.

Repeat this step until just before $T_{ik} > B_{ik}$ holds for some i and k. For each link L_j, compute

$$F_j = \frac{\sum\limits_{i,\,k} [(T_{ik}^- - T_{ik})/B_{ik} \mid T_{ik}^- \le B_{ik} \text{ and } L_j \in P_i]}{D_j - D_j^-}$$

Find the link with minimum value of F_j, and assign it the capacity C_{jo}^-.

7. EXC Here, two link capacities are changed simultaneously, within the delay constraints and only if there is a cost reduction. For any two links L_i and L_j, reassign $C_i \leftarrow C_i^+$, $C_j \leftarrow C_j^-$, which results in $D_i \leftarrow D_i^+$, $D_j \leftarrow D_j^-$, $T_{ik} \leftarrow T_{ik}^+$, and $T_{jk} \leftarrow T_{jk}^-$, for all k, if it does not violate any delay constraints and if $D_i + D_j > D_i^+ + D_j^-$.

The algorithm is executed by employing one of several possible combinations of the above steps. The most desirable algorithm, considering solution optimality and computational efficiency, as proposed by Maruyama and Tang [3], is shown in Fig. 4-12. RESETHIGH pro-

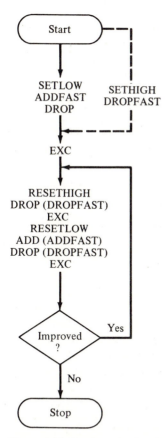

Figure 4-12 A composite heuristic algorithm for the discrete capacity assignment. (From K. Maruyama and D. T. Tang, "Discrete Link Capacity Assignment in Communication Networks," *Proceedings of the Third International Conference on Computer Communication*, Toronto, August 1976, p. 94.)

vides an interface to DROP or DROPFAST, and resets the currently assigned capacity C_j to C_j^+ for all j. Similarly, RESETLOW provides an interface to ADD or ADDFAST, and resets the currently assigned capacity C_j to C_j^-, for all j.

Given the network message traffic, links, and link capacities, the next step is to assign traffic on the links. The goal is to distribute the network traffic such that delay is minimized or throughput maximized. As pointed out earlier, this is a subproblem of overall topological design and is treated in Sec. 6-1. Next, we proceed to address reliability issues in topological design.

4-4 DISJOINT ROUTE TOPOLOGY

In the beginning of this chapter, we identified the topological design requirement for a desired number of exclusive or disjoint paths. In this section, we describe this requirement along with some relevant results.

For reasons of security or reliability, a network may be required to provide a minimum specified number of link (or node) disjoint routes for every node pair. A simple case is that of requiring at least two routes for every node pair, with no link or node shared between the two routes. This requirement is easily satisfied by connecting all network nodes in a loop. Consider the general problem of disjoint route topology: Given the node locations, determine a topology (link assignments) to permit a specified number of disjoint routes for every node pair. This problem has been addressed in Berge [17] and Ahuja [10]. To begin with, a disjoint route topology may be obtained by repeatedly trying various topologies and obtaining the number of disjoint routes. Clearly, such an approach is computationally unmanageable. However, this problem is directly related to several existing graph theory results. In order to describe these results, some definitions are required. A graph $G = (X, A)$ is *connected* if for each pair of nodes (x_1, x_2) in X, there exists a set $(a_i, \ldots, a_j)$ of arcs in A such that x_1 is the beginning node of arc a_i and x_2 is the terminating node of arc a_j, and that the terminating node of each arc a_k in the set is the beginning node of arc a_{k+1}. For a given connected graph $G = (X, A)$, its *connectivity* $C(G)$ is the minimum number of vertices whose removal disconnects G or reduces G to a single node. Finally, a graph G is *k-connected* if its connectivity $C(G) \geq k$.

According to a theorem by Menger [17, p. 167; 18, pp. 47–49], if a graph is k-connected, then there are k node disjoint paths between any two distinct nodes. Thus, our problem is reduced to obtaining a

k-connected graph. Now a k-connected graph is obtained by providing a specified minimum number of arcs (or links) connected to each node. We present two results described in [17, pp. 173–174]:

1. A graph $G = (X, A)$ is k-connected if for each node x in X, $D_g(x) \geq (n + k)/2 - 1$, where $D_g(x)$ is the degree of x defined by the number of arcs having one endpoint in x, n is the number of nodes in X, and k is not greater than n. A stronger condition is described next.
2. A graph $G = (X, A)$ is k-connected if (1) for each integer $h \leq (n - k)/2$, the number of vertices with degree less than $h + k - 1$ is less than h, and (2) the number of vertices with degree less than $(n + k)/2 - 1$ is less than $n - k + 1$.

Thus, sufficient links must be assigned so that one of the above two sets of conditions are satisfied. Then, as stated earlier, such a graph has at least k node disjoint routes for each pair of nodes.

Instead of nodes, a network designer may desire link disjoint routes. Each of the above results will satisfy link disjointness. It can be readily seen that if two routes are node-disjoint, they are also link-disjoint; the converse is not true. Finally, there is the problem of preserving the route disjointness properties of a network when modifying its topology, such as addition or deletion of a link or a node. The reader is referred to [10] for a discussion of this problem. The problem of determining maximum message routes for a given node or link disjoint topology is discussed in Chap. 7.

SUMMARY

In the last few years, the topological design of networks has received considerable attention. Several algorithms have been developed and proposed, and some are presented in this chapter. These algorithms assign links and link capacities while satisfying a variety of requirements, such as link costs, message traffic, message delays, throughput, and connectivity. We have presented algorithms to transform a given set of terminal locations into a communication network through the selection of terminal concentrators, and the assignment of links and link capacities for connecting terminals and terminal concentrators. Optimal algorithms are of interest only for large networks; heuristic algorithms should suffice for networks with a few nodes. The topological design effort for **ARPANET** has resulted in several useful publications on this topic [1, 2, 20].

PROBLEMS

4-1 For the terminals shown in Fig. 4-4, apply the Dysart-Georganas algorithm for $k = 4$.

4-2 For the network shown in Figs. 4-7 and 4-8, assume that the cost for executing an operation (addition, multiplication, or comparison) is one-fiftieth of the cost units used in Fig. 4-8. Then, use (*a*) the Esau-Williams algorithm and (*b*) the Kruskal algorithm to estimate the total cost—sum of link costs and computational cost. Which one is desirable in this case, and why? At what cost ratio would your choice of the algorithm change? (That is, if at 1 : 50 cost ratio, the Esau-Williams algorithm is less expensive, then for what cost ratio would the Kruskal algorithm be less expensive?)

4-3 Consider the following topology:

4 msg/s

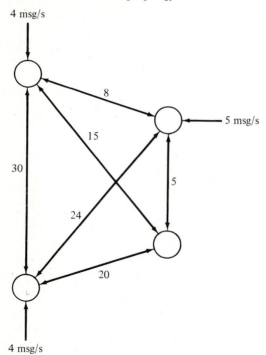

5 msg/s

4 msg/s

Distances are shown in miles along with the number of input messages entering the nodes per second. Let message size be 800 bits, and link costs per mile be $1 for 2400 bps, $1.80 for 9600 bps, and $3.30 for 56,000 bps.

(*a*) Use the Kruskal algorithm to find a minimum spanning tree employing only 9600 bps links.

(*b*) Use any heuristic algorithm to provide the least expensive multipoint layout of this network, assuming all links to be of the same speed and that every 1 second of delay is equivalent to $300 cost.

4-4 What are the underlying differences in phases 2 and 3 of the topological design described on p. 117? Can we use the same algorithm for both phases? Can we combine the algorithms, and thus obtain an improved solution? Support your claims with arguments.

4-5 Consider the problem of designing a network with the node locations and message traffic shown below. The message size is fixed at 800 bits, and all distances are shown in miles. Message routes should be based on the minimum number of links to reach the destination node. Message delay on the links (neglecting the queuing delays in the nodes and propagation delays on the links) through the network should not exceed 2 s, and link costs should be minimized. (Use the link cost values for prob. 4-3.) Assign links and link capacities for these nodes.

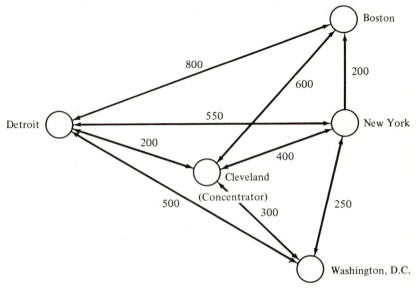

Message rate (messages/second)

From \ To	Detroit	Boston	New York	Washington, D.C.	Cleveland
Detroit	—	1	1	1	2
Boston	2	—	2	1	—
New York	1	2	—	1	—
Washington, D.C.	1.5	1	2	—	1
Cleveland	1	1	1	1	—

4-6 Apply the Esau-Williams and Kruskal algorithms to the configuration shown in Figs. 4-7 and 4-8. Explain, in detail, why the two algorithms give different results.

REFERENCES

1. H. Frank and W. Chou, "Network Properties of the ARPA Computer Network," *Networks*, vol. 4, 1974, pp. 213–239.
2. H. Frank, I. T. Frisch, and W. Chou, "Topological Considerations in the Design of the ARPA Computer Network," *Proceedings of the Spring Joint Computer Conference*, Atlantic City, N. J., 1970, pp. 581–587.
3. K. Maruyama and D. T. Tang, "Discrete Link Capacity Assignment in Communication Networks," *Proceedings of the Third International Conference on Computer Communication*, Toronto, August 1976, pp. 92–97.
4. M. Gerla, H. Frank, W. Chou, and J. Eckl, "A Cut Saturation Algorithm for Topological Design of Packet Switched Communication Networks," *Proceedings of the IEEE National Telecommunications Conference*, San Diego, December 1974, pp. 1074–1085.
5. H. G. Dysart and N. D. Georganas, "NEWCLUST: An Algorithm for the Topological Design of Two-level, Multidrop Teleprocessing Networks," *IEEE Transactions on Communications*, vol. COM-26, no. 1, January 1978, pp. 55–61.
6. I. Rubin, "On Reliable Topological Structures for Message-Switching Communication Networks," *IEEE Transactions on Communications*, vol. COM-26, no. 1, January 1978, pp. 62–74.
7. H. Dirilten and R. W. Donaldson, "Topological Design of Distributed Data Communication Networks Using Linear Regression Clustering," *IEEE Transactions on Communications*, vol. COM-25, no. 10, October 1977, pp. 1083–1091.
8. L. R. Esau and K. C. Williams, "A Method for Approximating the Optimal Network," *IBM Systems Journal*, vol. 5, no. 3, 1966, pp. 142–147.
9. K. M. Chandy and R. A. Russell, "The Design of Multipoint Linkages in a Teleprocessing Tree Network," *IEEE Transactions on Computers*, vol. C-21, no. 10, October 1972, pp. 1062–1066.
10. V. Ahuja, "Approaches for Disjoint Routing in Communication Networks," *Proceedings of Trends and Applications*, Gaithersburg, Md., May 1979, pp. 36–40.
11. K. Paton, "An Algorithm for Finding a Fundamental Set of Cycles of a Graph," *Communications of the ACM*, vol. 12, no. 9, September 1969, pp. 514–518.
12. J. C. Tiernan, "An Efficient Search Algorithm to Find the Elementary Circuits of a Graph," *Communications of the ACM*, vol. 13, no. 12, December 1970, pp. 772–726.
13. H. Weinblatt, "A New Search Algorithm for Finding the Simple Cycles of a Finite Directed Graph," *Journal of the ACM*, vol. 19, no. 1, January 1972, pp. 43–56.
14. A. Kershenbaum and W. Chou, "A Unified Algorithm for Designing Multidrop Teleprocessing Networks," *IEEE Transactions on Communications*, vol. COM-22, no. 11, November 1974, pp. 1762–1772.
15. J. B. Kruskal, Jr., "On the Shortest Spanning Subtree of a Graph and the Traveling Salesman Problem," *Proceedings of the American Mathematical Society*, vol. 7, 1956, pp. 48–50.
16. L. Kleinrock, *Queueing Systems, Volume II: Computer Applications*, Wiley, New York, 1976.

17. C. Berge, *Graphs and Hypergraphs*, American Elsevier, New York, 1973.
18. F. Harary, *Graph Theory*, Addison-Wesley, Reading, Mass., 1972.
19. M. Schwartz, *Computer-Communication Network Design and Analysis*, Prentice-Hall, Englewood Cliffs, N. J., 1977.
20. H. Frank and W. Chou, "Topological Optimization of Computer Networks," *Proceedings of the IEEE*, vol. 60, no. 11, November 1972, pp. 1385–1397.

CHAPTER
FIVE

NETWORK PROTOCOLS

CHAPTER OUTLINE

A network consists of a collection of interconnected nodes that permit exchange of units of information, or data, among each other. An orderly exchange of data requires that each node conform to some preestablished agreements or rules. These rules specify the formats and relative timings of messages to be exchanged among the nodes. A *network protocol* establishes these rules, standards, or conventions. Network protocols essentially consist of three elements: (1) syntax, or the structure of data and control messages; (2) semantics, or the set of control messages to be issued, actions to be performed, and responses to be returned; and (3) timing, or specification of the order of event executions.

A *network architecture* specifies the precise functions that a network and its components should perform, while providing the framework in which nodes with possibly different software and hardware structures may participate in the network. As such, network architectures are often specified in terms of the implicit network protocols, including message formats. Over the last decade, several network architectures have emerged, some of which specify such protocols. In Sec. 5-1, we introduce the underlying concepts and functions of a network protocol. Section 5-2 provides a survey of some network architectures and protocols, namely, the ARPANET protocols, the reference model for open systems interconnection, the CCITT recommendation X.25, the Systems Network Architecture of IBM, and the Digital Network Architecture of DEC. Finally, in Secs. 5-3 and 5-4, we review the various techniques to specify and validate network protocols.

5-1 CONCEPTS IN PROTOCOL DESIGN

The primary purpose of a protocol is to establish orderly information exchange among processes, and to efficiently manage network resources. Thus, as pointed out earlier, a protocol may also be conceived as a set of agreements between two communicating processes. For purposes of illustration, consider the exchange of messages between two processes, A and B. The sequence that leads to the initiation and termination of data transmission is shown in Fig. 5-1. To begin with, process A sends a Ready to Send control message to process B. Process B responds by transmitting a Ready to Receive control message to process A. This initiates data transmission from process A to process B. The data messages are sent by process A and

153

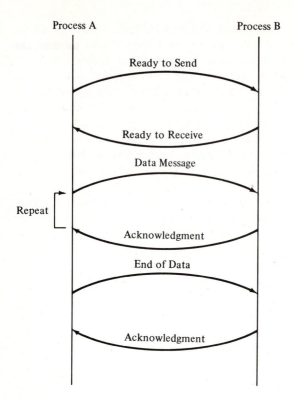

Figure 5-1 A simple protocol to send messages from process A to process B.

acknowledged by process B. In order to terminate the exchange, process A sends an End of Data control message to process B, which is also acknowledged by process B.

The protocol for this simple data exchange must also specify the format of each control message (such as a Ready to Receive, or an Acknowledgment), the header for data messages, and the relative timings (for example, the implicit order that a data message should be sent after receipt of Ready to Receive). Furthermore, processes A and B must agree, a priori, on these rules.

The need for establishing protocols may be appreciated when one considers that there may be more than one, perhaps several, types of nodes in a network. Consider the network shown in Fig. 5-2. The network consists of seven nodes. There are three types of nodes—*A*, *B*, and *C*—depending on the convention required to communicate with another type of node. In order for the network to provide communication of information (data) among these nodes, there are as many as six unique ways for the nodes to exchange information. The six distinct pairwise combinations, as shown in Figs. 5-2 and 5-3, are *AA*, *AB*, *AC*, *BB*, *BC*, and *CC*. This problem can be simplified by establishing one common protocol that is to be followed by each type of node, as shown in Fig. 5-3.

There are three logical components that constitute a network protocol. The first is an entity such as the application programs (residing in a computing system), or a terminal operator. The second component is some form of pairing or binding for these entities that provides a logical communication path between the two entities. This binding may be permanent or may exist only for the duration that the two entities desire to communicate with each other. Finally, there is

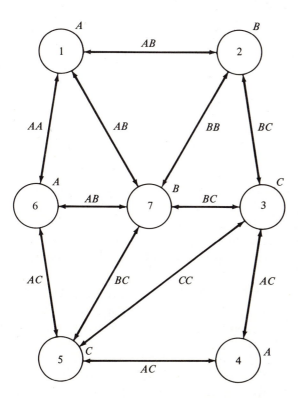

Figure 5-2 A network with seven nodes of three types: A, B, and C. (The pairwise interactions between nodes are labelled on the arcs.)

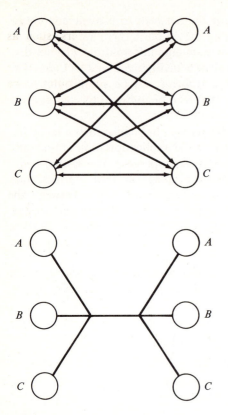

Figure 5-3 Reduction in the ways to exchange messages between three terminal types.

the need for a mechanism to transport information between the two entities that are paired, as shown in Fig. 5-4.

Given the above three entities, the protocol designer must es-

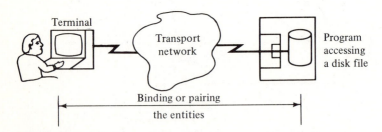

Figure 5-4 Entities for a network protocol.

tablish several rules for using and managing the transport network. These rules should not be exposed to the network users, such as terminal operators. Instead, such rules should reside within the transport network and be transparent to the communicating entities. The rules for the transport network may define the message routes to be followed, the segmenting of messages into smaller fixed-size packets, or the procedures to prevent congestion within the network. Such an approach leads to the concept of *layering*, as shown in Fig. 5-5.

As shown in that figure, the network user accesses the network through some logical entity; let us call it a *process*. The session layer receives a message from the process layer and takes the necessary action, such as establishing or managing the dialogue between the network users. The session layer sends messages to the next lowest layer, or the transport system, which delivers messages to the session layer at the destination node. The underlying principle is that a given layer in a node logically exchanges messages with its corresponding layer in another node, and that the processing at other layers is transparent to it. There are peer-to-peer protocols for communication between the corresponding layers in different nodes. A given layer also communicates with an adjacent layer above or below it through an interface protocol, as shown in Fig. 5-6. This concept of

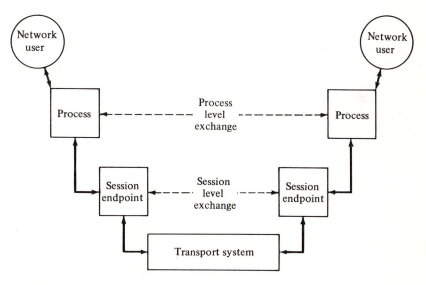

Figure 5-5 Protocol layers.

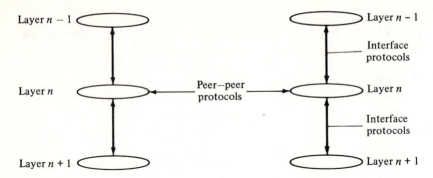

Figure 5-6 Protocols and interfaces.

layering is generally followed in designing protocols. It yields several advantages:

It allows interactions between functionally paired layers in different nodes.

It lends the protocol software to simpler descriptive, development, and testing processes.

It permits changes or modifications to a given layer without affecting other layers.

It provides simpler management of, and smoother enhancements to, the protocols.

Layered protocols must permit certain control information for each layer to be carried by each data message. This information is provided in the message header, often constituting a subheader for each layer. Thus, the layering structure may impose the additional cost of certain message header bits resulting from information that is common to more than one layer. Another negative aspect of layering is that it requires interfaces and control signals between adjacent layers. These costs, in general, are considered negligible when compared to the savings outlined earlier.

Functions of Protocols

Network nodes exchange two types of messages: control and data. Data messages, or simply *messages*, are units of information exchanged between network users, such as operators or application programs. Control messages are used to exchange information among the layers at different nodes to facilitate transmission of data messages.

Compared to data messages, control messages are not known to the network user and are transmitted within the network. Some of the numerous functions served by network protocol are:

1. Orderly exchange of data messages
2. Management of priorities at both the network entry and transmission levels within the network
3. Process synchronization
4. Session establishment between network users
5. Session termination between network users
6. Means for protocol validation
7. Routing—establishment and assignment of message routes and routing information
8. Flow control and congestion prevention
9. Sequencing—sequenced transmission and delivery of messages
10. Addressing of network components and users
11. Efficient network resource utilization
12. Resource management, monitoring, and protection
13. Layered transparency between network users and nodes
14. Reliable message transmission, including error control and recovery
15. Testing of network resources, such as links and routes
16. Security and privacy
17. Optional packet switching through message segmenting and pipelining

Protocols can also satisfy such unique requirements as providing a broadcast mode (transmission of certain messages to more than one network node), transferring large files, or handling long propagation delays for satellites. Each layer in a node supports its own protocols to communicate with the corresponding layer in another node. The protocols for layers that are relatively farther from the transmission link layer match the application functions, while the protocols for layers closer to the link layer contribute to the communication mechanism of the network.

5-2 NETWORK ARCHITECTURES AND PROTOCOLS

In the preceding section, we outlined the underlying concepts of network protocols. In this section, we describe some network architectures and protocols.* These protocols provide functions specific to their respective environments, but a functional similarity may be found in the various protocol layers of each architecture.

Protocols for ARPANET

ARPANET was developed by the Advanced Research Project Agency of the U.S. Department of Defense to allow interconnection of dissimilar computers at widely separated ARPA-sponsored research projects. Since its inception, the network has provided an environment for research in several fields, such as topological design, routing and flow control, computer-to-computer protocols, resource sharing, and satellite communications. ARPANET consists of a collection of interconnected hosts and network nodes. The host processors are the computer systems of different manufacturers, such as the International Business Machines Corporation and the Digital Equipment Corporation. The network nodes are called the *interface message processors* (*IMPs*). The original IMPs, the Honeywell DDP-516 computers, provided host access into the network. Later IMPs were modified to permit direct access from a terminal to the network and IMP, instead of through a host processor and IMP. These modified IMPs are called *terminal interface message processors* (*TIPs*). The following description of ARPANET protocols is based on two papers [1, 11] and two reports [20, 24].

ARPANET protocols are structured into two levels. The higher level, to be discussed later, provides user-level functions. The lower level, shown in Fig. 5-7, consists of three layers. The lowest layer provides for exchanges between two IMPs. The IMP-IMP protocol permits reliable communication among IMPs. It provides transmission error detection and correction, routing, and flow control for preventing congestion. The IMP-HOST protocol provides for exchanges between hosts and IMPs. It allows a host to send messages to specified hosts, and informs the originating host of the disposition of these messages. Next, the HOST-HOST protocol permits hosts to establish and maintain communication between processes, or user jobs, in remote computers.

Several higher-level protocols have been introduced. The layered relationship of these protocols with the lower layers is shown in Fig.

---

* Sometimes, a network architecture is distinguished from a network protocol by the fact that the former includes network protocols as well as the specification of various fields in control messages and headers of data messages.

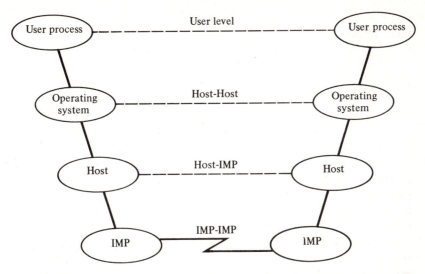

Figure 5-7 Layers of the ARPANET protocol. Solid line = actual communication; dashed line = virtual communication. (From S. D. Crocker, J. F. Heafner, R. M. Metcalfe, and J. B. Postel, "Function-Oriented Protocols for the ARPA Computer Network," *Proceedings of the Spring Joint Computer Conference*, May 1972, p. 274. Published by AFIPS Press, Arlington, Va.)

5-8. The *initial connection protocol* (ICP) provides the protocol for a remote user (or process) to attract the attention of a network host before using the host. A direct analogy is a terminal user pressing the attention key to obtain service from a host.

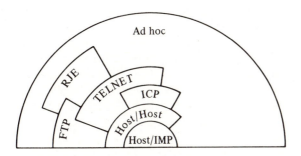

Figure 5-8 Layered relationship of the ARPANET protocols. (From J. Davidson, W. Hathaway, J. Postel, N. Mimno, R. Thomas, and D. Walden, "The ARPANET TELNET Protocol: Its Purpose, Principles, Implementation, and Impact on Host Operating System Design," *Proceedings of the Fifth Data Communications Symposium*, Snowbird, Utah, 1977, p. 4-10.)

An important user-level protocol is that for remote use of interactive systems. The purpose of the telecommunications network (TELNET) protocol is to provide a general, bidirectional, character-oriented communication facility. A given user at a terminal, connected to the local host, controls a process in a remote host as if the user were a local user of the remote host. The local host transfers characters between the user terminal and the TELNET connections over ARPANET. At the local host, the user may perform the following functions through the TELNET user process: initiate and terminate a pair of connections to a serving host (or remote host), send and receive characters to and from the serving host, and send a HOST-HOST interrupt signal. The TELNET protocols employ a *network virtual terminal* (*NVT*) [11]. An NVT is an imaginary device for providing a standard intermediate representation of a terminal throughout the network. Each host maps its local device characteristics and conventions as if it were communicating with the NVT. It eliminates the need for local and remote hosts to retain information regarding the characteristics and conventions of each other's terminals.*

The *file transfer protocol* (*FTP*) allows a user to transfer files of data between two host systems. *Remote job entry* (*RJE*) allows a user at some host system to run a batch job on some other server-host system.

As of June 1977, the ARPANET had 57 nodes and 113 host systems, including CDC 6600 and 7600, IBM System/360 and System/370, DEC PDP-10, and others [24].

Reference Model for Open Systems Interconnection

The International Organization for Standardization (ISO) is working toward an architecture for interconnecting systems, such as computers and terminals.† In so doing, a model for the architecture to permit systems interconnection is being developed; this model is called the *reference model for open systems interconnection* or, simply, the OSI

---

* This concept has also been used in CYCLADES, TELENET, and DATAPAC networks [11].

† This description of the reference model for open systems interconnection is based on [17]. The architecture, under development at the time of writing, may finally result in a form that is somewhat different from what is described here. Several aspects of the layers described here are being refined or are under further study. Some other papers related to this topic are [16, 25, 26, 27, 28].

model. The OSI model is based on three basic elements: the application processes, the connections joining these processes to provide information exchange, and the systems supporting the application processes.

The OSI model consists of seven layers, as shown in Fig. 5-9. Each layer, with the exception of the physical layer, uses the services of the layer beneath it. *Entities* within certain layers are defined to represent the notion of an endpoint and are used to provide services to the next highest layer. A *connection* in a given layer is an association established for communication between two or more entities of the higher layer.

The *application layer*, the highest layer, provides communication between two application processes, such as for application programs or operators. It provides application-specific aspects of communication between the network users.

The *presentation layer* provides services for the application layer to interpret the meaning of the data exchanged. It includes management of the entry, exchange, display, and control of structured data.

The *session layer* provides two classes of functions: (1) binding

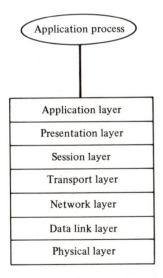

Figure 5-9 Functional layers of the reference model for open systems interconnection. (From V. Ahuja and J. E. Merkel, "Recent Developments in Systems Network Architecture," *Proceedings of the Online Conference on Data Networks: Developments and Use*, London, June 1980, p. 469.)

and unbinding of two presentation entities (that exist in the presentation layer) for a relationship and (2) control of data exchange, delimiting, and synchronization of operations between two presentation entities. Thus, this layer provides session initiation and termination, session recovery, data delimiting, and dialog control. Dialog control pertains to the order in which messages may flow between the end users. In providing dialog control, messages can flow in both directions simultaneously (two-way simultaneous), in only one of two directions at any given time (two-way alternate), or in one given direction (one-way interaction).

The *transport layer* provides the transparent transfer of data between two session entities. (Session entities are the endpoints defined in the session layer.) This layer assigns a unique transport address to each user. All protocols at this layer have end-to-end significance and are to be interpreted at respective transport entities. This leads to the notion of a *transport connection.* One or more transport connections can exist between a pair of transport addresses. The transport layer also includes such functions as class of service (varying levels of transport service), sequencing of messages (first-in first-out, or FIFO, delivery) and flow control. It also permits an expedited flow of messages on a transport connection. Such a flow is useful when normal data flow is blocked, and some control message must be sent to relieve the congestion.

The *network layer* provides message routing; that is, it determines whether the message should be sent to the transport layer in the local node or through the data link layer to another node. Besides routing, this layer also segments and blocks messages to facilitate transmission. A message between two network users transverses the lowest three layers in each of the transit nodes in the network.

The *data link layer* establishes and maintains one or more data links between network entities, and provides sequencing and link flow control. Current examples of standards for this layer include the Advanced Data Communications Control Procedures (ADCCP) in the United States and the ISO High Level Data Link Control (HDLC).

The *physical layer* supports the mechanical, electrical, and functional procedures for creation, maintenance, and release of data circuits between link entities. Examples of standards for this layer are CCITT recommendations V.24 for telephone networks and X.21 for data networks (Sec. 2-3).

The OSI model appears to be progressing toward a flexible layered architecture while permitting a variety of functions in each layer. Several details are being addressed or noted for further study.

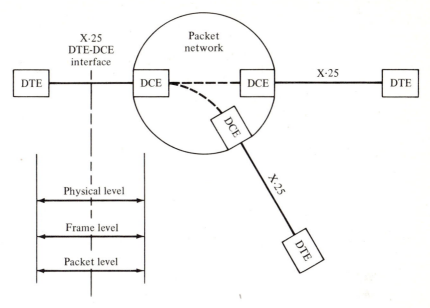

Figure 5-10 X.25 DTE-DCE interface.

X.25

The CCITT recommendation X.25 specifies the interface protocols for a DTE* to attach to a packet-switched network. In essence, it describes the interface between a DTE and a DCE,* as shown in Fig. 5.10. This recommendation was originally adopted by the International Telegraph and Telephone Consultative Committee (CCITT) in 1976, and a revised version was approved in 1980.

In order to allow data transfer between a DTE and a DCE, the CCITT recommendation X.25 uses the notion of a *virtual circuit*, which is defined as a bidirectional association between a pair of DTEs over which all data transfer takes place in the form of packets. The virtual circuit is identified by using the logical channel group number and the logical channel number, which is included in the packet header, as shown in Fig. 5-11(*a*). As shown in Fig. 5-10, more than one virtual circuit can use the same DTE-DCE interface. Since there are 12 bits designated in the packet header for identifying the logical channels, there may be as many as 4096 virtual circuits associated

* The terms *DTE* and *DCE* are defined in the description of CCITT recommendation X.21 in Sec. 2-3. The following description of X.25 uses [3, 13, 14, 16, 19, 36, 37, 38].

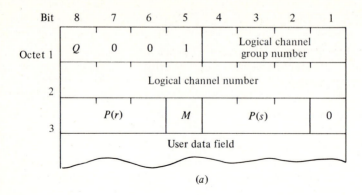

(a)

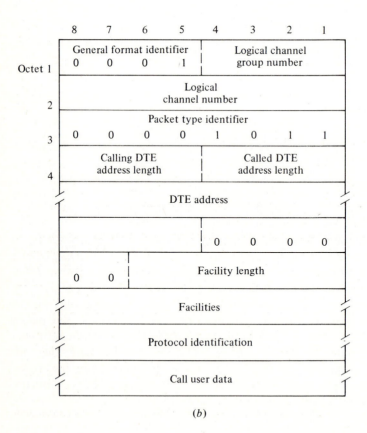

(b)

with a DTE. Two types of virtual circuits are defined. A *permanent* virtual circuit implies a fixed DTE-DTE connection and requires no call establishment or call-clearing. A *switched* virtual circuit, or *virtual call*, requires call establishment and call clearing to establish a connection for communication.

The X.25 protocol consists of three levels: physical, frame, and packet, as illustrated in Fig. 5-10. In terms of the OSI model, the X.25 protocols correspond to the physical, link, and network layers, respectively.

The *physical level* specifies the physical, electrical, functional, and procedural characteristics needed to establish, maintain, and disconnect the physical path between the DTE and DCE. This level specifies the settings of the physical circuits to communicate conditions, such as Receive or Send. It conforms to CCITT recommendation X.21 (see Sec. 2-3).

The *frame level*, or *link level*, specifies the link access procedure (LAP) for exchanging data between the DTE and DCE. LAP was adopted in 1976 to conform to the ISO HDLC, but turned out to be not fully compatible with ISO HDLC. LAP was revised in 1977 to conform to the asynchronous balanced mode of operation in HDLC. In this mode, a given station combines the control attributes of both a primary and a secondary station. This version of the X.25 frame level is called *LAP B*. While LAP remains as originally specified, LAP B is the preferred specification.

The *packet level* pertains to the format and exchange of packets containing control data and user data between the DTE and the network. A data packet usually consists of a 3-byte header and a network-defined limit of data bytes. (Thus, the packet size for the DTE is defined by the X.25 network.) The format of a data packet, shown in Fig. 5-11(a), includes a Q bit, or a data qualifier bit, indicating existence of more than one data level. It is used to specify some special processing for that packet, such as device control. The format

---

Figure 5-11 (a) Format of X.25 data packet. (Adopted from A. Rybczynski, B. Wessler, R. Despres, and J. Wedlake, "A New Communication Protocol for Accessing Data Networks—The International Packet-Mode Interface," *Proceedings of the 1976 National Computer Conference*, vol. 45, p. 480, fig. 3. Published by AFIPS Press, Arlington, Va.)

(b) Format of call request and incoming call packet. (From H. C. Folts, "Status Report on New Standards for DTE/DCE Interface Protocols," *IEEE Computer*, September 1979, p. 18.)

identifier field, excluding the Q bit, has a value of 001 for packet sequence numbers [$P(s)$ and $P(r)$, described later] for modulus 8, and 010 for modulus 128. The $P(r)$ and $P(s)$ fields are assigned 3 bits each for modulus 8 and 7 bits each for modulus 128. Modulus 128 is also called the *extended modulus*. Each virtual circuit is assigned a logical channel group number (≤ 15) and a logical channel number (≤ 255). These numbers hold significance only at the DTE-DCE interface.

The packet-receive and packet-send counts, $P(r)$ and $P(s)$, respectively, are analogous to Nr and Ns counts for a link in SDLC (Chap. 2). However, there is an important difference; the $P(r)$ and $P(s)$ counts pertain to each virtual circuit, and there may be several virtual circuits using the same link. The $P(r)$ and $P(s)$ counts are used to provide flow control* on each virtual circuit by controlling the value of $P(r)$ sent by the receiver and the value of $P(s)$ by the sender. The sender increments the value of $P(s)$ by one in each packet that it transmits. Since flow control is exercised in both directions, the sender or the receiver can be either the DTE or DCE. Thus, the $P(r)$ and $P(s)$ counts help restrict the total number of packets in a virtual circuit. Specifically, let W be the window size for a given virtual circuit. The window size is the maximum number of outstanding packets in that virtual circuit. The receipt of a given value of $P(r)$ from the DCE to the DTE allows packets with a $P(s)$ number of up to $P(r) + W - 1$ to be transmitted by the DTE. Conversely, a DCE may send packets with a $P(s)$ of up to $P(r) + W - 1$, where $P(r)$ is the count the DCE received in the last packet from the DTE. Shah [4] has described line utilization considerations in selecting window size.

In their deliberations, the CCITT considered use of $P(r)$ to provide the end-to-end, or DTE-to-DTE, packet acknowledgment. Such an option may be specified in the delivery confirmation bit (D bit), which is designated to be bit 7 in byte 1 of the data packet header.

The M bit is used to indicate in a full data packet if there is a logical continuation of data in the next data packet on a particular virtual circuit. The last bit in byte 3 is set to 0 for all data packets. For each control packet, such as the call request packet shown in Fig. 5-11, this bit is always set to 1. In the case of control packets, the byte 3 defines the type of packet.

X.25 procedures Several X.25 procedures are described in [13]; we will briefly outline some of them here—Call Establishment and Call Clearing, Flow Control, Interrupt, Reset, Restart, Fast Select, and

---

* The general class of end-to-end flow control techniques is presented in Chap. 7.

Datagram. These procedures employ several types of control packets; see [13] for the formats of these packets.

A simplified call-establishment, data transfer, and call-clearing sequence is shown in Fig. 5-12. The call-establishment and call-clearing sequences are required only in the case of switched virtual circuits. Note that a control packet is sent for each of the signals shown, such as for call request [Fig. 5-11(*b*)] or call accepted. Furthermore, this procedure is executed for each virtual circuit.

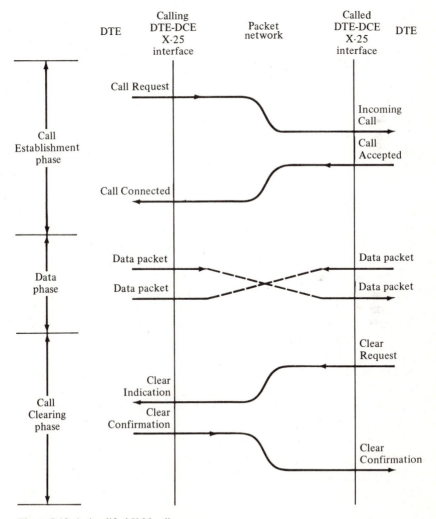

Figure 5-12 A simplified X.25 call sequence.

1. The calling DTE indicates a call request by transfering a Call Request packet across the DTE-DCE interface. This packet includes the address of the called DTE. The destination DCE indicates that there is an incoming call by sending an Incoming Call packet to its DTE. A logical channel number is assigned to the call at both ends of the virtual circuit.
2. The called DTE enters the data transfer phase after sending a Call Accepted packet. The calling DTE receives a Call Connected packet.
3. In the data phase, packets flow in either direction under the constraints of virtual circuit window sizes and other X.25 procedures.
4. Either of the two DTEs may request that the call be cleared by sending a Clear Request packet.
5. The partner DTE receives a Clear Indication packet and sends a Clear Confirmation packet.

The X.25 Flow Control procedure uses the $P(r)$ and $P(s)$ counts to control the flow of packets from the DTE to the network, and from the network to the DTE. The window scheme for this flow control has been outlined earlier.

The Interrupt procedure permits a DTE to transmit 1 byte of data to the remote DTE without following the Flow Control procedure. This procedure begins with a DTE transferring a DTE Interrupt packet across the DTE-DCE interface. The DCE confirms it by sending a DCE Interrupt Confirmation packet to the DTE. The originating DTE cannot send another interrupt packet until it receives the DCE Interrupt Confirmation packet.

The Reset procedure is used to reinitialize a permanent virtual circuit or a switched virtual circuit. In so doing, it removes all the data and Interrupt packets in each direction. The Reset procedure is initiated by the DTE transferring a DTE Reset Request packet to the DCE. The DCE presents a DCE Reset Indication packet to the remote DTE. Finally, the DCE transfers a DCE Reset Confirmation packet to the DTE that originated the DTE Reset Request packet.

The Restart procedure is used to simultaneously clear all switched virtual circuits and reset all permanent virtual circuits on a given DTE-DCE interface.

The X.25 Fast Select facility and Datagram services are part of the revisions being made to X.25. Fast Select facility [36] permits 128 bytes of data in the call user data field of the Call Request/Incoming Call packet [Fig. 5.11(b)]. Furthermore, the Call Accepted/Call Connected, and the Clear Request/Clear Indication packets may also include 128 bytes of data. Thus, exchange of a few bytes of data between the DTEs may be accomplished by only transferring Call Establishment and Call Clearing packets that also include the data.

For X.25 Datagram service, neither call setup nor call clearing is required. Such service is desirable for transfer of short independent units of data without requiring the establishment and clearing of a virtual circuit. The DTE transfers a Datagram packet across the DTE-DCE interface. The DCE delivers the packet to the destination DTE. The first 2 bytes of the user data field are reserved for a Datagram ID to uniquely identify a Datagram with the destination DTE.

CCITT recommendation X.25 is being increasingly supported (or planned to be supported) as an interface for several networks, such as DATAPAC (Canada), TRANSPAC (France), DDX (Japan), and TELENET (U.S.). However, as pointed out by Hess et al. [14], there are noticeable differences in the various X.25 implementations. The DDX network allows the user to contract for a logical channel group number and a logical channel number within each group. DATAPAC, TRANSPAC, and TELENET use the two fields as a contiguous 12-bit field. The maximum length of the user data field in data packets is not the same for all networks, as shown in Table 5-1.

Table 5-1 Maximum data packet sizes*

Network	16	32	64	128	256	512	1024
DATAPAC	n.a.	n.a.	n.a.	Opt	Def	n.a.	n.a.
DDX	n.a.	n.a.	n.a.	n.a.	Def	n.a.	n.a.
TELENET	n.a.	n.a.	n.a.	Def	Opt	Opt	Opt
TRANSPAC	n.a.	Opt	n.a.	Def	n.a.	n.a.	n.a.

* Differences in ways to request the packet sizes are not shown. Opt indicates optional; Def, default; n.a., not available.

Source: M. L. Hess, M. Brethes, and A. Saito, "A Comparison of Four X.25 Public Network Interfaces," *International Conference on Communications*, Boston, 1979, p. 38.6.4, table 9.

Systems Network Architecture

IBM introduced the Systems Network Architecture (SNA) in 1974. SNA has evolved from supporting a single-host configuration to supporting a multihost mesh network [12, 15].* SNA provides the means

* Several publications describe the concepts and details of SNA [7, 12, 18, 19, 21, 30].

for end-users to communicate using network components. An end-user can be a person using a terminal or an application program residing in a host.

In order to describe the layered structure, some definitions are first required. A *network addressable unit* (NAU) is a resource managed by the network. Each end-user accesses the network through a NAU. Specifically, this is called a *logical unit* (LU), one of three kinds of NAUs. The other two kinds are the *system services control point* (SSCP), which controls a portion or domain of a network, and the *physical unit* (PU), which carries out commands from the SSCPs and controls resources within the node. PUs are divided into four types—1, 2, 4, and 5—based on the further subdivision of domains into addressing *subareas* and the capabilities of the nodes containing each PU. The SNA network address consists of a *subarea* and an *element* address component. Each PU type 4 or 5 is assigned a unique subarea address, and is referred as a *subarea node*. In terms of the communication products, PU type 4 and 5 nodes are the IBM communication controllers and host processors, respectively; PU type 1 and 2 nodes are the terminal and cluster controllers (terminal concentrators). An SNA network permits attachment of PU type 1 or 2 nodes to an adjacent subarea node. A subarea node manages some of the network functions, such as addresses, for its attached PU type 1 or 2 nodes. There may be one or more NAUs in a network node. A formally bound pairing, called a *session*, is established between two NAUs before their corresponding end-users can communicate. Each end of a session (in which a NAU is located) is called a *half session*.

The functional layers of SNA are shown in Fig. 5-13. The *services manager layer* provides end-user coordination for the NAU, as well as any device control. *Presentation services* provide the data stream and format control. The next layer, *data flow control*, provides functions for sequence numbering and logical chaining of data messages, for correlation of requests and responses between the end-users, and for control of send and receive concurrency between end-users. *Transmission control* enforces the end-to-end control of message traffic between end-users in accordance with the storage and processing available for it.

The *path control layer* supports message routing throughout the network. Path control for PU types 1 and 2 simply permits routing on the link to and from the associated subarea node. SNA provides alternate routes between a PU type 5 and another PU type 4 or 5 node [12]. A bidirectional logical connection is established between

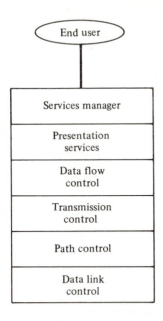

Figure 5-13 Functional layers of SNA.

two such nodes. This connection, called a *virtual route*, is then mapped to a physical path, or *explicit route*, between the two nodes. The explicit route consists of an ordered set of *transmission groups*. A transmission group, in turn, is defined by one or more links connecting a given pair of adjacent PU type 4 or 5 nodes. A *transmission priority* determines the order of message transmission on a transmission group. There may be up to eight virtual route numbers and three transmission priorities, thereby allowing up to 24 virtual routes between two PU type 4 or 5 nodes. A session is assigned to 1 of 24 possible virtual routes. The path control layer for PU type 4 or 5 node may be further divided into three sublayers, as shown in Fig. 5-14. Virtual route control provides end-to-end control between two PU type 4 or 5 nodes. Network flow control* is exercised on each virtual route through an end-to-end window scheme [12]. Explicit route control provides transit routing through the network using routing tables. Transmission group control provides the management of multilink protocols for links attached to the node.

* See Sec. 6.2 for a description of SNA flow control on virtual routes.

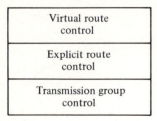

Virtual route control
Explicit route control
Transmission group control

Figure 5-14 Sublayers of path control layer for SNA physical unit types 4 or 5.

The *data-link control layer* provides message transfer across each of the links, using a unique data-link control element for each link.

Digital Network Architecture

Digital Network Architecture (DNA) is the architecture model used by the Digital Equipment Corporation for the DECNET family of implementations [6, 31, 39]. An important goal of this architecture is to support heterogeneous hardware and software components through layering, modularization, extensible (variable-length) fields, and exchange of version levels. DNA uses multilevel hierarchical addressing to address the nodes of the network.

As shown in Fig. 5-15, the highest layer of DNA* is the *user* or *application layer*. This layer provides data exchanges between application programs and input-output devices or file systems. An example of the protocol at this level is the *data access protocol* (DAP). DAP provides users with application-specific (location-independent) communication with files and devices. The user has the following functions available at the DAP interface:

1. Open device or file.
2. Get data.
3. Put data.
4. Control device or file.
5. Get device or file status.
6. Close device or file.

---

* The layered structure of DNA is described in [6, 39].

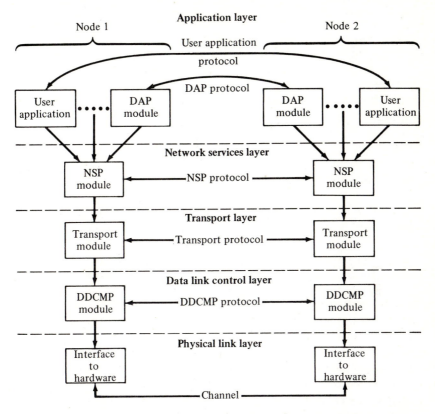

Figure 5-15 Peer layer communication in the DNA hierarchy. (From S. Wecker, "DNA: The Digital Network Architecture," *IEEE Transactions on Communications*, April 1980, vol. COM-28, no. 4, p. 516.)

The *network services layer* establishes and maintains logical link paths for network users. It is concerned with flow control and buffer management. This layer uses the transport layer to move messages from the source node to the destination node. Within a node, this layer forwards the messages to the appropriate logical link path. The protocol at this level is called *network services protocol* (NSP). NSP establishes and deletes logical links upon command from the communication processes. NSP provides sequential delivery with no loss or duplication. NSP also provides the functions of flow control, such that data is sent only on arrival of a request from the receiver, and message segmentation into smaller data units and reassembly.

The *transport layer* routes messages from a source node to a destination node. The protocol at this layer is called the *transport protocol*. Messages are forwarded using a routing table. The routing algorithm employs the best path based on the number of hops and the cost, which is based on the delay, throughput, and error rate of the path. Thus, each node maintains the HOPS and COST information to each destination node through each outgoing link. Whenever a change to the COST or HOPS information occurs (such as a node failure), the node computes new values (of COST and HOPS) and forwards them to each adjacent nodes. Upon receiving these new values, each node updates its routing information appropriately.

The *data-link control layer* creates a sequential error-free communication path between adjacent nodes. The standard protocol at this layer is the *digital data communications message protocol* (DDCMP). The DDCMP message consists of a header, header block check, user data field, and data field block check. The message header consists of a count field for framing, the transmit sequence number of the message, a piggybacked acknowledgment number, and a polling flag and station address for link management. Details of this protocol are given in [39].

The *physical link layer* manages the transmission of data over a channel. It is concerned with the physical characteristics of the transmission channel, and uses protocols for interface standards, such as RS-232C.

The layers of the architectures described above are roughly analagous. The three levels of X.25 provide the interface for the three lowest layers of the OSI model. The functional relationship between the OSI model and SNA layers is [16, 25]: OSI model data link layer to SNA data link layer; OSI model network, transport, and session layers to SNA path control, transmission control, and data flow control layers; and OSI model presentation and application layers to SNA presentation services and services manager layers. The functional similarity between SNA and DNA may also be readily observed [31].

5-3 PROTOCOL DESCRIPTION TECHNIQUES

Network protocols should be described clearly and concisely. A detailed and complete description can provide clarity but often lacks the brevity needed to study network protocols. A brief overview, on the other hand, often lacks the details needed to implement the protocols. Thus, there are requirements for protocol description techniques that may not be satisfied simultaneously. Because of the increasing complexity of network protocols, protocol description techniques must be extendable to permit automatic protocol analysis. Thus, it seems desirable that the protocol description be available in a machine-readable form. Some protocol analyses of interest include:

1. Observing protocol behavior, such as detection of network congestion and freedom from protocol lockups.
2. Checking protocol completeness, or the capability to handle all possible conditions.
3. Checking stability, or the verification that the network components return to a normal state after temporary errors.
4. Measuring protocol performance, such as message overhead due to network protocols.
5. Investigating reachability of each defined state of the network.
6. Verifying protocol freedom from a cyclic behavior resulting in no useful activity.
7. Studying event scheduling in the network.
8. Studying the extent of parallel execution as allowed in the network protocol.

We now present some techniques for describing network protocols. To begin with, perhaps the simplest technique is the description of protocols in text form. An example of this technique is the description of DNA and SNA in Sec. 5-2. A description in text form can be incomplete, however, since it may not address each possible condition and the corresponding action. Next, the technique of flowcharting has been used to describe protocols since their inception. Flowcharts provide a process description at a desired level of detail. Although flowcharting is quite common, it lacks the capability of conveniently transforming the description to machine-readable form. Also, an enormous number of flowcharts is required to completely describe a network protocol. A flowchart for a simple message and reply exchange (receive and send) is shown in Fig. 5-16. This flowchart requires 12 blocks to represent a simple message exchange protocol. Finally, flowcharts do not provide a convenient means to represent concurrency in processing.

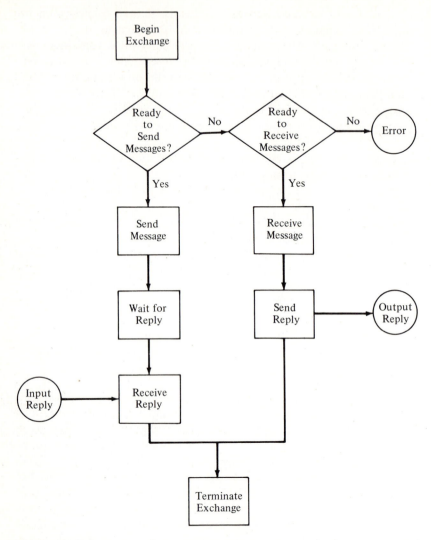

Figure 5-16 Flowchart for a message exchange protocol.

State Diagrams

Certain network protocols can be described in terms of *network states* and *state transitions*. A network state is generally defined by the state, or condition, of each of the network components. A state transition depicts the change from one network state to another, along with the required inputs and any resulting outputs. Thus, a network protocol can be described in terms of the states and state transitions of the participating network components. The state diagram for the protocol of Fig. 5-1 is shown in Fig. 5-17. State diagrams tend to provide a concise representation of simple protocols. However, the number of states for a complex protocol increases rapidly and renders this ap-

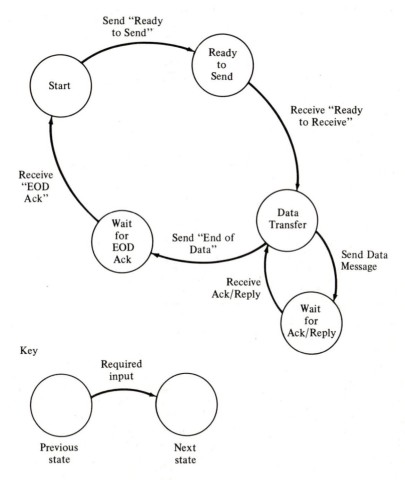

Ack = Acknowledgment
EOD Ack = End of Data Acknowledgment

Figure 5-17 State diagram for process A in the protocol shown in Fig. 5-1.

proach impractical. Further details on the use of state diagrams appear in [22].

Protocols can also be described by sequence diagrams. Sequence diagrams show the order of exchanges between network entities. In a sequence diagram, the state of each entity can be shown on a vertical line. Sequence diagrams are not suitable when the number of entities exceeds three. Sequence diagrams are used in this book to describe several protocols (Figs. 2-20, 5-1, and 5-12).

Petri Nets

Petri nets, developed by Carl Adam Petri and further elaborated by Anatol Holt, offer an alternative way to describe and study protocols.* In Petri nets, conditions are represented by arcs, and events are represented by transition bars. A token is placed on the arc that represents an existing condition. A transition bar (event) can fire (occur) only if each input arc to that bar holds a token. A transition bar fires (or an event occurs) when a token is removed from each input arc and placed on each output arc. A Petri-net graph for a simple message exchange is shown in Fig. 5-18. Petri nets also allow complex arcs in which an arc is initiated by several transition bars, terminated by several transition bars, or both.

Backus Normal Form

The Backus Normal Form (BNF), or Backus-Naur Form, is a notation used for writing grammars that, in turn, specify the rules of programming languages. The notation uses the symbols ::= and | to mean "is replaced by" and "or," respectively. BNF has been extensively used to describe the syntax rules for programming languages. In the context of network protocols, it has been used to describe the syntax rules for character strings, such as the Call Progress signals for X.21 protocols [29]. Here, we present a possible use to describe network protocols through an example of the simple message exchange sequence of Fig. 5-1. The following expressions generate the character strings that, in turn, specify the rules of the message exchange protocol to be followed by process A in Fig. 5-1.

---

* A detailed description of Petri nets is given in [33]. Postel [23] shows their use in communication protocols.

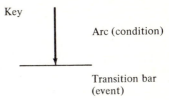

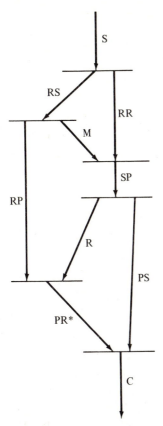

Key

Arc (condition)

Transition bar
(event)

S = Ready for Exchange
RS = Ready to Send Message
RR = Ready to Receive Message
RP = Ready to Receive Reply
M = Message is Available
SP = Ready to Send Reply
R = Reply Available
PR = Reply Received
PS = Reply Sent
C = Exchange Completed

*Problem 5-3

Figure 5-18 Petri net of a simple message exchange protocol. (From J. B. Postel, "A Graph Model Analysis of Computer Communications Protocols," Report no. AD777506, National Technical Information Service, U. S. Department of Commerce, Springfield, Va. 22151, 1974, p. 42.)

$$S ::= \langle SRS \rangle$$

$$\langle SRS \rangle ::= \text{"Send Ready to Send"}, \langle RRR \rangle$$

$$\langle RRR \rangle ::= \text{"Receive Ready to Receive"}, \langle SD \rangle$$

$$\langle SD \rangle ::= \text{"Send Message"}, \langle ACK \rangle$$

$$\langle ACK \rangle ::= \langle AK \rangle, \langle SD \rangle \mid \langle ED \rangle$$

$$\langle ED \rangle ::= \text{"Send End of Data"}, \langle AK \rangle$$

$$\langle AK \rangle ::= \text{"Receive Acknowledgment"}$$

A complete expansion of the above expressions gives:

S = "Send Ready to Send", "Receive Ready to Receive",

"Send a Message", "Receive Acknowledgment",*

"Send End of Data", "Receive Acknowledgment"

Perhaps the most promising protocol description technique is the use of a programming language. This approach provides the protocol in machine-readable form. We briefly describe two languages that have been used to specify network protocols.

Format and Protocol Language

The IBM Systems Network Architecture has been described (partially, at the time of writing) in Format and Protocol Language (FAPL). The architecture uses a set of finite-state machines (FSMs) for each network node, and provides state transitions through FAPL code. FAPL augments the programming language PL/I to provide representations of FSMs and references to them. It defines general list-handling capabilities, and includes features for queued dispatching of procedures (FAPL programs) as well as for operations on queues. A finite-state machine (FSM) is represented in the form of a state-transition matrix. Inputs and outputs are represented in mnemonic form, and defined outside the matrix. The matrix form, as compared to a state-transition diagram, provides easy visual verification and facilitates consideration of all possible combinations of states and inputs. FSMs are referenced in several ways. First, an FSM may be called along with an input for a possible state transition:

CALL FSM_fsmname [(fsm_input)];

Secondly, the state of an FSM may be tested as follows:†

IF FSM_fsmname = state_name   THEN___;

RSPL

RSPL is the language developed and used to specify protocols by Schindler et al. [32]. The RSPL code for X.25 LAPB‡ is given in [32].

---

* Can be repeated.

† Additional details on FAPL, its representation of FSMs, and its use in describing SNA are given in [7, 21].

‡ See Sec. 5-2 for a description of LAPB.

The language combines various actions and options in single statements. A *protocol sequence expression* (PSE) consists of one or more functions. An example of the RSPL code taken from [35] is described below.

PSE   X.25/LAPB: = (ABM → IT_P* OR IT_S* → DIS)+;

This statement implies the following actions.

ABM
: Execute the ABM phase of X.25 Level 2 exactly once.

→ IT_P*
OR IT_S*
: Next, execute the phase IT_P for 0, one or more times, or IT_S for 0, one or more times. IT_P is the information transfer phase for primary, and IT_S is the information transfer phase for secondary.

→ DIS
: Next, it must execute the DIS (for link disconnect) phase exactly once.

(– – –) +
: Repeat the sequence in parenthesis any number of times.

Timeouts are allowed by repeating the execution of an expression within parenthesis a given number of times. For example, (– – – – +)#N2 specifies the execution of the statement within parenthesis for N2 times. Exits are allowed to perform special checking in case of unexpected events.

5-4 PROTOCOL VALIDATION TECHNIQUES

Protocol validation determines if a protocol is complete, well-behaved, and error-free.† Validation of communication protocols is becoming increasingly difficult because of the complexity of network protocols. Although it is not difficult to check a simple protocol such as the one shown in Fig. 5-1, it is understandably impractical to manually validate protocols that provide communication among sev-

---

† Sunshine [34] provides the status and an overview of the various protocol specification and verification techniques.

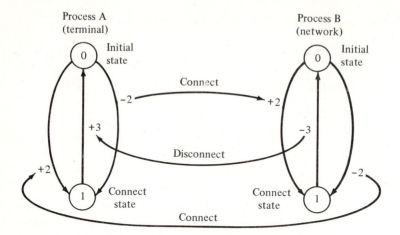

Figure 5-19 A simplified connection-establishment protocol for protocol validation. (From P. Zafiropulo, "A New Approach to Protocol Validation," *Proceedings of the International Conference on Communications*, Chicago, 1977, p. 30.2-259.)

eral processes, manage orderly information exchange, and recover from error conditions. Next, we present two techniques on protocol validation: *duologue matrix theory* [9] and the *state perturbation approach* [7, 8]. These techniques provide automated validation of the logical structure of a network protocol.

Duologue Matrix Approach

In order to explain the concept of a duologue matrix,* we consider the protocol shown in Fig. 5-19. Communication between the two processes (terminal and network) is achieved by events. Each event is represented by an integer. A negative value implies event transmission; a positive value implies event reception. We assume that each process shown in Fig. 5-19 begins and ends in the intial state 0. The connect event is represented by -2 for its transmission and $+2$ for its reception. Similarly, the disconnect event is represented by -3 for its transmission and $+3$ for its reception. Then, the event sequences for processes A and B are shown in Fig. 5-20. Now a *unilogue* is a path beginning and ending in state 0, but not traversing state 0. The sequence A_1 and B_1 shown in Fig. 5.20 are each a unilogue. The tuple $\langle A_1, B_1 \rangle$ is called a *duologue*. The duologue

* This description of the duologue matrix theory is based on [9].

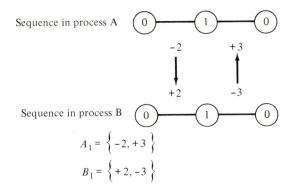

Sequence in process A

Sequence in process B

$$A_1 = \left\{ -2, +3 \right\}$$

$$B_1 = \left\{ +2, -3 \right\}$$

Figure 5-20 Interaction sequences for protocol shown in Fig. 5-19. (From P. Zafiro-pulo, "A New Approach to Protocol Validation," *Proceedings of the International Conference on Communications*, Chicago, 1977, p. 30.2-260.)

matrix is the set of all conceivable duologues for a given protocol. For processes A and B in Fig. 5-19, there are also the unilogues $A_2 = (+2, +3)$, and $B_2 = (-2, -3)$. Thus, the duologue matrix in this case is:

$$\left\{ \begin{array}{ll} (A_1, B_1) & (A_1, B_2) \\ (A_2, B_1) & (A_2, B_2) \end{array} \right\}$$

A validation function on a duologue (A_i, B_k) is defined to yield one of three values:

$+1$ if (A_i, B_k) is well-behaved

0 if (A_i, B_k) is nonoccurable

-1 if (A_i, B_k) is erroneous

The conditions that determine the above values are described next. First, suppose that one process is not designed to receive outputs from the other. This erroneous condition is detected by checking the duologue for the conditions that every event transmitted by A_i is subsequently received in B_k, and vice versa. This condition is called the *post-transmission condition*. Next, a deadlock can occur when both processes remain in a state and cannot exit from it. This can happen when an input required for a process to exit a state is not sent by the other process. It is corrected by requiring that every event received in A_i must be previously transmitted by B_k, and vice versa. This is called the *prereception condition. Completeness* conditions are defined when every state traversed by B_k (or A_i) that can potentially receive an event, transmitted by A_i (or B_k), is designed to receive that event. A duologue is *occurable* if it satisfies post-transmission and prereception conditions. Finally, a duologue is *well-behaved* if it is occurable and satisfies completeness conditions.

The above approach has been automated in the form of a computer program. It was used to validate the X.21 protocols (at that time) and detected some points where the interface state diagram did not completely define interface behavior [5]. As observed by West [8], the duologue matrix theory has two limitations:

1. It is restricted to protocols in which the interacting processes must return together to their initial states after a finite number of initial steps.
2. It only addresses protocols between two processes.

We next describe an approach that addresses these limitations.

State Perturbation Approach

This approach, developed by West [8], removes the limitations of the duologue matrix approach. It is based on defining an initial state (comprising the states of all components of the system), generating all states accessible from it, and then checking all system state transitions and their possible interaction sequences. Consider two processes in the initial state that communicate by two simplex channels. The system state is then defined by the state of the two processes and the two channels. (A channel state is defined by the messages it is carrying at a given time.) A *perturbation* of a system state is defined as the execution of a single transiton in one process in the system, resulting in a change of state of a channel if an event (or message) is transmitted or received.

Consider the example of the read-write protocol shown in Fig. 5-21 and the system states described in Fig. 5-22. The only perturbation of the initial (Reset) state occurs when process A transmits a write instruction to process B. This leads to system state 1, with process A in PEND.WRITE state and the channel from A to B containing the event write. The system changes from state 1 to state 2 when process B receives the write instruction. Both processes are now in the PEND.WRITE state, and two different perturbations of the

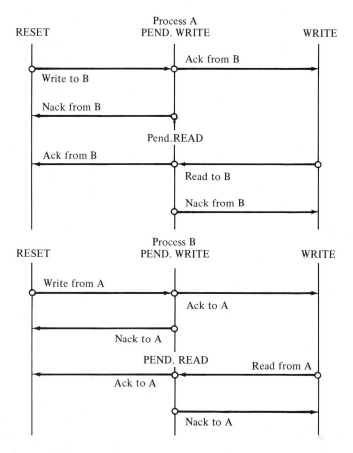

Figure 5-21 A loop example for a write/read protocol. (From C. H. West, "General Technique for Communications Protocol Validation," *IBM Journal of Research and Development*, vol. 22, no. 4, July 1978, p. 394. Copyright 1978 by International Business Machines Corporation; reprinted with permission.)

system state are possible, depending on whether B transmits a positive or negative acknowledgment. The execution tree shown at right in Fig. 5-22 indicates the execution paths possible in the system.

West provides the description of a formal communications system model [8]. Here, we skip that portion and briefly describe his validation algorithm.

1. Define a set S of system states beginning with only the initial state $S(0)$ of the system.

System state	State of A	Channel A to B	State of B	Channel B to A	Execution tree
0	RESET	–	RESET	–	
1	PEND.WRITE	Write	RESET	–	
2	PEND.WRITE	–	PEND.WRITE	–	
3	PEND.WRITE	–	RESET	Nack	
0	RESET	–	RESET	–	
4	PEND.WRITE		WRITE	Ack	
5	WRITE	–	WRITE	–	
6	PEND.READ	Read	WRITE	–	
7	PEND.READ	–	PEND.READ	–	
8	PEND.READ	–	WRITE	Nack	
5	WRITE	–	WRITE	–	
9	PEND.READ	–	RESET	Ack	
0	RESET	–	RESET	–	

*Indicates a state already validated.

Figure 5-22 Analysis of the loop example of Fig. 5-21. (From C. H. West, "General Technique for Communications Protocol Validation," *IBM Journal of Research and Development*, vol. 22, no. 4, July 1978, p. 396. Copyright 1978 by International Business Machines Corporation; reprinted with permission.)

2. Find an element $S(N)$ from the set of system states such that its perturbations have not been determined. If no such element exists, the algorithm terminates since the validation is complete.
3. Derive the set of system states Sp that can be reached by a perturbation of $S(N)$. There will be an element of Sp for each executable transition from state $S(N)$.
4. If Sp is an empty set, then $S(N)$ is a deadlock state.
5. Remove all states leading to an error, after recording the errors generated by them.
6. Add all remaining elements of Sp that are not already elements of S to the set S.
7. Return to step 2.

By an example [8], West shows how to apply this approach to more than two processes. In [7], the validation of the SNA data flow control protocols, using the state perturbation approach, is described.

SUMMARY

At the beginning of this chapter, we described the functions and design concepts of a network protocol, and then surveyed five network protocols and architectures. There is a noticeable similarity between the functional layers of various protocols. There are other network protocols, including those for local area networking, that are not included here. The second part of this chapter addressed two important areas of protocols: description and validation. The increasing complexity of network protocols is imposing new requirements on description techniques such as to permit machine readability and representation of protocol entities and states. Protocol validation is an area of emerging interest and recent research. We feel that further work is needed to develop and refine specialized tools for validating as well as describing protocols.

PROBLEMS

5-1 Compare the functions provided at each layer of SNA, DNA, and the OSI model. Identify their similarities and differences.

5-2 Compare the merits of different protocol description techniques, if it were to be used to describe the (a) X.25 protocol and (b) the OSI model.

5-3 Assume that the condition PR is not coded correctly for the system in Fig. 5-18. Thus, the transition bar that requires PR (* in the figure) never fires. Write a validation algorithm that detects the error.

5-4 One possible protocol validation scheme is to develop a state transition diagram for the protocol and, beginning with the initial state, to check each possible sequence of state transitions. If the sequence results in a state other than the one designed, it is in error. Also, if it is in a state (other than termination) such that it cannot proceed, it is in a deadlock. In case of an invalid input to a state, an error should be generated.

  (a) For each of the two examples of validation schemes described in Sec. 5-4, use the above approach to validate the sequences. Identify the sequences (inputs for various states) that are invalid.

  (b) Compare the above scheme with the duologue matrix and state perturbation approaches.

5-5 Trace the various states and the execution tree for processes A and B shown in Figs. 5-21 and 5-22.

REFERENCES

1. S. D. Crocker, J. F. Heafner, R. M. Metcalfe, and J. B. Postel, "Function-Oriented Protocols for the ARPA Computer Network," *Spring Joint Computer Conference*, May 1972, p. 271–279.
2. C. S. Carr, S. D. Crocker, and V. G. Cerf, "HOST-HOST Communication Protocol in the ARPA Network," *Spring Joint Computer Conference*, May 1970, pp. 589–597.
3. A. Rybczynski, B. Wessler, R. Despres, and J. Wedlake, "A New Communication Protocol for Accessing Data Networks—The International Packet-Mode Interface," *National Computer Conference*, 1976, pp. 477–482.

4. A. Shah, "On Flow Control Mechanism in Packet-Switching Networks—An Analytical Approach," *Proceedings of Trends and Applications*, Gaithersburg, Md., 1976, pp. 37–41.

5. C. H. West and P. Zafiropulo, "Automated Validation of a Communications Protocol: The CCITT X.21 Recommendation," *IBM Journal of Research and Development*, vol. 22, no. 1, January 1978, pp. 60–71.

6. G. E. Conant and S. Wecker, "DNA: An Architecture for Heterogeneous Computer Networks," *Proceedings of the Third International Conference on Computer Communication*, Toronto, 1976, pp. 618–625.

7. G. D. Schultz, D. B. Rose, C. H. West, and J. P. Gray, "Executable Description and Validation of SNA," *IEEE Transactions on Communications*, vol. COM-28, no. 4, April 1980, pp. 661–677.

8. C. H. West, "General Technique for Communications Protocol Validation," *IBM Journal of Research and Development*, vol. 22, no. 4, July 1978, pp. 393–404.

9. P. Zafiropulo, "A New Approach to Protocol Validation," *Proceedings of the International Communications Conference*, Chicago, 1977, pp. 30.2-259 to 30.2-263.

10. C. H. West, "An Automated Technique of Communications Protocol Validation," *IEEE Transactions on Communications*, vol. COM-26, no. 8, August 1978, pp. 1271–1275.

11. J. Davidson, W. Hathaway, J. Postel, N. Mimno, R. Thomas, and D. Walden, "The ARPANET TELENET Protocol: Its Purpose, Principles, Implementation and Impact on Host Operating System Design," *Fifth Data Communications Symposium*, Snowbird, Utah, 1977, pp. 4–10 to 4–18.

12. V. Ahuja, "Routing and Flow Control in Systems Network Architecture," *IBM Systems Journal*, vol. 18, no. 2, 1979, pp. 298–314.

13. International Telegraph and Telephone Consultative Committee, "CCITT Provisional Recommendations X.3, X.25, X.28 and X.29 on Packet-Switched Data Transmission Services," Geneva, 1978.

14. M. L. Hess, M. Brethes, and A. Saito, "A Comparison of Four X.25 Public Network Interfaces," *International Conference on Communication*, Boston, 1979, pp. 38.6.1–38.6.8.

15. J. P. Gray and T. B. McNeill, "SNA Multiple-System Networking," *IBM Systems Journal*, vol. 18, no. 2, 1979, pp. 263–297.

16. F. P. Corr and D. H. Neal, "SNA and Emerging International Standards," *IBM Systems Journal*, vol. 18, no. 2, 1979, pp. 244–262.

17. International Organization for Standardization, "Reference Model of Open Systems Interconnection," document no. ISO/TC97/SC16 N227, June 1979.

18. IBM Corporation, "Systems Network Architecture: General Information," no. GA27-3102.

19. R. J. Cypser, *Communications Architecture for Distributed Systems*, Addison-Wesley, Reading, Mass., 1978.

20. Network Analysis Corporation, "ARPANET: Design, Operation, Management, Performance," Glen Cove, N.Y., April 1973.

21. IBM Corporation, "Systems Network Architecture Format and Protocol Reference Manual: Architecture Logic," no. SC30-3112-1, 1978.

22. Z. Kohavi, *Switching and Finite Automata Theory*, McGraw-Hill, New York, 1970.

23. J. B. Postel, "A Graph Model Analysis of Computer Communications Protocols," Ph.D. thesis, University of California, Los Angeles, 1974. Published as report no.

AD-777506, National Technical Information Service, Springfield, Va., January 1974.

24. J. A. Payne, "ARPANET Host to Host Access and Disengagement Measurements," National Technical Information Service, Springfield, Va., no. 78-3, accession no. PB 283 554, May 1978.

25. V. Ahuja and J. E. Merkel, "Recent Developments in Systems Network Architecture," *Proceeding of Online Conference on Data Networks: Developments and Use*, London, June 1980, pp. 463–474.

26. C. Bachman and M. Canepa, "The Session Control Layer of an Open System Interconnection," *Proceedings of the COMPCON*, 1978, pp. 150–156.

27. M. Gien and H. Zimmermann, "Design Principles for Network Interconnection," *Proceedings of the Sixth Data Communications Symposium*, Pacific Grove, Calif., pp. 109–119.

28. D. Basu, "A Data Communications Architecture for Centralized Telephone Operations," *Proceedings of the National Telecommunications Conference*, 1979, pp. 32.1.1–32.1.6.

29. "CCITT Draft Recommendation X.21," Geneva, April 1979.

30. E. H. Sussenguth, "Systems Network Architecture: A Perspective," *Proceedings of the International Conference on Computer Communications*, Kyoto, 1978, pp. 353–358.

31. P. E. Green, "An Introduction to Network Architectures and Protocols," *IBM Systems Journal*, vol. 18, no. 2, 1979, pp. 202–222.

32. S. Schindler, "X.25 Considered Harmful?" *IEEE Computer*, December 1979, pp. 120–121.

33. J. L. Peterson, "Petri Nets," *Computing Surveys*, vol. 9., no. 3, September 1977, pp. 223–252.

34. C. Sunshine, "Formal Techniques for Protocol Specification and Verification," *IEEE Computer*, September 1979, pp. 20–27.

35. S. Schindler, T. Luckenbach, and W. Schroeder, "Formal Specifications of the X.25 Layer 2 Protocols," Technical University of Berlin, August 1979.

36. H. C. Folts, "Status Report on New Standards for DTE/DCE Interface Protocols," *IEEE Computer*, September 1979, pp. 12–19.

37. A. Rybczynski, "X.25 Interface and End-to-End Virtual Circuit Service Characteristics," *IEEE Transactions on Communications*, vol. COM-28, no. 4, April 1980, pp. 500–510.

38. H. C. Folts, "X.25 Transaction Oriented Features—Datagram and Fast Select," *IEEE Transactions on Communications*, vol. COM-28, no. 4, April 1980, pp. 496–500.

39. S. Wecker, "DNA: The Digital Network Architecture," *IEEE Transactions on Communications*, vol. COM-28, no. 4, April 1980, pp. 510–526.

CHAPTER
SIX

FLOW CONTROL

CHAPTER OUTLINE

6-1 NETWORK CONGESTION

Networks consist of finite resources, such as the message buffers that reside in network nodes. An unrestricted flow of messages into the network may lead to *congestion*. A network is considered to be congested when messages are experiencing longer than expected delays through it. A close analogy to network congestion is the traffic condition during the rush hour in a downtown district. In this case, the cars correspond to the messages, and the car spaces in the streets correspond to the message buffers. As the traffic increases, a traffic jam results that, in turn, proliferates to other adjacent streets. Correspondingly, when the network becomes congested, it transmits few, if any, messages and the congestion rapidly spreads. Network congestion can ultimately lead to a deadlock in which no message flow takes place. Thus, network congestion, if not prevented, progressively degrades performance, and the rate of such degradation increases rapidly with congestion. Although it may be argued as to exactly when a network becomes congested, the general network performance under increasing loads is predictable, as shown in Fig. 6-1. The network behavior is undesirable in the range when throughput declines with an increase in

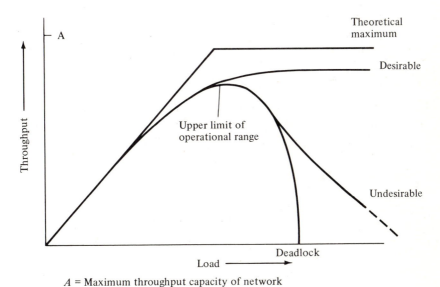

A = Maximum throughput capacity of network

Figure 6-1 Network throughput versus load.

load. Thus, the best operating range is just below the load at which network throughput begins to decline.

As noted above, an unexpected high rate of message arrivals into the network can lead to congestion. If no remedy is applied, network congestion can eventually result in a buffer deadlock, thereby blocking all message movement. A simple buffer deadlock is shown in Fig. 6-2. In this case, it is assumed that a node can transmit a message only after a buffer for the message has been assigned in the next node, that each node has one message to send (along the arrow), and that there is no message buffer available in any node. Then, nodes *A*, *B*, and *C* are waiting for each other to release a buffer. The wait in this case cannot be resolved and, consequently, deadlock in the network results. This deadlock is sometimes called a *circular* or *indirect store-and-forward deadlock*. If there are only two nodes, it is called a *direct store-and-forward deadlock*.

Flow Control

Simply stated, *flow control* is a mechanism for preventing congestion in networks. Congestion arises when the nodes that are sending messages to a particular receiving node exceed the capacity of that re-

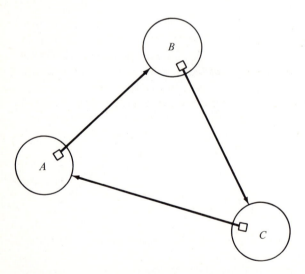

Figure 6-2 A simple buffer deadlock. (The node on the trailing edge of an arrow is waiting for a buffer in the node on the leading edge; each node has a single buffer that is already in use by a message waiting for transmission.)

ceiving node to process, or forward, messages. Thus, the problem reduces to one of providing each given node with mechanisms to control the rate at which it receives the messages from other nodes. As such, flow control is the process of regulating the rate at which a sender generates messages so that the receiver can process them. From a network user perspective, flow control is a mechanism that prevents those messages from entering the network that cannot be delivered in a predefined time.

Network flow control can also be used as a mechanism for distributing the traffic equally among network nodes. As such, flow control can reduce message delays during normal network operations and prevent any part of the network from becoming overloaded relative to the rest of the network.

We present various flow control strategies in the next section. Because of weaknesses in some flow control mechanisms, or conditions unique to a network, some networks can be exposed to a buffer deadlock. A network may result in a deadlock when its protocols are in an indefinite wait. In Sec. 6-3, we describe the problems of protocol deadlock and buffer deadlock along with some approaches to address them.

6-2 FLOW CONTROL TECHNIQUES

A flow control mechanism operates on a network-wide basis to prevent congestion and deadlocks, and attempts to equitably distribute network traffic. Flow control requires imposing some form of control over the flow of network messages. This control can reside in a designated node of the network, or be distributed over each of the network nodes. We have chosen to group flow control techniques into two classes. If the network flow control is exercised from a single node in the network, it is called *centralized flow control*; otherwise, it is called *distributed flow control*.

Centralized Flow Control

Centralized flow control is administered in three basic steps:

1. Gather information on current message traffic patterns in a designated (network control) node.
2. Execute some algorithm in the network control node to compute message flow assignments (described below) for each node.
3. Communicate the new message flow assignments to each node or,

preferably, only to those nodes for which the flow assignments have changed.

If the message flow exceeds network capacity, then impose constraints on the rate of message input to the network.

By message flow assignment, we mean the allocation of the number of messages a node is permitted to accept from network users for transmission through the network, as well as the number of messages arriving from other nodes that pass through this node toward their destination nodes. Clearly, the critical part of a centralized flow control scheme is the algorithm that assign flows so as to prevent congestion. An outline of the algorithms that provide centralized flow control is given in four steps:

1. Record or estimate the number of messages per time unit through each node.
2. Check each node or link to determine if its message rate exceeds the acceptable rate. If such a node or link exists, proceed to step 3; otherwise, terminate the algorithm.
3. For each node or link on which the message traffic exceeds a predefined limit, compute a new set of message flows so that the excess traffic on overloaded links and nodes is directed through the less heavily loaded nodes and links.

   When such a flow assignment is not feasible, then clearly the network cannot handle the message traffic. In such a case, satisfactory performance requires an increase in the link capacities, addition of new links, or initiation of some form of a shutoff procedure by the network to reduce new traffic entering the network.
4. Transmit new message flow assignments to each node.

One possible approach to determining an acceptable message rate on a link is to restrict the rate to a level below the predefined limit. This would prevent congestion by restricting the message delay across a link. For purposes of analysis, a given link can be considered as an exponential server. We also assume that message arrivals are random, described by the Poisson distribution. The Poisson distribution provides easily obtainable results and, in most cases, adequately approximates processes, such as the number of messages entering the network. Then, as will be outlined in Chap. 8, the average queue size of messages waiting for transmission is $\rho/(1 - \rho)$, where ρ is the average link utilization. As ρ approaches the value of 1 in this expression, the average queue size increases rapidly, thereby increasing the message delay. Then the desired message rate for a link corresponds to the level of link utilization (typically, 70 to 80 percent) that does not result in excessive message delays.

Next, we outline another approach for assigning message flows on the links. Flows can be based on link capacities and message routes between each source node and destination node pair [3, pp. 231–233]. We use the following notation: M is the number of links, λ_i is the average message rate per second on the ith link, C_i is the capacity of the ith link in bits per second, $1/u$ is the average message size in bits, and γ is the total external traffic entering the network per second. Suppose there are R pairs of source-destination nodes in the network. Then, we can map this problem to a minimum-cost multiple-commodity flow problem, stating that there are R commodities to flow through the network. The message delay through the network may be estimated by:*

$$T = \sum_{i=1}^{M} \frac{\lambda_i}{\gamma(uC_i - \lambda_i)} \qquad (6\text{-}1)$$

The objective is to determine the flow on each link for each commodity such that the average message delay through the network is minimized. The *cost* on each link in the multiple-commodity flow problem corresponds to the time delay on each link. If $f_{i,k}$ is the flow on link i due to commodity k, $k = 1$ to R, then

$$F_i = \sum_{k=1}^{R} f_{i,k}$$

where F_i is the flow on link i.

Also, the total incoming traffic to a node must be equal to the total outgoing traffic. Thus, the traffic caused by commodity (i, j) at a given node l must satisfy

$$\sum_{k=1}^{n} f_{i,j:k,l} - \sum_{m=1}^{n} f_{i,j:l,m} = \begin{cases} -r_{i,j} & \text{if } l = i \\ r_{i,j} & \text{if } l = j \\ 0 & \text{otherwise} \end{cases}$$

where $r_{i,j}$ is the total traffic generated at node i and destined for node j, n is the number of nodes, and $f_{i,j:k,l}$ (or $f_{i,j:l,m}$) is the traffic for commodity (i, j) on the link connecting nodes k and l (or l and m).

Similar equations must be written for each node and for each of the R commodities. Then, the objective is to establish values for each

* Derived in Chap. 8.

$f_{i,j:k,l}$ in the network that minimize network delays and satisfy the above constraint equations, as well as the constraints imposed by link capacities, namely, $F_i < C_i$. For an n node network, there can be as many as $n(n-1)$ commodities, thus resulting in a total of $n^2(n-1)$ equations for n nodes. This requires solving a large number of equations for a moderate-size network. (A 10-node network can require solving as many as 900 equations; a 50-node network, as many as 122,500 equations.) Furthermore, this approach is attractive only if the message routes are defined a priori for each source-destination node pair, and the message flow does not change significantly during network operation. If the message rate changes at a slow rate, then the preceding algorithm can be used by executing it and incorporating its results at sufficiently longer time intervals.

Flow control in TYMNET An example of centralized flow control is the scheme employed by TYMNET [3, pp. 26–27; 6; 20; 21]. TYMNET is a computer communication network developed by Tymshare. The network is centrally directed and, as of 1978, consisted of nearly 300 nodes [21]. One of the network nodes is assigned the task of establishing message routes. Such a node is called the *supervisor*, and there are other nodes in the network that can take over the supervisory task if the supervisor node fails. When a user requests a connection, the supervisor selects a path based on the link speeds, node capacities, and message traffic. It uses the shortest-path or least-cost routing (a modified version of the Floyd's algorithm* [21]) in which the cost for a path is obtained by adding a certain cost for each link. The user is assigned the virtual circuit with minimum cost, and the assignment holds for the duration of the connection. A summary of the cost factors used in TYMNET is shown below:

Link speed, bps	Cost normal	Cost overloaded, one way	Cost overloaded, both ways
9600	10	26	42
7200	11	27	43
4800	12	28	44
2400	16	32	48

Source: J. Rinde, "Routing and Control in a Centrally Directed Network," *Proceedings of the National Computer Conference*, AFIPS Press, 1977, vol. 46, p. 604.

* Floyd's algorithm is described in Chap. 7.

As shown in the preceding table, three factors are considered in computing the cost: (1) the cost decreases with an increase in link speed, (2) a penalty cost (of 16) is added for the overloaded link, and (3) an infinite cost (that is not shown in the table) is added if a link is inoperative or not to be used. Thus, the above algorithm tends to minimize congestion by spreading network traffic over all links and nodes.*

Flow deviation method A useful approach to assign flows has been described by Fratta, Gerla, and Kleinrock [22]. Their algorithm, called the *flow deviation method*, is based on minimizing network delay. The algorithm assigns flows within a network so as to minimize cost, delay, or both for a given topology and external flow requirements.†

The message delay T through a network can be estimated as

$$T = \sum_{i=1}^{M} \frac{\lambda_i}{\gamma(uC_i - \lambda_i)}$$

where M, λ_i, γ, $1/u$, and C_i have been defined earlier; see eq. (6-1). Then, to obtain the flow for minimum delay through the network, differentiate the delay T by the flow λ_i/u.

$$\frac{\partial T}{\partial\left(\dfrac{\lambda_i}{u}\right)} = \frac{C_i}{\gamma(C_i - \lambda_i/u)^2} \qquad i = 1, 2, \ldots, M$$

The algorithm uses this derivative to determine the minimum delay paths through the network. We describe the fixed routing flow algorithm,‡ based on the flow deviation algorithm. To start the algorithm, assume that a feasible fixed routing flow of $f^{(k)}$ can be obtained.

1. Let

$$f^{(k)} = \left(\frac{\lambda_1^{(k)}}{u}, \frac{\lambda_2^{(k)}}{u}, \ldots, \frac{\lambda_M^{(k)}}{u}\right)$$

be the flow through M links, as determined on the kth iteration.

---

* Details on TYMNET are given in App. A.

† A detailed description of the algorithm, along with its supporting results, is given in [2, pp. 341–348; 22].

‡ An optimal routing flow algorithm is given in [2, p. 343–346].

2. For each link i, $i = 1, 2, \ldots, M$, compute a *length*

$$l_i = \frac{C_i}{\gamma \left(C_i - \frac{\lambda_i^{(k)}}{u} \right)^2}$$

where $\lambda_i^{(k)}$ is the flow on kth iteration. Treating $\partial T / \partial(\lambda_i / u)$ as a length helps determine a total path with a minimum total delay.

3. Obtain the shortest routes based on l_i. Let $G = f^{(k)}$, as defined in step 1.

4. For each flow requirement γ_{jk}, proceed as follows:

   (*a*) Create a vector **V** that represents the new flow obtained from G by directing all the traffic γ_{jk} for node pair (j, k) through the shortest j–k route.

   (*b*) If **V** is feasible, and if the value T of the delay obtained by using vector **V** is strictly less than that obtained by using G, then let $G = $ **V**. Check whether all γ_{jk} flows have been examined. If so, proceed to step 5; otherwise return to step 4(*a*).

5. If $G = f^{(k)}$, the algorithm terminates since no improvement is possible. Otherwise, let $f^{(k+1)} = G$, $k = k + 1$, and return to step 3.

This algorithm was applied to a 21-node ARPANET configuration [2, p. 347], using 1.187 kbps as γ_{jk} for each of the distinct-ordered node pairs. The network included 26 full-duplex links, and thus $M = 52$. The algorithm, programmed in Fortran and run on an IBM 360/91, required an execution time of 4 s. It yielded a message delay of .2438 s in 12 shortest-route computations. Details on the use of this algorithm are given in [22].

In general, a centralized flow control scheme requires each given node to periodically collect data on message flow through the node, and to update a designated *control node* with this data. Furthermore, the control node must also periodically communicate new message assignments to each node. These updates must be sufficiently frequent so that the control node can change flow assignments in a timely fashion. However, too frequent updates can result in an excessive amount of control message traffic as well as additional processing of control messages, thereby degrading network performance. Thus, an important drawback of centralized flow control is the delay between the time the network traffic condition is sampled and the time the network nodes receive the new flow assignments. The centralized flow control scheme is attractive when network loads are nearly constant or change very slowly. In such cases, one may exercise the flow control algorithms at longer time intervals. A related benefit of centralized flow control is that it provides information on total network load at any given time.

Distributed Flow Control

In distributed flow control, the process of managing network flows is assigned to several (possibly to each) network nodes. Each node regulates the transit traffic passing through the node as well as that entering from outside the network. There are three approaches for providing distributed flow control in networks.

1. In *adaptive routing* algorithms, each node selects that adjacent node to forward messages such that the message delay through the network is minimized. The principle of adaptive routing is depicted in Fig. 6-3. Node *A* decides to forward a message for node *D* through node *C*, if node *B* has more traffic than node *C*. This approach, used in ARPANET, prevents local congestion by forwarding messages to appropriate adjacent nodes. Since this scheme relates to both flow control and message routing, we delay its treatment to Chap. 7, which addresses network routing.
2. Network congestion can be controlled by restricting the total number of messages in the network to a fixed value. One such scheme, *isarithmic flow control*, is described later in this section.
3. A network node can regulate message traffic entering the node from outside the network, thereby preventing congestion. Correspondingly, a given network node can also regulate transmission of messages destined for other nodes, depending on such conditions as

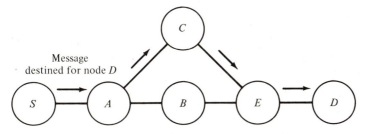

Figure 6-3 Principle of adaptive routing. Node *A* sends messages through node *C* when node *B* is handling relatively more message traffic than node *C*.

buffer depletion, at the nodes receiving the messages. Such schemes operate by coordinating the flow from source node to destination node for each message path. These schemes, called *end-to-end flow control*, are presented next.

End-to-end flow control This process regulates the rate at which a sending node generates message traffic, based on the condition of the receiving node. Sometimes, the sending node can also regulate message traffic based on the intermediate nodes as well as on the receiving node. We illustrate this approach through an example of a network.

Let us consider the network shown in Fig. 6-4. We are concerned with flow control being exercised at node A. Suppose that node A is expected to transmit messages only to nodes G, B, and E. This implies that there is a logical connection or a *virtual channel* for each of the node pairs A–G, A–B, and A–E. Let these virtual channels be labeled V_1, V_2, and V_3, respectively. Then, message traffic on virtual channel V_2 (from node A to B through nodes F and C) can be regulated by

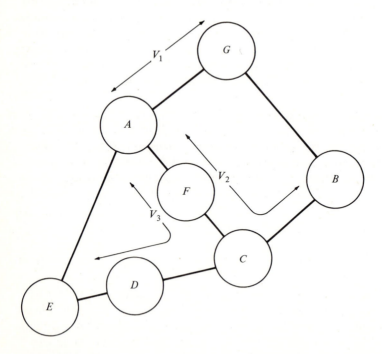

Figure 6-4 A network with seven nodes. Three virtual channels are shown, each with an endpoint in node A.

node A based on the capacity of node B. If B is overloaded, A reduces the rate of message transmission to B.

The number of messages on a virtual channel can be controlled by a *window* mechanism; a window represents a group of messages that a sending node can transmit each time the receiving node sends permission. Thus, with the window mechanism, a sending node may transmit a group of messages upon receiving permission from the receiving node. After transmitting the group of messages, the sending node must wait for another permission from the receiving node to send the next group of messages. The maximum possible number of messages in the message group is called the *window size*.

An example of end-to-end flow control for virtual channel V_3 is illustrated in Fig. 6-5. The window size in this case is 4, and every message is acknowledged. As shown, every message experiences a certain delay in passing through each transit node—F, C, and D. Permission to transmit a group of 4 messages can be sent, as shown here, as part of the message acknowledgments (A_1, A_5, and A_9). Note that if node E were congested, it could withhold permission until its buffers are freed. Alternatively, node E could request a reduction in window size. Such action can also be taken by node E when any transit node on virtual channel V_3 (such as node F, C, or D) is congested. In the desirable situation when there is no congestion along the virtual channel, the window size can be increased or left unchanged.

Window size selection Selection of an appropriate window size determines the behavior of network flow control and its immunity from congestion. An extremely small window size can impede performance by restricting throughput on a virtual channel, while a very large window size may not provide timely control to prevent congestion. We describe an approach by Ahuja [17] to select the window size for end-to-end flow control using network delays and link capacities. The delay through a given (ith) link in the network is estimated by

$$t_i = \frac{1}{uC_i - \lambda_i} \tag{6-2}$$

where $1/u$ is the average message size, C_i is the capacity of the ith link, and λ_i is the message rate on the ith link. (This expression will be derived in Chap. 8.) The approach is based on an iterative solution, since λ_i depends on the window size and network delay depends on $(uC_i - \lambda_i)$, as shown in eq. (6-2).

By using the independence assumption [2, p. 322], which will be

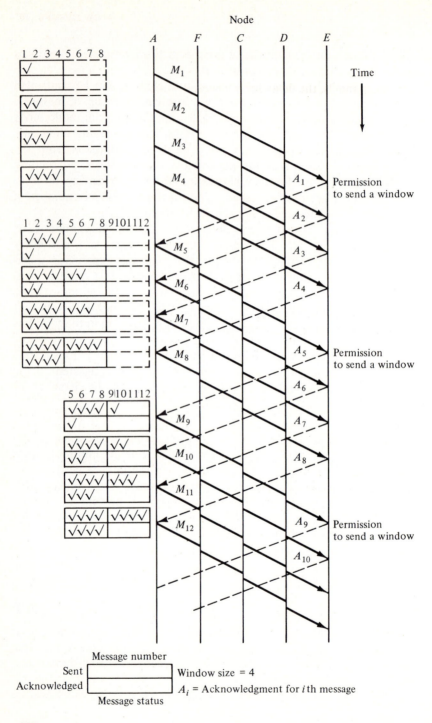

Node

A   F   C   D   E

1 2 3 4 5 6 7 8

1 2 3 4 5 6 7 8 9 10 11 12

5 6 7 8 9 10 11 12

M_1

M_2

M_3

M_4

M_5

M_6

M_7

M_8

M_9

M_{10}

M_{11}

M_{12}

A_1

A_2

A_3

A_4

A_5

A_6

A_7

A_8

A_9

A_{10}

Time

Permission to send a window

Permission to send a window

Permission to send a window

Message number

Sent

Acknowledged

Message status

Window size = 4

A_i = Acknowledgment for i th message

described in Chap. 8, each link on a virtual channel can be considered as an isolated M/M/1 system. Assuming there are M links and n virtual channels, the delay for a virtual channel V_j is

$$T_j = \sum_{\substack{a_i \in V_j}}^{\text{all } i} t_i$$

where the sum is taken over all a_i such that a_i is a link on virtual channel V_j. Using eq. (6-2),

$$T_j = \sum_{\substack{a_i \in V_j}}^{\text{all } i} \frac{1}{uC_i - \lambda_i} \tag{6-3}$$

where $\mathbf{V} = (V_1, V_2, \ldots, V_n)$ is the vector representing all the virtual channels and $\mathbf{W} = (W_1, W_2, \ldots, W_n)$ is the vector containing corresponding window sizes.

The message rate on the ith link is the sum of the message rates of all virtual channels using that link. The message rate on a given virtual channel V_k, with a sending node s and a receiving node d, is estimated as follows. Assume that the network is in a steady-state condition, and that W_k messages are transmitted for each permission received from the receiving node d. The message delay on virtual channel V_k, using earlier notation, is T_k. The total time required for the first of W_k messages to reach node d, and for the permission to transmit from node d to node s, is $T_k + T_k = 2T_k$, assuming that message traffic is the same in the two directions of flow on a virtual channel. If we assume that W_k messages have been entered into the network by node s before permission is received, the message rate on virtual channel V_k is $W_k/2T_k$.

Let $V_k \simeq a_i$ define that virtual channel V_k that uses link a_i. Thus,

$$\lambda_i = \sum_{\substack{V_k \simeq a_i \\ \text{all } k}} \frac{W_k}{2T_k} \qquad k = 1, 2, \ldots, n \tag{6-4}$$

Substituting the value of λ_i from eq. (6-4) into (6-3),

$$T_j = \sum_{\substack{a_i \in V_j}}^{\text{all } i} \frac{1}{uC_i - \sum\limits_{\substack{V_k \simeq a_i \\ \text{all } k}} \dfrac{W_k}{2T_k}} \qquad j = 1, 2, \ldots, n \tag{6-5}$$

Figure 6-5 Window protocol for virtual channel V_3 (shown in Fig. 6.4) for messages from node A to node E.

Note that T_j and T_k represent the message delay on the jth and kth virtual channels, respectively. For a given set of values W_k ($k = 1, 2, \ldots, n$), one can begin by estimating the values of T_k; for example, estimate T_k by computing message transmission delay on each link of the virtual channel V_k. Then, eq. (6-5) provides an iterative solution for all T_k. When these values of T_k converge, then eq. (6-5) provides a relationship between window size W_k and message delay $T_k(k = 1, 2, \ldots, n)$.

The throughput is computed simply by using $\sum_{k=1}^{n} (W_k/2T_k)$. Using the preceding expressions, a general behavior of window size versus throughput and network delay is plotted in Fig. 6-6. It can be seen that an increase in window size increases throughput to a certain point. After that desirable operating point, throughput decreases and the response time starts increasing rapidly.

Different adaptations of end-to-end flow control using window scheme are employed in SDLC, HDLC, X.25, ARPANET, and IBM's SNA. In SDLC, up to 7 frames can be outstanding at a time, without acknowledgment. In HDLC, this limit can be extended to 127. In X.25, the data packet header transmitted on a virtual channel includes a packet-send and a packet-receive number to regulate flow control. As described in Sec. 5-2, the values of window sizes are limited to the range 1 to 7 in normal mode and 1 to 127 in the extended mode. Shah [14] develops results for the effect of window size and acknowledgment width on link utilization.

Flow control in SNA SNA employs an end-to-end window flow control mechanism, described in [18]. This flow control is exercised over virtual routes, which are defined as end-to-end bidirectional logical connections between certain types of SNA nodes.* The protocol uses three entities in implementing an adaptive window scheme:

1. Virtual Route Pacing Response (VRPRS): Permission from the receiver to send K more messages, where K is the window size. The receiver can withhold this permission depending on the availability of buffers to receive messages. Before sending this response, the receiver should have gotten a request from the sender for sending more messages.

---

* See Sec. 5-2 for details on SNA. For purposes of this discussion, a virtual route is similar to a virtual channel, described earlier in this section. In SNA, flow control is also exercised on each session. The session flow control, called *pacing*, regulates the flow in each direction for a session.

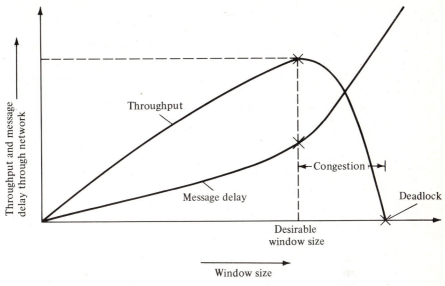

Figure 6-6 Window size versus throughput and message delay.

2. Change Window Reply Indicator (CWRI): A bit indicating a change of 1 in window size without violating the predetermined limits of the window size. If this bit is set to 1, the window size can be decreased; otherwise, it can be increased. Depending on the number of available buffers and the size of the message queue at the node, any node on the virtual route can request the receiving node to set this bit to 1.

3. Reset Window Indicator (RWI): A bit used to request reduction in window size to a preestablished minimum limit (described below).

For each virtual route, minimum and maximum window size limits are established. Based on network performance studies [18], minimum window size limit is assigned a default value of h, and maximum window size limit is assigned a default value of $3h$, where h is the number of links (or hops) in the virtual route. The adaptive window algorithm is shown in Fig. 6-7, and works as follows:

1. At the time the virtual route is initialized, window size k is set to the minimum limit.

2. The window size is changed at the sending node as follows:

(*a*) *k* is replaced by *h* if the RWI bit is set to 1. Any node on the virtual route can set this bit to 1 if severe congestion exists in the node. Upon receiving this bit set to 1, the transmitting node resets window size to the minimum limit of *h*.

(*b*) *k* may be incremented by 1 if the CWRI bit is set to 0 and messages are waiting for transmission.

(*c*) *k* is decremented by 1 if CWRI is set to 1. The CWRI bit may be set to 1 only by the receiving node. However, any given node on the virtual route can request setting this bit to 1 if the node is moderately congested. (Moderate and severe congestion are determined by the individual product that is implementing this architecture.) Upon receiving the CWRI bit set to 1, the window

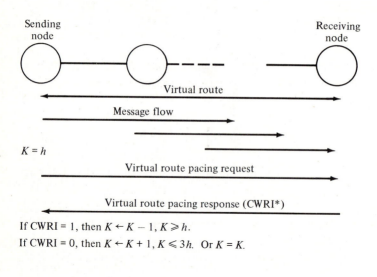

$K = h$

If CWRI = 1, then $K \leftarrow K - 1, K \geqslant h$.
If CWRI = 0, then $K \leftarrow K + 1, K \leqslant 3h.$ Or $K = K.$

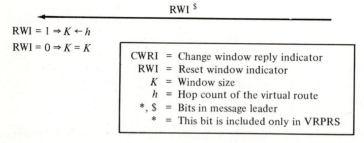

RWI = 1 $\Rightarrow K \leftarrow h$
RWI = 0 $\Rightarrow K = K$

CWRI	= Change window reply indicator
RWI	= Reset window indicator
K	= Window size
h	= Hop count of the virtual route
*, $	= Bits in message leader
*	= This bit is included only in VRPRS

Figure 6-7 End-to-end window control is IBM Systems network architecture. (For simplicity, message flow in only one direction is shown.)

size is decreased by 1 at the sending node unless it is already at its minimum value h.

A modification of the window scheme, the *rate flow scheme*, is analyzed by Pujolle [25]. In this scheme, the sending node accepts messages for the network at a predefined rate per unit time. Then, this rate is changed depending on the state of the network. The scheme requires a system of control packets to monitor network conditions, and an appropriate rate adjustment scheme for maximum throughput.

Isarithmic Flow Control

Network congestion can also be prevented by restricting the total number of messages that are permitted to exist in the network at any time. Such a network is called *isarithmic*. In isarithmic flow control, as proposed by Davies [12], the total number of messages (*data* messages and *empty* messages) in the network is kept constant. An empty message is created as soon as a data message leaves the network. A data message can enter the network after finding and destroying an empty message. An empty message first becomes available for a data message that is entering the same node where the empty message was created. In the simplest case, when there is no data message in that node, the empty message is routed to a random destination node.

The performance of an isarithmic network depends largely on an appropriate selection of the total number of messages in the network. Davies [12] describes the results of simulation of a particular isarithmic network design. Let P be the number of messages per node obtained by dividing the total number of messages allowed in the network by the number of nodes, and let the performance be characterized by C, the total data-carrying capacity of the network in terms of messages per second. Then, for small values of P, the capacity C is proportional to P. As P increases, C reaches a constant value limited by network capacity, and then decreases as congestion occurs.* Davies studied the relation between P and C for an 18-node network through simulation experiments. His results for maximum node output queue sizes of 3 and 8 are shown in Fig. 6-8. For a maximum queue size of 3, maximum throughput occurs at $P = 2$; for a queue size of 8, it occurs at $P = 4$. This implies that, for the simulated network, the number of messages (data or empty) in the network

---

* As one would expect, this is similar to the behavior of end-to-end window flow control shown in Fig. 6-6.

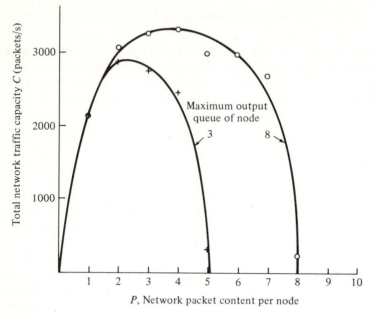

Figure 6-8 Characteristics of an isarithmic network with 18 nodes. (From D. W. Davies, "The Control of Congestion in Packet-Switching Networks," *IEEE Transactions on Communications*, vol. COM-20, no. 3, June 1972, p. 549.)

should be approximately $2N$ or $4N$ for a maximum node output queue size of 3 or 8, respectively, where N is the number of nodes in the network. Although the throughput can be improved by better network design, the general shape of these characteristics is thought to be the same [12].

Comparison of Flow Control Techniques

In isarithmic flow control, overhead for sending empty messages can be minimized by piggybacking an empty message onto a data message, possibly by using a bit in the message header that indicates inclusion of an empty message. This scheme tends to control overall network congestion, especially when messages are routed adaptively. Among the other flow control strategies described earlier, end-to-end window flow control is preferable for dynamic adaptation to network loads. Centralized flow control provides a focal point for controlling network traffic, and is desirable for networks in which message traffic does not vary significantly. Isarithmic flow control is, in principle, similar to end-to-end flow control, since both schemes attempt to control messages into the network. However, it is exercised at a network-wide level, while end-to-end flow control is operated at a virtual channel level. Finally, end-to-end flow control requires a mechanism to coordinate flow control among various virtual channels to control network-wide congestion.

6-3 DEADLOCKS

A communications network can be viewed as a set of resources shared by a collection of processes that exchange information with each other. Consider a situation in which two or more processes are waiting for resources to be released by each other. It is then possible for these processes to block each other's progress; such a condition is generally known as a *deadlock*. Two types of deadlocks can occur. One can result from a logical resource such as a signal or a permission to perform some action, and is called *protocol deadlock*. The second type can result from a physical resource, usually the message buffers, and is defined by the physical resource causing the deadlock. Since message buffers are the commonly used resource for moving messages, this type of deadlock is called *buffer deadlock*.

Protocol Deadlocks

Protocol deadlocks result when two or more tasks are waiting on each other for some type of control message, such as an acknowledgment or a permission. Generally, this wait manifests itself as a condition in which no further message transmission can take place. Protocol deadlocks prevent any further movement of messages, and should be eliminated to obtain smooth network operation. One possible deadlock, caused by out-of-sequence arrival of control messages, was shown in Fig. 3-3. The software logic in the sender assumes it is in session, but that in the receiver does not.

Consider the network shown in Fig. 6-9. Additional transit nodes can exist between nodes *B* and *D*, and nodes *J* and *K*. Node *A* sends a request to initiate a session (dialog) with node *P*. In the meantime, link *D–J* fails. A link-failure notification is sent to the two nodes attached to the link. This failure notification, when appropriately propagated to other nodes, updates each of the affected nodes with

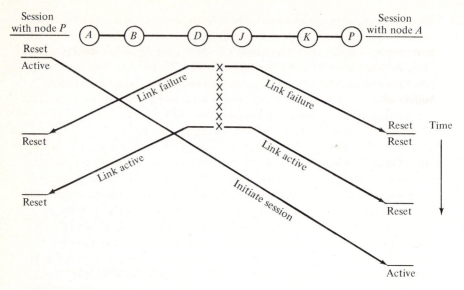

Figure 6-9 A hang condition (or deadlock) resulting from messages crossing each other during transmission.

information on the failed link. Let us assume that subsequently the link recovers, and that a link-active notification is sent to each node. With this notification, node A has been reset to a condition representing that node A has not initiated any session activation request with node P. However, the session initiation request from node A eventually arrives at node P, after the arrival of link-failure and subsequent link-active notification. Therefore, node P assumes that it is in session with node A. Thus, nodes A and P are in a "hang" or deadlock condition. The problem has resulted from notification messages crossing the session initiation request during transmission. This particular deadlock can be prevented by requiring failure notification messages to discard any session activation messages encountered on their way. By doing so, the link-failure notification would have discarded the session initiation request (in node B), thereby preventing it from reaching node P. Then, after the exchange, both nodes (A and P) would be in the same (reset) condition.

Several protocol deadlocks have been discovered and resolved during network design time. In [18], Ahuja discusses a possible protocol deadlock and its resolution in SNA design. This deadlock could occur if a network link fails during the activation sequence of a network route.

Reassembly lockup In ARPANET, a message can be segmented into fixed-size packets at the source node, and reassembled at the destination node. Kahn and Crowther describe a reassembly deadlock in [10]. A node in ARPANET is called an *interface message processor* (*IMP*). There are two types of buffers in each IMP: *store-and-forward buffers* and *reassembly buffers*. The former in a given IMP A are used for packets passing through IMP A toward another IMP. The reassembly buffers in IMP A are used for packets destined for IMP A. Thus, the reassembly buffers provide storage for packets in order to reassemble them into messages. For illustration of the underlying principle in a reassembly lockup, consider the hypothetical network shown in Fig. 6-10, in which each node represents an IMP. Assume that all reassembly buffers in node B are waiting for packets of partially reassembled messages. Furthermore, assume that each node adjacent to B (nodes A, C, and L) has all its store-and-forward buffers assigned to packets that comprise parts of the messages destined for node B, and requires use of its reassembly buffers to reassemble new messages. Then, node B cannot accept these new packets since it does not have new reassembly buffers to allocate them. At the same time, there could be packets in other nodes, such as nodes D or M, that might complete the partially assembled messages currently in node B, and thus free some reassembly buffers of node B. But nodes, A, C, and L cannot accept these packets since all their store-and-forward buffers are occupied, as explained above. In such a case, a deadlock can occur since no movement of packets is possible from nodes A, C, or L. This lockup can be avoided by permitting IMP B to discard any packets that it cannot accept for reassembly, and to notify the sending node of its disposal. Alternatively, the source IMP can request the destination IMP to allocate sufficient reassembly buffers for assembling a complete message before transmitting the packets for the message into the network.

Protocol deadlocks affect network performance and should be detected at protocol design time. Protocol validation techniques, presented in Sec. 5-4, are the only approaches known to this author for preventing these deadlocks.

Buffer Deadlocks

As pointed out at the beginning of this section, congestion can lead to a situation when some network nodes are in a buffer deadlock. A buffer deadlock occurs when two or more nodes have no free buffers, and each node is waiting for some other node to provide a buffer.

Consider the network shown in Fig. 6-10. Let us assume that nodes A, B, and C have no buffers available to store new messages. Furthermore, assume that each message in node A requires assignment of a buffer in node B before the message can be transmitted. If messages in node B are also waiting for a buffer in node C, and those in C are waiting for a buffer in A, then nodes A, B, and C are in a store-and-forward buffer deadlock. Now, consider another buffer deadlock in the same network. Again assume that there is no free buffer in any node in the set $X = (F, G, H, J, K, M)$ of nodes in the network of Fig. 6-10. If messages in each of these nodes are waiting for buffers in one

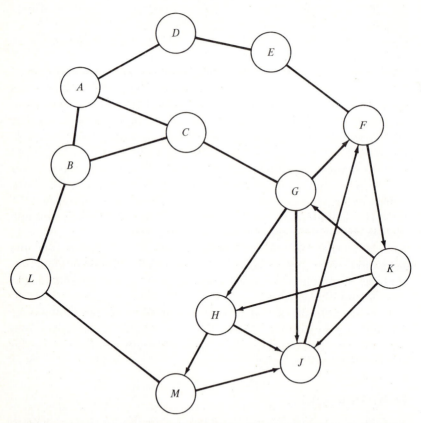

Figure 6-10 A network with two buffer deadlocks—(1) nodes A, B, and C, store-and-forward wait deadlock ($A \rightarrow B$, $B \rightarrow C$, $C \rightarrow A$); (2) nodes F, G, H, M, J, and K: mutual wait deadlock.

or more nodes in X, then the set of nodes X is in a buffer deadlock. This deadlock results from the mutual wait among nodes in set X.

There are two important points to be made here. First, the set of nodes in a deadlock must be connected. For example, in Fig. 6-10, the set $X = (F, G, H, J, K, M)$ is connected, since each node in X is linked to every other node in X through nodes in X. Secondly, the above deadlocks can occur only if each message in the network follows a fixed route. On the other hand, if the message routes are adaptive,* it is possible that the above two deadlocks may not occur. For example, consider messages in node M destined for node A. Assuming that there is no free buffer in nodes H or J, the message can be directed through node L. Thus, for adaptive routing, local congestion can be prevented, at least for short periods of time. In cases with adaptive routing, a buffer deadlock usually occurs only when most of the network nodes have no free buffers. For the remainder of this chapter, we restrict our treatment to networks with fixed routing.

The problem of detecting deadlocks in networks continues to receive considerable attention. The difficulty in developing viable algorithms, their inherent computational complexity, and the associated processing overhead have resulted in a lack of commonly used algorithms for checking network deadlocks. Although we will now report some research work in this field, the reader should keep in mind the practical difficulties in incorporating the results.

Buffer deadlocks can be detected at network design time [19, 23]. These algorithms, because of their computational cost (described later), may be useful only for networks with a small number of nodes. Alternatively, one may implement an algorithm to avoid circularity in the wait [13]. We first describe approaches for examining network design, and then present the deadlock-free buffer allocation scheme.

State enumeration approach Given a network design, one can enumerate each network state, and check it for buffer deadlock. This approach uses a formal model of networks and provides an efficient algorithm to check a given network state for deadlock [19]. We begin by describing a model for networks, followed by the algorithm and an example.

A model Nodes, links, and buffers in a network can be represented as a graph on which each node is labeled with the number of message

---

* See Sec. 7-4 for discussion of adaptive routing.

buffers in it. We assume that each message occupies exactly one buffer. Thus, we can define a network in terms of the nodes, links, message buffers, network routes, and message-carrying capacity of each network route. Thus, a *network* is a quintuple $N = (X, A, B, R, M)$, where X is the set of nodes, A is the set of links of the network, B is defined such that $B(x_i)$ or, simply, b_i is the number of buffers in node x_i, R is the set of routes (directed paths) of the network, and M is a function that provides the maximum number of messages on each route.* Each directed arc in A represents one direction of link flow. A buffer is either *free* (available) for a message or *allocated* to one. It is assumed that a message in a node is transmitted to the next node only after a buffer has been allocated for it in the next node.

Network activity is defined by the allocation of and request for resources. A unit of activity, or *task*, has one buffer allocated to it in a node, and can request one additional buffer in an adjacent node. A buffer index is included to distinguish tasks in the same node. Thus, a task is defined by a triple $\langle x_i, p, x_j \rangle$, where x_i and x_j are two adjacent nodes and p is a positive integer not greater than b_i. The index p uniquely identifies each task associated with each of the b_i buffers. For a task $t = \langle x_i, p, x_j \rangle$, we call x_i the allocated node $A(t)$, p the buffer index of t, and x_j the requested node $R(t)$. We can now define a network state and deadlock. A *network state* is defined by a set T' of tasks such that there is no more than one task with the same allocated node and buffer index. This definition permits at most one task to be allocated to any given buffer.

Consider a set of connected† nodes such that their tasks are waiting for each other for a buffer, and that there is no free buffer. Then, the tasks in those nodes are in an unresolvable wait, or *mutual wait*, that leads to buffer deadlock; the set (F, G, H, J, K, M) of nodes in Fig. 6-10 has been shown to be in a mutual wait. Formally, in a state T' of a network, a nonempty‡ set $T'' \subseteq T'$ of tasks is in a mutual wait if (1) for each task $t = \langle x_i, r, x_j \rangle$ in T'', the tasks in set $\{\langle x_i, p, x_j \rangle \mid p \le b_i, x_j \in X\}$ are in T'' and x_j is in set $\{A(t') \mid t' \in T''\}$ of nodes; and (2) there is no free buffer in the set $\{x_i \mid x_i \in A(T'')\}$ of nodes.

The first part of this definition provides that if there is some task of a node in T'', then all tasks residing in that node are in T'', and that the requested node of each task in T'' is also in the set of nodes that

---

* A formal description of this model is given in [19, 23, 24].

† A set of nodes is connected if there exists a path consisting of one or more links from each node to every other node.

‡ A nonempty set of tasks is a set that must have at least one task in it.

have tasks in T''. The second part of the definition implies that there is no free buffer in the nodes that have tasks in T''.

Then, in a network, a *buffer deadlock state* is a state T' such that there exists a nonempty set $T'' \subseteq T'$ of tasks that is in a mutual wait.

Ahuja [19] has used this model to establish results for an algorithm to check a network state for deadlock. Before presenting that algorithm, we describe the result that is used to determine the nodes with tasks in a buffer deadlock. First, some definitions are needed. A relation W is defined among any two tasks, t_1 and t_2, in such a manner that W holds only if task t_2 occupies a buffer in a node from which task t_1 is waiting for a buffer. Thus, $t_1 W t_2$ implies $t_2 = \langle R(t_1),$ $p, x \rangle$, where p is the buffer index and x is any network node. Next, a relation W^* is defined between any two tasks t_1 and t_n such that W^* holds if there exists a sequence $t_1 W t_a, t_a W t_b, \ldots, t_u W t_n$. Thus, $t_1 W^* t_n$ is true if either (1) $t_1 W t_n$ or (2) $t_1 W^* t_u$ and $t_u W t_n$ holds. So, the relation W^* holds between any two tasks t_1 and t_n if t_1 requires, directly or indirectly through other tasks, a buffer in the node with task t_n.

Let $X' \subseteq X$ be a set of nodes in a network such that, for a given state, the set X' of nodes has no free buffers. Now, let $X'' \subseteq X'$ be a set of all those nodes in X' such that at least one task t in each node in X'' satisfies the relation $t W^* t'$, where t' is in a node with one or more free buffers. (By definition, then, task t' is in a node that is not in X'). Thus, although there is no free buffer in any node in X'', the wait by the tasks t occupying the buffers is resolvable. This is true since there are one or more free buffers available for these tasks, directly or indirectly, through other nodes. At the same time, nodes in the set $X' - X''$ cannot have the wait for their tasks resolved.† This is true since each task in the nodes $X' - X''$ is waiting, both directly and indirectly, for nodes without any free buffers. Thus, the tasks in nodes $X' - X''$ are in a mutual wait, and the state is a deadlock. This proves the following theorem.

Theorem 6-1‡ Let $N = (X, A, B, R, M)$ be a network and T' be a state of N such that there is no free buffer in the set $X' \subseteq X$ of nodes, and let $T'' \subseteq T'$ be the set of all those tasks such that for each task t in T'', $t \ W^* \ t'$ holds and the node $A(t')$ has a free buffer. Then, the set of tasks in the nodes $X' - \{A(t) | t \in T''\}$ is in a mutual wait.

† $X' - X''$ equals the set of nodes in X' that are not in X''.
‡ From [19].

The above theorem provides the basis of the following algorithm to check a network state for deadlock.

Algorithm This algorithm requires generating each network state and then checking the state for deadlock. The network states can be enumerated by obtaining all feasible mappings from the set of tasks (on all routes) to the set of nodes. Each state is then checked as follows.

Let $N = (X, A, B, R, M)$ be a network and T' be its state to be checked. The nodes in X are referred to as x_i, $i = 1, \ldots, n$, where n is the number of nodes in X. Variables i, j, k, and p are used as indices.

1. Define an $n \times n$ matrix M^* and an n-element vector $\mathbf{V}$.
2. (a) Initialize vector $\mathbf{V}$ such that, for each node x_i, element V_i is 0 if node x_i has no free buffer and V_i is 1 if x_i has at least one free buffer.

    (b) Check vector $\mathbf{V}$ for elements with a 0. If the number of elements with a 0 is less than 2, then the state is not a deadlock and the algorithm terminates.†
3. Initialize the matrix M so that, for each node, x_i, $M(i, j) = 1$ if there is a task in node x_i that has requested a buffer in node x_j; otherwise, $M(i, j) = 0$.
4. (a) Create a vector $\mathbf{Y}$ consisting of the indices of all those nodes x_i for which V_i has a value of 1. (If none, proceed to step 5.) Set k to the value of the first element in $\mathbf{Y}$.

    (b) For each row p, check if $M(p, k)$ is 1 and V_p is 0. If so, set V_p to 1 and add p to the vector $\mathbf{Y}$, since node x_p should also be examined.

    (c) Set k to the next element of $\mathbf{Y}$ and return to step 4(b). Continue until all entries in vector $\mathbf{Y}$ have been checked.
5. Check vector $\mathbf{V}$ for an element with a 0. If there is at least one such element, then and only then is the state a buffer deadlock. (These elements represent the nodes that have no free buffer and also have tasks for which the wait cannot be resolved, directly or indirectly, through other nodes with free buffers).

The computational complexity of this algorithm is determined primarily by steps 3 and 4. Assuming there are m tasks in the state, step 3

---

* This matrix M is to be distinguished from the message rates M used in definition of a network N.

† It can be easily verified that a buffer deadlock requires the participation of at least two nodes, each with no free buffers.

requires $0[m]$ comparison operations. In step 4, the algorithm sets to 1 those nodes (indices) of **V** that need not be checked for mutual wait (Theorem 6-1). To vector **Y**, the algorithm adds those nodes (indices) that have no free buffers but have some tasks in them that are waiting for a node that either has a free buffer or is, in turn, waiting for a node that can free a buffer. Since only those indices for which V_i is 0 are added to **Y**, therefore, by construction, vector **Y** cannot have more than n elements. For each entry in vector **Y**, the algorithm checks no more than n entries of the corresponding column in M, thus requiring $0[n^2]$ comparisons. Therefore, the computational complexity, in terms of comparison operations, is $0[m + n^2]$ for each network state.

Example* Consider the network shown in Fig. 6-11, with each node containing two buffers. The set of tasks in state T' (to be examined) are assumed to be:

$$T' = \begin{bmatrix} (1, & 1, & 4), & (1, & 2, & 2), \\ (2, & 1, & 1), & (2, & 2, & 4), \\ (3, & 1, & 2), & (3, & 2, & 4), \\ (4, & 1, & 1), & (4, & 2, & 5), \\ (5, & 1, & 1), & (5, & 2, & 3) \end{bmatrix}$$

The notation for describing each task was defined earlier, and is repeated here by an example. A given task in T', say (3, 1, 2), specifies that node 3 has a task waiting for a buffer in node 2. The index 1 specifies that this task occupies buffer 1 (of the two buffers) in node 3.

The algorithm is applied as follows.

1. The matrix M and vector **V** are initialized with zeros.
2. Nodes 1, 2, 3, 4, 5 have no free buffers so $\mathbf{V} = (0, 0, 0, 0, 0, 1)$. There are more than two elements with a 0 in vector **V**, so proceed to step 3.
3. Initialize matrix M using tasks in T', as follows:

$$M = \begin{pmatrix} 0 & 1 & 0 & 1 & 0 & 0 \\ 1 & 0 & 0 & 1 & 0 & 0 \\ 0 & 1 & 0 & 1 & 0 & 0 \\ 1 & 0 & 0 & 0 & 1 & 0 \\ 1 & 0 & 1 & 0 & 0 & 0 \\ 0 & 0 & 0 & 0 & 0 & 0 \end{pmatrix}$$

* This example is taken from [19, pp. 83–85].

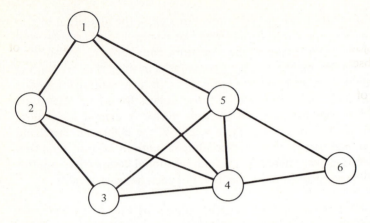

Figure 6-11 A network with six nodes for checking deadlock. Each node has two message buffers. (From V. Ahuja, "Algorithm to Check Network States for Deadlock," *IBM Journal of Research and Development*, vol. 23, no. 1, January 1979, p. 83. Copyright 1979 by International Business Machines Corporation; reprinted with permission.)

4. (a) $Y = \{6\}$, $k = 6$; (b) $p =$ none; (c) there are no more entries in **Y**.
5. There are five elements with a 0 in vector **V**. Therefore, the state T' is a deadlock.

Approach using network flows This approach [23] does not require enumerating each network state. Instead, it uses results from graph theory (described later) to examine network design for deadlock. Simply stated, the approach maps message buffers in each subset of nodes to the messages on the routes in the network. If, for some subset of nodes, each buffer is occupied in such a way that the next node for each message is also within this subset, then the nodes are in a buffer deadlock. This is true since messages in that subset of nodes are waiting for each other to free message buffers, and there is no free buffer. We first elaborate this concept by defining some entities, followed by the description of the underlying algorithm and an example.

We extend the network model described in the preceding section. A deadlock set $X' \subseteq X$ of a network $N = (X, A, B, R, M)$ is defined as a set* of nodes such that tasks in each of its nodes are in a mutual wait. Thus, a *deadlock set* is simply the subset of nodes that, for some

---

* This set of nodes must be nonempty and connected.

network state, is in a deadlock. Next, a *bipartite graph* $H = (X_1, X_2, E)$ is a graph $(X_1 \cup X_2, E)$ in which nodes have been partitioned into two disjoint subsets X_1 and X_2, whereby no two nodes in any one of the subsets are adjacent. If X' is a subset of nodes of a network $N = (X, A, B, R, M)$, its bipartite graph is $H = (X', R, E)$, where E is the set of edges such that the number of edges connecting a node x_i in X' and a route r_j in R is (1) Min (b_i, m_j), if node x_i is on route r_j and the next node after x_i on r_j is in X', and (2) 0 otherwise. The function Min(b_i, m_j) provides the lesser of b_i and m_j. Here m_j is the number of messages allowed on route r_j.

Note that any mapping of tasks (corresponding to messages in the set R of routes) to buffers (in the set X of nodes) must correspond to a feasible state. Thus, there cannot be more than b_i (number of buffers in node x_i) edges connected to a node x_i and no more than m_j (maximum number of messages on route r_j) edges connected to a route r_j. Such a mapping is called the *weighted matching of H*. It is defined by a set $E' \subseteq E$ of edges of H within the above constraints. A weighted matching is *maximum* if no additional edges can be added to E'; it is *complete* if, for each node $x_i \in X'$, the number of edges in E' connected to x_i is equal to b_i. A complete matching is also a maximum matching.

We have defined a weighted matching in such a way that the next node for each task is within the set X' of nodes. Thus, the existence of a complete weighted matching should imply that the set X' of nodes is a deadlock set. This is true since there is no free buffer in any node in X', and all tasks are waiting for buffers in X'. We state the corresponding theorem without proof.*

> **Theorem 6-2** In a network $N = (X, A, B, R, M)$, a nonempty connected set $X' \subseteq X$ of nodes is a deadlock set if and only if there exists a complete weighted matching of the bipartite graph $H = (X', R, E)$ for X'.

The above theorem provides the basis for checking connected sets of nodes for complete weighted matchings. Thus, we can determine whether a given connected set of nodes will be in a deadlock by checking its corresponding bipartite graph for a complete weighted matching.

> **Algorithm** The algorithm checks each connected subset of nodes for a deadlock set. The first two steps generate each set of con-

---

* A formal proof is described in [23, 24].

nected nodes. The subsequent steps check the subset of nodes for a deadlock set. Let n represent the number of nodes in the network.

1. By traversing the network graph, obtain the sets of nodes adjacent to each node. Thus, create an adjacency matrix of all nodes.

2. (*a*) Create a new n-bit binary number every time this step is entered, and proceed to step 2 (*b*). (The binary numbers range in value from 1 to $2^n - 1$.) If all n-bit binary numbers have been generated and checked, the procedure terminates and the network has no deadlock.

   (*b*) For a given binary number β from (*a*), let X' be the set of nodes defined by the node indices for which the corresponding bits in β are 1. Here, we check whether the set X' of nodes is connected. Begin at some node, say x_a in X', by initializing $\mathbf{Y} = \{x_a\}$. Using the adjacency matrix, add those nodes to $\mathbf{Y}$ that are adjacent to x_a and are also in X'. For every new node so included in $\mathbf{Y}$, repeat this process of adding adjacent nodes to $\mathbf{Y}$ until no more nodes can be added to the vector $\mathbf{Y}$. If the resulting vector $\mathbf{Y} = X'$, then X' is connected and proceed to step 3. If $\mathbf{Y} \neq X'$, then X' is not connected and return to step 2(*a*).

3. This step determines whether the bipartite graph $H = (X', R, E)$ has a complete weighted matching, as described below. If so, the set X' of nodes is a deadlock set; otherwise, return to step 2.

Existence of a complete weighted matching is checked by obtaining a maximum weighted matching (defined earlier). A maximum weighted matching of a bipartite graph can be obtained by using network flow theory, as follows. Let $H = (X', R, E)$ be the bipartite graph. Add a source node s and a sink node t to the set $X' \cup R$ of nodes. Include each arc (x_i, r_j) for which there are one or more edges $(x_i\text{-}r_j)$ in E. We transform this network to one with fixed capacities for each arc. To each arc (x_i, r_j), we assign a capacity that is not less than the number of buffers b_i in node x_i and the number of messages m_j allowed on route r_j. Add an arc from node s to each node in X', and an arc from t to each route in R. Assign a capacity of b_i (number of buffers in node x_i) to each arc from node s to x_i in X'. Assign a capacity of m_j (maximum number of messages allowed on route r_j) to each arc from route r_j to node t. Then, the maximum flow of this network, from node s to t, provides the maximum weighted matching. The maximum flow on arc (x_i, r_j) is also the number of edges in the maximum weighted matching. Algorithms to provide a maximum flow for such networks are given in [1, 4, 7, 8, 9]. For completeness, the simple, well-known labeling algorithm [4, 7, 9] is described below.

Labeling algorithm This algorithm addresses the problem of obtaining maximum flow from one point to another when there is a network of paths between two points. For example, consider a railway that connects two cities s and t. Each link of the railway network has a certain fixed capacity to carry the traffic. Assuming a steady-state condition, this algorithm determines the maximum flow from s to t.

In order to review the labeling algorithm, assume that $N = [X \cup (s, t), A \cup (ts)]$ is a network, where s is a new source node, t is a new sink node, and ts is a special arc. In the context of the above algorithm for checking deadlocks, the set X of nodes consists of two disjoint sets of nodes X_1 and X_2 for the bipartite graph described above. Node s is jointed to each node in X_1, and node t is joined to each node in X_2. $F(x_i, x_j)$ is the flow on arc (x_i, x_j) such that $F(x_i, x_j) \leq C(x_i, x_j)$, where $C(x_i, x_j)$ is the capacity of arc (x_i, x_j). Also, for each node x_i,

$$\sum_{\substack{x_j \in X \\ j \neq i}} F(x_i, x_j) - \sum_{\substack{x_j \in X \\ j \neq i}} F(x_j, x_i) = 0$$

The algorithm finds the maximum flow from node s to node t.

Algorithm Let a path P be defined by $(x_1, x_2, \ldots, x_i, \ldots, x_p)$, where either (x_{i+1}, x_i) or (x_i, x_{i+1}) is in the set of arcs A. Consider a path P, and proceed as follows.

1. If (x_i, x_{i+1}) is in A, and (x_{i+1}, x_i) is not in A, then obtain $d_i = C(x_i, x_{i+1}) - F(x_i, x_{i+1}) > 0$.
2. If (x_i, x_{i+1}) is not in A, and (x_{i+1}, x_i) is in A, then obtain $d_i = F(x_{i+1}, x_i) > 0$.
3. If both (x_i, x_{i+1}) and (x_{i+1}, x_i) are in A, then obtain

$$d_i = C(x_i, x_{i+1}) - F(x_i, x_{i+1}) + F(x_{i+1}, x_i) > 0*$$

---

* In applying the labeling algorithm to checking network deadlock, all arcs are unidirectional so that step 3 is not used.

Now compute $d = \text{Min}(d_i) > 0$ for the path P, and change the flow as follows: increase the flow on arc ts by d; add flow d to $F(x_i, x_{i+1})$ for case 1, reduce flow $F(x_{i+1}, x_i)$ by d for case 2, and reduce flow $F(x_{i+1}, x_i)$ by $\text{Max}[0, d - C(x_i, x_{i+1})]$ for case 3.

Thus, a new flow F' is obtained. Continue to improve the flows until the maximum flow is obtained. A simple example that illustrates the use of the labeling algorithm is shown below.

* The Min and Max functions provide the lowest and the highest value out of its arguments.

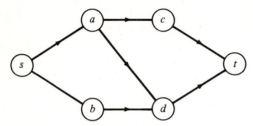

No flows; each arc has a capacity of 5.

Using step 1 and path *sadt*,

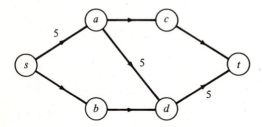

Using steps 1 and 2 and path *sbdact*

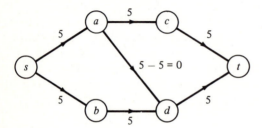

Example We illustrate the composite algorithm of checking a network for deadlock by an example. Figure 6-12(a) shows a network with four nodes, where each node has two buffers. The set of arcs and the message routes are described in Fig. 6-12(a). For simplicity we only consider the connected set (x_1, x_2, x_3) of nodes. The bipartite graph for this set is shown in Fig. 6-12(b). In this bipartite graph, the nodes x_1, x_2, and x_3 are connected to the routes depending on whether the next node on that route is also in the set (x_1, x_2, x_3). For example, node x_1 is connected to route r_1 since node x_2, the next node after node x_1 on route r_1, is in the set (x_1, x_2, x_3). The flow network, obtained by assigning appropriate capacities and including a new source node s and a sink node t, is shown in Fig. 6-12(c). A maximum flow from s to t, corresponding to a maximum weighted matching, is identified by dark lines in Fig. 6-12(c). Since this matching is also complete (each buffer in nodes x_1, x_2, and x_3 is mapped to some message on a route), the set of nodes (x_1, x_2, x_3) has a deadlock.

Let us consider the computational complexity of the above approach. For an n-node network, there cannot be more than 2^n subset of nodes. Dinic's algorithm [8] requires $0[v^2 c]$ operations, where v is the number of vertices and c is the number of arcs in the flow network. Thus, the computational complexity of this algorithm is $0[2^n(n+r)^2 c]$, where r is the number of routes. The state enumeration approach requires $0[m+n^2]$ operations for each state, where m is the number of tasks in the state. The important factor contributing to the improvement in computational complexity (for the above approach) is that there are usually fewer connected subsets of nodes than network states. Nevertheless, these algorithms are useful only for networks with fixed routing. Furthermore, because the computational complexity of these algorithms grows exponentially with number of nodes, these algorithms can only be useful for small networks.

Deadlock-free buffer allocation Finally, we consider the approach of Raubold and Haenle [13] that provides a buffer allocation algorithm to be exercised while the network is in operation. Buffers in each node are divided into an ordered set of buffer classes. (One can assign as few as one buffer to each class in an intermediate node, and keep the remaining buffers in a pool for dynamic allocation to buffer classes. This is true since only one free buffer is needed to avoid a circular wait.) As a message traverses the network, its buffer class index in-

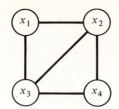

$$N = (X, A, B, R, M)$$
$$X = (x_1, x_2, x_3, x_4)$$
$$A = \text{As shown above}$$
$$B = \{b_i \mid b_i = 2 \quad \text{for } i = 1 \text{ to } 4\}$$
$$R = \{r_1 = [(x_1 - x_2), (x_2 - x_4)]$$
$$r_2 = (x_2 - x_3)$$
$$r_3 = (x_3 - x_1)$$
$$r_4 = [(x_2 - x_1), (x_1 - x_3)]\}$$
$$M = \{m_i \mid m_i = 2 \quad \text{for } i = 1 \text{ to } 4\}$$

(a)

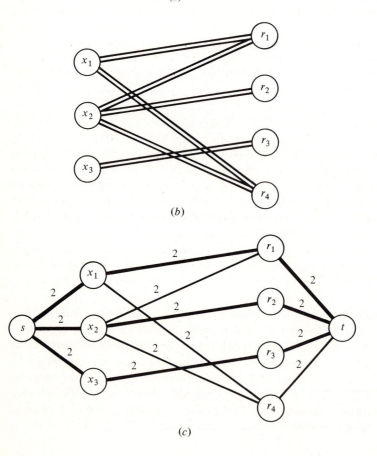

(b)

(c)

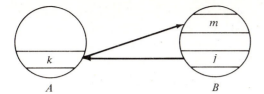

Figure 6-13 Deadlock prevention using buffer allocation scheme due to Raubold and Haenle. (This buffer allocation scheme is described in [13]. The above figure is taken from a description of their scheme in V. Ahuja, "On Congestion Problems in Communication Networks," *Proceedings of Trends and Applications*: 1978, May 1978, Gaithersburg, Md., p. 45.)

creases. A message with a buffer class index i has buffers available from buffer classes with an index less than or equal to i. The deadlock prevention is demonstrated by an example.

> **Example** Consider two adjacent nodes in a network (Fig. 6-13), so that certain messages in each node are waiting on the other node for a buffer. We assume that messages in class j of node B are waiting for a buffer in class k of node A. Therefore, if we show that messages in class k are waiting for a buffer in a class other (in fact higher) than j, then the circularity in the wait is prevented. Since the buffer class increases as a message traverses the network, $k = j + 1$. Now, messages in class k are waiting for buffers in a class, say, m. Then $m = k + 1$, which implies $m > j$. Therefore, the circular wait is avoided. This is true since, as we pointed out earlier in this chapter, circular wait results when messages in two classes are waiting on each other, either directly or indirectly, through other message classes.

SUMMARY

In this chapter, we have provided algorithms and approaches for flow control and deadlock prevention in networks. The congestion problem continues to attract greater attention as network size increases in

Figure 6-12 (*a*) A network to be examined for deadlock. (*b*) Bipartite graph for nodes (x_1, x_2, x_3). (*c*) Flow network for bipartite graph of Fig. 6-12(*b*).

terms of the number of nodes and links. Large networks lead directly to more complex network behavior, both for computational and analytical purposes. In the area of network flow control, additional references on analytical models and simulations are [11, 15, 16], and the proceedings of a symposium [5].

PROBLEMS

6-1 Develop an end-to-end flow control protocol that would prevent the reassembly lockup described in Sec. 6-3.

6-2 Develop an algorithm that enumerates each state for the state enumeration algorithm. Use the network model $N = (X, A, B, R, M)$ described for that algorithm.

6-3 Write a computer program to estimate the window size using the algorithm described in Sec. 6-2.

6-4 Consider a 100-node star-connected network that is experiencing message traffic fluctuations and congestion during certain peak hours. The network uses adaptive routing and employs no flow control scheme. You can make any other reasonable assumptions, after stating them explicitly. Specify the possible congestion problem and its remedy, including any topological changes.

6-5 Consider the network shown below.

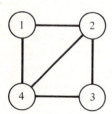

The number of message buffers in the four nodes 1, 2, 3, and 4 are 20, 20, 30, and 30, respectively. The message routes are clockwise and use the shortest path in terms of the number of links traversed. Assume that there are at most 10 messages allowed to flow simultaneously from each node to every other node.

(a) Check the network for exposure to buffer deadlock, and recommend a new buffer allocation that would prevent deadlock.

(b) Design a minimum number of buffers such that the same number of buffers is needed for each node. You may change the message routes to obtain this minimum number of buffers.

(c) For your new buffer allocation, determine the maximum message rate permissible on each route without any exposure to buffer deadlock.

6-6 For the network described in prob. 6-5, there exists a buffer deadlock among nodes 1, 2, and 4. Detect the deadlock and propose an alternative set of message routes to prevent it.

REFERENCES

1. D. R. Fulkerson, "An Out-of-Kilter Method for Minimal-Cost Flow Problems," *Journal of the Society of Industrial and Applied Mathematics*, vol. 9, no. 1, March 1961, pp. 18–27.

2. L. Kleinrock, *Queueing Systems*, vol. II: *Computer Applications*, Wiley, New York, 1976.

3. M. Schwartz, *Computer-Communication Network Design and Analysis*, Prentice-Hall, Englewood Cliffs, N.J., 1977.

4. L. R. Ford, Jr., and D. R. Fulkerson, *Flows in Networks*, Princeton University Press, Princeton, N.J., 1962.

5. *Proceedings of the International Symposium on Flow Control in Computer Networks*, Versailles, France, North-Holland, 1979.

6. M. Schwartz, R. R. Boorstyn, and R. L. Pickholtz, "Terminal-Oriented Computer Communication Networks," *Proceedings of the IEEE*, vol. 60, no. 11, November 1972, pp. 1408–1423.

7. J. Edmonds and R. M. Karp, "Theoretical Improvements in Algorithmic Efficiency for Network Flow Problems," *Journal of the Association for Computing Machinery*, vol. 19, no. 2, April 1972, pp. 248–264.

8. E. A. Dinic, "Algorithm for Solution of a Problem of Maximum Flow in a Network with Power Estimation," *Soviet Math. Dokl.*, vol. 11, no. 5, 1970.

9. L. R. Ford, Jr., and D. R. Fulkerson, "Maximum Flow through a Network," *Canadian Journal of Mathematics*, vol. 8, 1956, pp. 399–404.

10. R. E. Kahn and W. R. Crowther, "Flow Control in a Resource-Sharing Computer Network," *IEEE Transactions on Communications*, vol. COM-20, no. 3, June 1972, pp. 539–546.

11. M. C. Pennotti and M. Schwartz, "Congestion Control in Store and Forward Tandem Links," *IEEE Transactions on Communications*, vol. COM-23, no. 12, December 1975, pp. 1434–1443.

12. D. W. Davies, "The Control of Congestion in Packet-Switching Networks," *IEEE Transactions on Communications*, vol. COM-20, no. 3, June 1972, pp. 546–550.

13. E. Raubold and J. Haenle, "A Method of Deadlock-Free Resource Allocation and Flow Control in Packet Networks," *Proceedings of the Third International Conference on Computer Communication*, Toronto, 1976, pp. 483–487.

14. A. Shah, "On Flow Control Mechanism in Packet-Switching Networks—An Analytical Approach," *Proceedings of Trends and Applications*, Gaithersburg, Md., 1976, pp. 37–41.

15. H. Rudin and H. Müller, "On Routing and Flow Control," *Proceedings of the International Symposium on Flow Control in Computer Networks*, Versailles, France, North-Holland, 1979, pp. 241–256.

16. G. A. Deaton, Jr., "Flow Control in Packet-Switched Networks with Explicit Path Routing," *Proceedings of the International Symposium on Flow Control in Computer Networks*, Versailles, France, North-Holland, 1979, pp. 405–427.

17. V. Ahuja, "On Congestion Problems in Communication Networks, *Proceedings of Trends and Applications: Distributed Processing*, Gaithersburg, Md., May 1978, pp. 40–46.

18. V. Ahuja, "Routing and Flow Control in Systems Network Architecture," *IBM Systems Journal*, vol. 18, no. 2, 1979, pp. 298–314.

19. V. Ahuja, "Algorithm to Check Network States for Deadlock," *IBM Journal of Research and Development*, vol. 23, no. 1, January 1979, pp. 82–86.
20. J. Rinde, "Routing and Control in a Centrally Directed Network," *Proceedings of the AFIPS National Computer Conference*, 1977, vol. 46, pp. 603–608.
21. A. Rajaraman, "Routing in TYMNET," *Proceedings of the European Computing Congress*, 1978.
22. L. Fratta, M. Gerla, and L. Kleinrock, "The Flow Deviation Method: An Approach to Store-and-Forward Communication Network Design," *Networks*, vol. 3, 1973, pp. 97–133.
23. V. Ahuja, "Determining Deadlock Exposure for a Class of Store and Forward Communication Networks," *IBM Journal of Research and Development*, vol. 24, no. 1, January 1980, pp. 49–55.
24. V. Ahuja, "Exposure of Routed Networks to Deadlocks," Ph.D. dissertation, University of North Carolina, Chapel Hill, 1976. Reprinted as IBM Technical Report TR 29.0150, 1976.
25. G. Pujolle, "Comparison of Some End-to-End Flow Control Policies in a Packet-switching Network," *Proceedings of the National Computer Conference*, 1979, AFIPS vol. 48, pp. 893–903.

CHAPTER
SEVEN

ROUTING

CHAPTER OUTLINE

7-1 INTRODUCTION

A computer communications network can be viewed as a network graph $N = (X, A)$, where X is the set of network nodes and A is the set of transmission links connecting the nodes. A directed path of a network joins two network nodes through a collection of connected links. Thus, a directed path through a network is a sequence of arcs $(a_i, a_{i+1}, a_{i+2}, \ldots, a_n)$ such that the ending node of arc a_{i+k} is the same as the beginning node of arc a_{i+k+1}. These directed paths through the network are also called *network routes* or *message routes*. A message starting from its origination node follows the network route to reach its destination node. Thus, the routing algorithms are the rules that determine the directed path for each message from its originating node to its destination node.

Consider the network shown in Fig. 7-1, and assume that there is a message originating in node A that is destined for node M. There are several possibilities. It may traverse one of the following paths, such as $ABCM$, $ABEM$, $ADEM$, $ADFGM$, or $ADFGEM$. In the simplest case, once a path has been selected by the originating node for a given destination node, each network node directs the corresponding messages to follow that route. Thus, network routing pertains to the process of establishing and selecting an appropriate path for a message, and directing the message to follow that path through the network.

Several aspects of network design are inseparably related to the routing algorithms. The topological design of a network can be affected by the number of disjoint routes required for each node pair, as we will discuss in Sec. 7-3. The centralized flow control schemes, discussed in Sec. 6-2, determine the message routes based on network loads. The flow deviation method, described in Sec. 6-2, is an illustrative example of exercising flow control by changing message routes.

Before we proceed to present various routing algorithms, a review of some preliminary concepts may be useful. Network routing can be incorporated through a message header or a routing table. In the case of message header implementation, all nodes in the message route are included in the header. Consider a message to be sent from node A to node M for the network shown in Fig. 7-1. Let us assume that the message will follow route $ABCM$. Then, we can include these four node and link identifications in the message header. The order in which these node and link identifications appear in the message header is the same as that in which the nodes are traversed by the

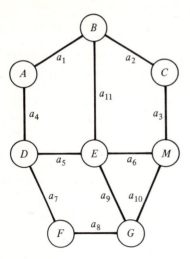

Figure 7-1 A network $N = (X, A)$; $X = (A, B, C, D, E, F, G, M)$; $A = (a_1, a_2, a_3, a_4, a_5, a_6, a_7, a_8, a_9, a_{10}, a_{11})$.

message. This is shown in Fig. 7-2(a). At each node, the message is forwarded on the transmission link that connects to the next node indicated in the message header. A modification to this approach is when the routing header simply contains node identifications. Then any given node should include the identification of each adjacent node and the corresponding transmission link connecting to that node. Thus, each node, except for the destination node, uses this correspondence to determine the appropriate link for forwarding a message.

Alternatively, the routing information can be stored in a routing table in each node, such as the one shown in Fig. 7-2(b). In this implementation, all routes are included in the routing table. The row and column indices of the routing table represent the origination and destination nodes of the route. A routing table entry identifies the link that connects to the next node on the route. At each node, the table is accessed, using the origination and destination node identifications, to determine the link on which to forward the message. The process continues at each node on the route until the message arrives at the destination node. The message header can include origination and destination node identifications, although the need for the originating node identification in this approach depends on the design of the algorithm. Finally, a message header can include a virtual channel

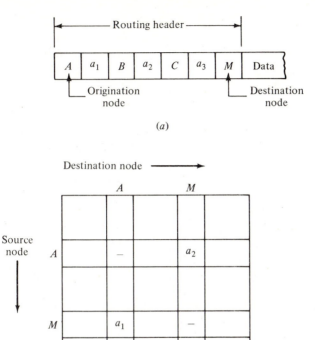

Figure 7-2 (*a*) Routing header for a message originating in node *A* and destined for node *M*. (The network is shown in Fig. 7.1.) (*b*) Routing table for node *B*. Entries identify links for routing messages between nodes *A* and *M*. Other entries are not shown. (Inclusion of entries for originating node depends on the design of routing algorithm.)

number, such as in X.25 (described in Sec. 5-2), thereby allowing more than one route for the same origination and destination nodes.

Several variations of the above two concepts are possible, depending on network design and the extent to which a node participates in determining message routes. For the above approaches, a tradeoff occurs between transmission link cost (for message header)

---

* Some additional processing is required to access and update the routing table.

and memory cost (for routing table).* Let us assume that transmission
link costs decrease at a slower rate than memory costs. Then, it appears that, assuming everything else to be equivalent, the routing table
implementations should be cost-effective. In case of a given network
design, the selection of a given implementation would depend on such
factors as message header size and memory requirements for the routing table. For message routes that traverse several nodes, the message
header can become lengthy and uneconomical as compared to use of
routing tables.

Routing algorithms have been classified in several ways. A
common approach is to classify them depending on whether routes
are (frequently) adapted to network traffic patterns. Fixed or deterministic routing algorithms are based on network topology and average
network delays. Once selected, the routes are generally not adjusted to
changes in traffic patterns. We present this class of algorithms in Sec.
7-2. In Sec. 7-3, we present the algorithms that address the reliability
aspects of deterministic routing. Approaches that adapt routes to network loads are described in Sec. 7-4.

7-2 DETERMINISTIC ROUTING

The deterministic, or fixed, routing approach establishes message
routes based on network topology, average message delays, or both
factors. Message routes are established as part of the network design
and usually do not change during message transmission and network
operation. In the simplest case, the message routes can be selected to
provide the shortest distance between two nodes. This approach is
simple to implement and provides the minimum distance. However, it
does not account for network traffic or overloads on a link or a node.
For low network loads, however, this approach should provide satisfactory performance.

Shortest Path Algorithms

Shortest path algorithms have been a subject of research in graph
theory for a long time. Several publications have appeared on these
algorithms [5, sec. 3.7, Chap. 6; 14; 16; 19]. Comparison of these
algorithms is given in [14, 16, 19]. Dijkstra's algorithm provides the
shortest path from a network node to every other node. Algorithms
by Floyd and by Dantzig are considered efficient in providing shortest
paths for each node pair.

Floyd's Algorithm

This algorithm generates a series of matrices by successively including a new node to provide the shortest path for each node pair. In a given matrix D^k, the path between any two nodes uses only nodes 1 to k. Hence, true shortest paths are obtained when $k = N$, where N is the total number of nodes.

1. Label the nodes of the network from 1 to N, where N is the total number of nodes. Define an $N \times N$ matrix M, whose element $m_{i,j}$ represents the length of the directed arc connecting node i to node j. If there is no arc connecting i to j, then $m_{i,j}$ is set to infinity or, for computational purposes, $m_{i,j}$ is set to a very large value.
2. Successively generate an $N \times N$ matrix D^k, $k = 0, \ldots, N$, as follows. The matrix D^k can be interpreted as providing the lengths of the shortest paths for all node pairs (i, j) such that the path between node i and node j may include any nodes from the set $(1, 2, \ldots, k)$, as well as nodes i and j. (Thus, the matrix D^0 consists only of the end nodes for each path, which is the same as matrix M.)

   The matrix D^{k+1} is obtained from the matrix D^k by evaluating inclusion of the node $k + 1$ in the existing shortest paths as follows:

$$d_{i,j}^{k+1} = \text{Min}(d_{i,j}^k, d_{i,k+1}^k + d_{k+1,j}^k)$$

   where the Min function provides the least value from its arguments. That is, in the shortest path for each node pair, include the node $k + 1$ if the inclusion reduces the path as compared to the path in the matrix D^k.
3. The matrix D^N provides the shortest paths.

   Example Consider the network shown in Fig. 7-3. Matrices D^0 to D^5 are shown in Fig. 7.4. Note that the shortest path between nodes A and D is not through arc AD but through node E.

The Dantzig algorithm, described in [14, 16], generates matrices of increasing size. A $k \times k$ matrix, produced at the kth iteration, provides the shortest path between nodes i and j ($i, j = 1, \ldots, k$), using nodes from the set $(1, \ldots, k)$. Given the $k \times k$ matrix, the determination of the $(k + 1) \times (k + 1)$ matrix is left as an exercise (see prob. 7-2).

Computationally, Floyd's algorithm requires N^2 additions and N^2 minimizations to produce each matrix D^i. Thus, in all, this algorithm requires N^3 additions and N^3 comparisons, or $2N^3$ total operations. The Dantzig algorithm also requires $2N^3$ operations.

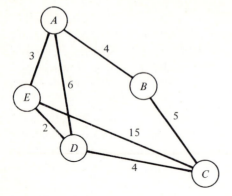

Figure 7-3 A sample network for determining shortest paths between nodes. (Arc lengths are shown as labels.)

Finally, within the context of shortest path algorithms, there can be a requirement to obtain the 2d, 3d, ..., or kth shortest path for a node pair. We do not address this here and suggest the reader refer to [16] for a treatment of this topic.

Minimum Delay Algorithms

As we observed earlier in this chapter, deterministic, or fixed, routing is established based on average network traffic. Thus, message routes are generally unaffected by fluctuations in network traffic. The fixed message routes are either never changed or changed infrequently. Such an approach lends itself to centralized route assignment. One possibility is to assign a route only on a user log-on basis. The route is assigned depending on the network traffic at that time, and does not change for the duration that the user is in a session. An example of route assignment at user log-on is TYMNET, which is described in Sec. 6-2 and App. A.

Messages can be assigned routes based on the current network traffic. The flow deviation method [24] assigns messages (flows) to nodes (routes) based on network traffic. We suggest that the reader review this algorithm in Sec. 6-2. The problem of assigning message routes for the node pairs to minimize delays can also be transformed

Figure 7-4 Application of Floyd's algorithm to network shown in Fig. 7.3.

	A	B	C	D	E
A	∞	4	∞	6	3
B	4	∞	5	∞	∞
C	∞	5	∞	4	15
D	6	∞	4	∞	2
E	3	∞	15	2	∞

$M =$ (above)

∞ = infinity

The matrix is symmetric (that is, $d_{i,j} = d_{j,i}$ for all i, j), since the links are bidirectional. Therefore, we can simply consider half of the matrix. For purposes of illustration here, each element includes the arcs for the shortest path, instead of the length.

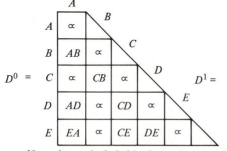

$D^0 =$

No nodes are included in the routes; except the two end nodes.

$D^1 =$

Includes node A in the routes.

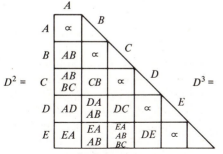

$D^2 =$

Includes nodes A and B in the routes.

$D^3 =$

Includes nodes A, B, and C in the routes.

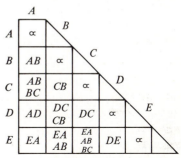

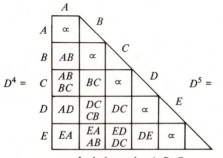

$D^4 =$

Includes nodes A, B, C, and D in the routes.

$D^5 =$

Includes all nodes in the network

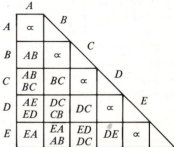

into a multicommodity network flow problem, as described in [2, pp. 231–233] and included in Sec. 6-2.

7-3 RELIABILITY IN DETERMINISTIC ROUTING

A reliable network should provide alternate routes for message transmission in order to handle such conditions as link or node failure. Reliability is an important consideration for networks that are exposed to node or link failures. It can also be important for business considerations, such as for an airline reservation network requiring 24-hour uninterrupted service. We describe some approaches to address network routing in the context of network reliability. These approaches basically exploit network topology to select alternate routes.

One class of deterministic routing algorithm employs the *flooding* technique [22]. Here, a message arriving in a node is transmitted to all neighboring nodes or to a group of selected neighboring nodes. The selected node group usually consists of the nodes closest to the destination node. Thus, as the name implies, the network is flooded with several copies of messages. Duplicate copies are discarded at the destination node. This technique is simple to implement, and the message almost always reaches the destination node. This approach should be more efficient for transmission of broadcast messages, as compared to transmission of messages destined for the same node. It is also useful for networks with light message loads. To entertain higher loads, the scheme should reduce duplicate messages by being more selective for the nodes on which copies of messages are forwarded. This, however, implies increased complexity in implementing the algorithm.

Disjoint Deterministic Routes

The disjoint route problem pertains to providing routes between two nodes so that no link or node is shared by any two routes. The route disjointness property is desirable for reliability, and maximizes backup capability. Disjointness can exist simply for links, or for both links and nodes on the route. We address the problem of obtaining the maximum number of disjoint routes for one or more node pairs of a given network. Specifically, let X be the set of nodes in the network and A the set of links connecting the nodes. Then, given the network topology $N = (X, A)$, we wish to derive routes $R = (r_i, \ldots, r_k)$ for a

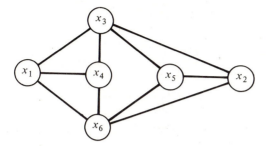

Figure 7-5 A network. (Figures 7.5, 7.6, and 7.7 from V. Ahuja, "Approaches for Disjoint Routing in Communication Networks," *Proceedings of Trends and Applications*, Gaithersburg, Md., May 1979, p. 37.)

given node pair (x_1, x_2) such that (1) no link exists in more than one route of R, and (2) the number of routes in R is maximum. This is the link-disjoint route problem. A similar problem for node disjoint routes is described later.

The link-disjoint route problem has been addressed in [3, p. 49; 21]. Consider the network shown in Fig. 7-5. Let (x_1, x_2) be the node pair for which the maximum number of link disjoint routes is desired. This is achieved by first assigning a capacity of 1 to each link. Then, the maximum flow from node x_1 to node x_2 gives the maximum number of link disjoint routes. This is true since no link is permitted a flow greater than 1; thus, no more than one route can use the same link. The maximum flow from node x_1 to node x_2, using the labeling algorithm (described in Sec. 6-3), is 3. Thus, there exists a maximum of three link disjoint routes between node x_1 and node x_2, as shown in Fig. 7-6.

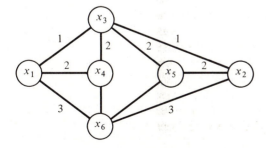

Figure 7-6 Link disjoint routes from node x_1 to node x_2 in the network shown in Fig. 7-5.) (The three link disjoint routes are labelled 1, 2, and 3.)

The node-disjoint route problem requires that no node appears more than once in any route for a given node pair. In other words, given a network $N = (X, A)$, the node-disjoint route problem is to determine the routes $R = (r_i, \ldots, r_k)$ for a given node pair (x_1, x_2) such that (1) there is no node in X (except, of course, x_1 and x_2) that is in more than one route in R, and (2) the number of routes in R is maximum. It can be readily seen that if two routes are node-disjoint, they are also link-disjoint; however, the converse is not true (prob. 7-3).

The node-disjoint route problem is addressed by transforming it into a network flow problem [21]. The approach described here uses a theorem by Menger [3, pp. 47–50; 17]. Let (x_1, x_2) be the pair of nodes in the given network for which the maximum number of node disjoint routes are desired. Then, the approach splits each node x_i (except for nodes x_1 and x_2) into nodes x_i' and x_i'', such that x_i' is connected to all incoming arcs to x_i, and x_i'' is connected to all outgoing arcs from x_i. The capacity of each arc joining x_i' or x_i'' is fixed at 1; thus, no more than one route can use node x_i. Every arc (x, x_i) is replaced by arc (x, x_i'), and every arc (x_i, x) is replaced by arc (x_i'', x). Nodes x_i' and x_i'' are connected by an arc with a capacity of 1; the capacity of all other arcs is also fixed at 1. Then, the maximum flow from node x_1 to node x_2 in this new *flow network* provides the maximum number of node disjoint routes from node x_1 to node x_2. This is intuitively obvious, since a flow of no more than 1 is allowed through any node in the network. Here again, we can use a maximum flow algorithm, such as the labeling algorithm (Sec. 6-3), to obtain maximum node disjoint routes.*

To illustrate the above procedure, again consider the network shown in Fig. 7-5. Each network node in Fig. 7-5 is replaced by a pair of nodes, as shown in Fig. 7-7 and as described above. For the flow network of Fig. 7-7, the maximum flow is 2. Thus, there are two node disjoint routes between nodes x_1 and x_2: $[(x_1, x_3), (x_3, x_2)]$ and $[(x_1, x_6), (x_6, x_2)]$. Although these routes are not necessarily unique, there are at most two node disjoint routes between nodes x_1 and x_2. Note that every arc in Fig. 7.5 is replaced by two arcs, one in each direction of flow.

The above disjoint routing approaches provide alternate routes when a node or a link fails. Such routes can also be used to distribute traffic during normal network operation. However, the above strat-

---

* Other references on maximum static flows include [1, 5, 6, 7, 10, 11, 12, 13, 18].

egies do not consider the problem of providing a primary route with the shortest path, and then a disjoint route that does not share any link or node with the primary route. That is, these approaches do not consider the lengths of routes in obtaining disjoint routes. Another problem of interest is to obtain a (shortest) route that avoids a given (failing) link or node. This problem can be addressed by applying a shortest path algorithm, such as Floyd's algorithm, on the modified network that excludes the failing link or node.

Fixed routing is attractive when network loads remain constant or change very slowly. The other extreme is, obviously, rapidly changing message traffic. The latter requires frequent changes in message routes to adapt to network traffic so as to minimize network delays and congestion. The fixed routing strategies, discussed above, permit changes to message routes only at infrequent intervals. Thus, there is a continuum between the totally fixed and completely adaptive routing schemes. As pointed out earlier, the primary advantages of fixed routing are minimal overhead cost in processing and communicating route assignments (incurred each time the routes are established), and simplicity in implementing the algorithms. In the next section, we present strategies in which routes are adapted dynamically to adjust to network traffic.

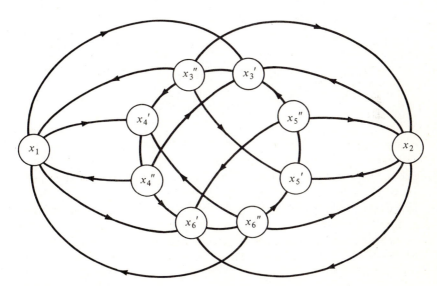

Figure 7-7 Flow network to determine node disjoint routes in the network of Fig. 7-5 for node pair (x_1, x_2).

7-4 ADAPTIVE ROUTING STRATEGIES

Adaptive routing strategies employ centralized or distributed schemes to forward messages based on some criterion that is usually not fixed over time. The message route is determined during message transmission to adapt to the current network traffic or other conditions, such as node or link failures. We begin this section by presenting a centralized adaptive routing scheme, followed by random routing and a description of adaptive routing in ARPANET.

Centralized Adaptive Routing

Adaptive routing, because of its requirement for adjustment to network conditions, is difficult to manage from a central point. Parameters such as message queue lengths and expected delays at each node have to be collected in the central node. The inherent delay in receiving and disseminating this information can result in addressing traffic conditions that existed some time ago instead of current traffic conditions. However, a centralized scheme is feasible and desirable in some situations.

Consider Fig. 7-8(a) in which several source nodes share one or more paths to the same destination node. A concentrator is located for each path, and each message is to be routed to a path so that the sum of message queues in all concentrator nodes is minimized. Then, the problem is to assign each message in a source node to one of the possible paths so as to minimize network delay. The intervening controller determines selection of the concentrator. A possible analogy is the telephone switching system, in which each call is routed through one of several possible paths. Schwartz and Brown have treated this problem [2*; 23]; and we summarize their approach below.

For simplicity, assume a single source [Fig. 7-8(b)] that can send messages to a fixed concentrator node during a time unit. The queue length information from each concentrator node is received in the controller at every T time units. The controller node, which assigns the message routes, must determine the path for a message. A message takes one time unit to be transmitted on the link.

* M. Schwartz, *Computer Communication Network Design and Analysis*, Prentice-Hall, Inc., Englewood Cliffs, N.J., 1977, pp. 223–226. Reprinted by permission.

C. W. Brown and M. Schwartz, "Adaptive Routing in Centralized Computer Communications Networks with an Application to Processor Allocation," *Proceedings of the IEEE International Conference on Communications*, San Francisco, June 1975, pp. 47-12 to 47-14. Adapted by permission of the IEEE and the authors.

Source node · Controller · Concentrator nodes · Destination node

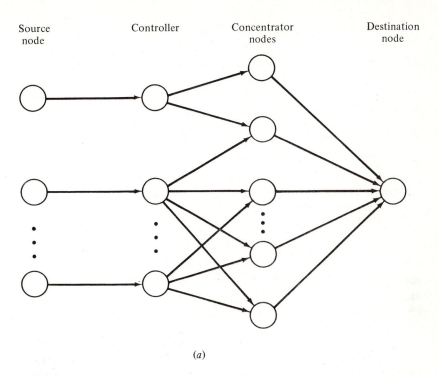

(*a*)

Source nodes · Controller · Concentrator nodes · Destination node

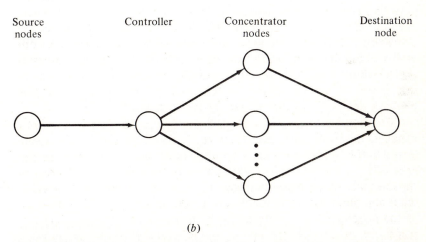

(*b*)

Figure 7-8 (*a*) Shared paths between source nodes and destination node. (*b*) Single source network. (From M. Schwartz, *Computer Communication Network Design and Analysis*, Prentice-Hall, Englewood Cliffs, N.J., 1977, pp. 222–223. Adapted by permission.)

Let there be Q concentrator nodes, and let the probability that there are m messages waiting in queue j ($j = 1, 2, \ldots, Q$) at the end of kth time unit be

$$p_{m,j}(k + 1) \qquad (7\text{-}1)$$

Then, the expected sum of queues at time slot k is

$$C(k) = \sum_{j=1}^{Q} \sum_{m=0}^{L} [m p_{m,j}(k + 1)]$$

where L is the maximum number of messages allowed in a concentrator, or the maximum queue size. The expected queue size at a given concentrator is

$$\sum_{m=0}^{L} m \, p_{m,j}(k + 1)$$

The objective is to minimize the average queue sum

$$C = \frac{1}{T} \sum_{k=0}^{T-1} C(k) \qquad (7\text{-}2)$$

This C function is related to message traffic and queue lengths as follows. Let $t_{im}^{j}[v(k)]$ be the transition probability that m messages are in queue j at time $(k + 1)$, given that there were i messages at time k. In this probability term, $v(k)$ represents the queue to which traffic is sent in time slot k; $v(k) = j$ implies the switch is connected to concentrator j in slot k. The term $v(k)$ is included in the transition probability, since the probability depends on whether the switch is connected to concentrator j. Then,

$$p_{m,j}(k + 1) = \sum_{i=0}^{L} p_{i,j}(k) \, t_{im}^{j}[v(k)]$$

That is, the probability that there are m messages in queue j at time $k + 1$ is the sum of products of probabilities that there are i messages ($i = 0, 1, \ldots, L$) at time k, multiplied by the transition probability that this number of messages changes to m in queue j. Thus, this recursive equation gives us the probabilities for queue lengths. Now, the transition probabilities are determined by message arrival rate at the concentrator nodes. Let $r(j, m)v(k)$ be the probability that m messages arrive at queue j during time unit k. Then, excluding the term $v(k)$, the transition probability $t_{im}^{j} v(k)$ can take on the values:

$$t^j_{im} = 0 \qquad\qquad\qquad \text{for } m < i - 1$$

$$t^j_{im} = r(j, m - i + 1)(v) \qquad \text{for } i > 0, i - 1 \leq m < L$$

$$t^j_{im} = r(j, m)(v) \qquad\qquad \text{for } i = 0, m < L$$

$$t^j_{im} = 1 - \sum_{n=0}^{L-i} r(j, n)(v) \qquad \text{for } i > 0, m = L$$

$$t^j_{im} = 1 - \sum_{n=0}^{L-1} r(j, n)(v) \qquad \text{for } i = 0, m = L$$

The basis of writing the above equations is straightforward. For example, in the case of the first equation, the probability that m messages are in queue j at time unit $k + 1$, given there were i at time unit k, is 0 for $m < i - 1$. This is true since queue size cannot reduce by more than 1 in a time unit. (A given concentrator node cannot transmit more than one message in a time unit.) For the second equation, there is one message transmitted and, consequently, there must be $m - i + 1$ arrivals. We leave it up to the reader to study the remaining equations.

Finally, we must determine the probabilities $r(j, m)(v)$. If the source is sending messages to the jth concentrator, then

$$r(j, n)(v) = \frac{\lambda^n e^{-\lambda}}{n!}$$

where λ is the average number of messages generated per slot. This is true when the controller is connected to the concentrator $[v(k) = j]$. If the controller is not connected to the concentrator $[v(k) \neq j]$, then $r(j, n)(v) = 0$ if $n \neq 0$, and $r(j, n)(v) = 1$ if $n = 0$. That is, no arrivals will take place in queue j if $v(k) \neq j$.

The above equations provide values to be used in eq. (7-2). Thus, each routing sequence (queue 1, 2, ..., Q for slot 0, 1, ..., $T - 1$) can be checked to obtain the one sequence that results in minimum queue size. For Q concentrators, Q^T sequences are to be checked. For $T = 10$ time units and $Q = 3$, it requires 3^{10} or approximately 60,000 sequences to be tested. Several suboptimal algorithms are possible. One possibility, a "shortsighted" algorithm [2, p. 229], saves computation by evaluating the best strategy for the next time unit only, based on the strategy used up to that time.

Random Routing

Random routing procedures determine routing to the next node based on a probability distribution over the set of neighboring nodes. For example, one random routing policy sends the message on any one of the links with equal probability. Random routing has been analyzed by Kleinrock [8, chap. 6].

   To study random routing, consider the ring configuration shown in Fig. 7-9. The probability that a message in node *A* is routed to node *B* is *p*, and to node *C* is $1 - p$. If each node had *n* neighboring nodes, the probability that a given message is sent to any given node is $1/n$. Kleinrock has considered a 13-node network with variable *k*, which defines the connectivity, or the number of neighboring nodes for each node. For the network shown in Fig. 7-9, *k* is 2 and $p = 1 - p = .5$. This network could be completely connected by increasing the connectivity such that $k = 12$. For $k = 2$, the shortest path algorithm gives

$$n' = \frac{1}{N}\left(2\sum_{i=1}^{N/2} i\right) = \frac{1}{2}\left(\frac{N}{2} + 1\right)$$

where *N* is the total number of nodes. Kleinrock has obtained the

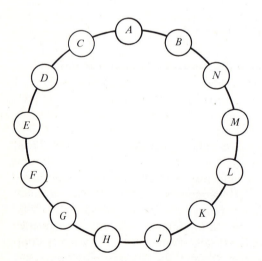

Figure 7-9 A 13-node ring network considered for random routing. (From L. Kleinrock, *Communication Nets: Stochastic Message Flow and Delay*, Dover, New York 1964, p. 105.)

average number of links n' traversed by each message, and has compared it with the shortest path algorithm. The following values pertain to the network shown in Fig. 7-9, but for varying values of k.

Table 7-1 Average number of links traversed

k	n' (random)	n' (shortest path)
2	30.3	3.5
3	14.65	2.25
4	14	1.67
12	12	1

Source: L. Kleinrock, "Communication Nets: Stochastic Message Flow and Delay," Dover, New York, 1964, p. 105.

As the values in Table 7-1 indicate, random routing procedures cause messages to traverse more nodes than other routing procedures. Based on analysis and simulation, Kleinrock [8, p. 106] observes that random routing is expensive in three ways: the number of nodes visited by each message is large, the time spent at each node is large, and the mean total traffic that the network can accept is small; each comment is relative to a fixed routing scheme described by Kleinrock. The main advantages of random routing are that the procedures are simple, little information about the rest of the network is required, and the network degrades slowly in the presence of fluctuating loads.

Adaptive Routing in ARPANET

The original ARPANET routing algorithm, described in [9; 26; 4, pp. 23–26], is based on adapting message routes to network load. The network uses packet switching and each packet is routed, in principle, to reach the destination node in a minimum amount of time. Specifically, the packet is routed from one node to the next, so that the total estimated delay to reach the destination node is minimized. Obviously, such a path will vary with time because of the stochastic nature of the traffic and link or node failures. Each IMP* periodically estimates the minimum expected delay route to every destination node,

* An ARPANET node is called an interface message processor (IMP).

and enters the corresponding outgoing link address in a table. The destination node and its most desirable link address are stored in a routing table. When a packet arrives in a node, it is sent on the link corresponding to its destination node entry in the routing table. Every IMP transmits to each of its neighboring IMPs an estimate of minimum delay for every destination node. The delay of each IMP to itself is set to 0. The delay vector is stored as entries in the delay table for the link on which it arrived. As shown in Fig. 7-10, IMP B sends its minimum delay vector to IMP A on link J. IMP A stores it in the delay table under link J. IMP A adds its own expected delay (from IMP A to IMP B) to these entries in the delay table. The minimum delay value for each destination IMP is then obtained by comparing the values of the entries for that destination IMP in the delay table. The link address corresponding to the minimum delay path is entered in the routing table. This minimum delay table is sent to each neighboring IMP every 128 ms.

The above algorithm equalizes network load while adapting to

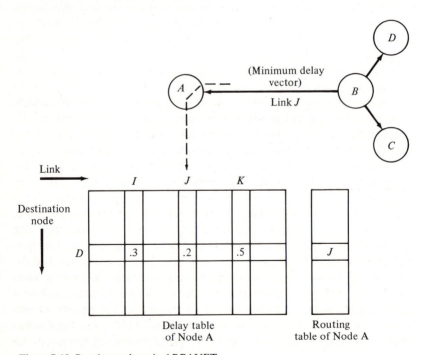

Figure 7-10 Routing updates in ARPANET.

changes in network topology. The algorithm computes and uses minimum delays for packets. However, because of routing updates and time delays, the delay information at a given instance could be a function of the traffic several seconds earlier. This time lag can lead to looping or oscillations, and can thus increase link utilization. To avoid these problems, the delay vector is biased toward the shortest path. Thus, the delay can be estimated to be proportional to the number of packets on the output queue, plus a fixed increment. In this way, even if a queue is empty, it represents some delay, thereby inducing the packets to follow the shortest path more often and avoid oscillations. The disadvantage of the bias is that it causes the algorithm to lose some sensitivity to network traffic. Another fault in the routing algorithm is that it maintains only one route per destination, thereby not permitting load splitting. The approach to estimate delay on a link is based on the number of packets on the link, but this does not account for differences in link speeds and propagation delays in the network. Finally, the routing-update packets grow in size with the number of network nodes, thereby posing a performance problem. The routing computation is proportional to the number of IMPs in the network, and takes only about 5 percent of the IMP's CPU capacity. The routing tables require about 3 percent of IMP storage, and the exchange of delay information requires about 3 percent of the bandwidth of the 50-kb links [9, p. 87].

A new routing algorithm [26], which addresses problems with the original routing algorithm, has been implemented in ARPANET. This algorithm also routes packets adaptively at each node, based on the shortest estimated delay path. However, in this algorithm, average delay is measured on each link by the attached nodes every 10 s. This delay estimate is received and propagated by each node on every outgoing link. Each node uses this estimate to compute its own shortest path to every other node. In order to perform this computation, each node now has a database that describes network topology and delays on each link. The update packet is small since it carries delay information for all links attached to a node, and is independent of the number of nodes in the network. Upon receiving an update, each node checks whether it has already received (and processed) this or a later update from the same node. If so, it discards the update. Otherwise, it immediately forwards it to all adjacent nodes. The fixed information in these packets implies fast propagation since the update need not be processed before forwarding.

Other Adaptive Routing Schemes

There are some variations pertaining to delay information and its use in adaptive routing. First, as we mentioned above, the queue size on each outbound link can be used as a measure for time delay. In another scheme, called *backward learning*, each node uses weighted values of the delay estimates of message flow in opposite directions [22, 25]. Clearly, it is assumed here that the traffic, and therefore the message delays, are symmetric in the two directions of message flow. Therefore, messages arriving in a given node *A* (Fig. 7-11) from node *G* provide the estimated delay in reverse direction to node *G*. Then, node *A* routes a message to node *B* or *C*, depending on whichever path provides the lowest estimate. Specifically, a *handover number* is used. This number, representing the time delay, is appended to the message and incremented at each node. The handover number can also be used to represent the number of hops by initializing the number to 0 at the source node and incrementing it by 1 at each intermediate node. By noting the origin and the handover number of arriving messages, each node identifies the neighbor for the shortest (or fastest) route to a destination node. Problems encountered with the backward-learning technique include poor adaptation to networks in which links or nodes fail, oscillations or looping of messages (in which messages revisit the same node), and the fact that the congestion in the backward direction (which is learned) may not be the same as in the forward congestion (direction or transmission).

Hierarchical Adaptive Routing

For a large number of nodes, network routing table sizes grow and require large amounts of storage. Consider the adaptive routing scheme for ARPANET. The routing table (Fig. 7-10) has one entry per node. For a network with several hundred nodes, table size will be quite large. Furthermore, the length of the minimum delay vector also increases linearly with the number of nodes. (This has been addressed by the new ARPANET routing algorithm.) This suggests some form of grouping of nodes. Kleinrock and Kamoun have published a study of hierarchical routing [15], which is briefly described here.

Network nodes can be divided into groups or clusters of nodes. Then, the routing table size in a node can be reduced by providing less information about nodes in other clusters. The information required for other nodes within the same cluster may not be reduced.

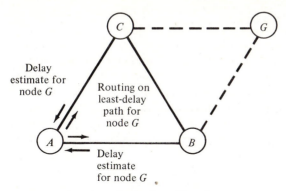

Figure 7-11 Routing using backward learning.

Thus, the routing table can provide one entry per destination for nodes within the same cluster, as well as one entry for every other cluster of nodes. An m-level hierarchical clustering of a set of nodes is defined by grouping network nodes, referred to as 0th-level clusters, into 1st-level clusters that may, in turn, be grouped into 2d-level clusters, and so on. The mth-level cluster is the highest-level cluster. An example of three-level clustering of a 24-node network is shown in Fig. 7-12.

As observed by Kleinrock and Kamoun, the size of a routing table is directly determined by the clustering structure. Let L be the fixed table size at every node for the network in Fig. 7-12(a). Then, the clustering of Fig. 7-12(a) leads to $L = 10$, as shown in the routing table for node 1.1.1 in Fig. 7-12(c). If clusters 1.1 and 1.2 are merged, L becomes 12, since the size of the largest cluster is increased by 3 and one cluster is eliminated.

Ideally, the clustering structure should minimize routing table size, but this can require increased message processing. Kleinrock and Kamoun have developed approaches for an optimal hierarchical clustering structure, providing table length reduction from N to $e \ln N$, where N is the number of nodes, and the number of levels is $\ln N$.

SUMMARY

Message routing in networks directly determines message delays through the network. The objective of a routing algorithm is to deliver messages in the shortest possible time. Routing schemes can be

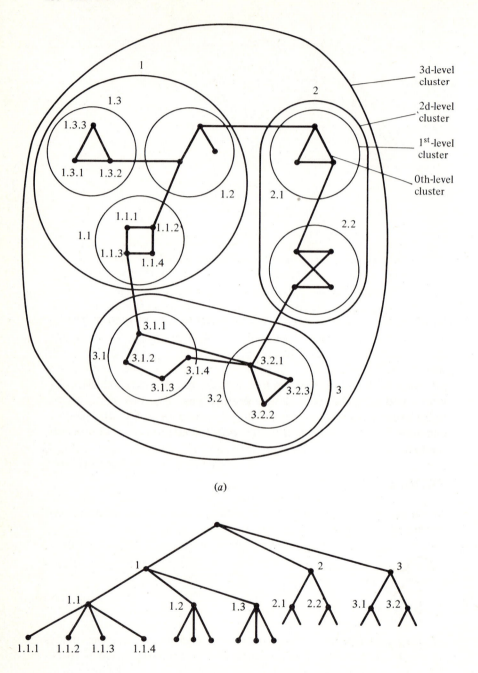

3d-level
cluster

2d-level
cluster

1st-level
cluster

0th-level
cluster

(a)

(b)

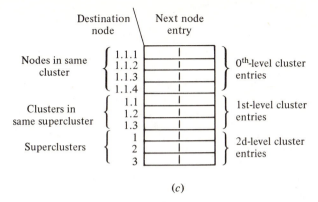

Destination node / Next node entry

Nodes in same cluster { 1.1.1 1.1.2 1.1.3 1.1.4 } 0th-level cluster entries

Clusters in same supercluster { 1.1 1.2 1.3 } 1st-level cluster entries

Superclusters { 1 2 3 } 2d-level cluster entries

(c)

Figure 7-12 (a) A three-level clustered 24-node network. (b) A tree representation of a three-level clustered network. (c) Routing table of node 1.1.1. (From L. Kleinrock and F. Kamoun, "Hierarchical Routing for Large Networks: Performance Evaluation and Optimization," *Computer Networks*, vol. 1, North-Holland Publishing Co., 1977, p. 158. Reprinted with permission.)

classified as fixed or dynamic, deterministic or adaptive, and centralized or distributed. However, fixed or deterministic routing strategies, which employ centralized techniques, are usually considered for networks with predictable loads. Dynamic or adaptive routing approaches often employ distributed techniques and are useful for networks with unpredictable loads. Within these two extremes, several hybrid schemes are possible. Finally, it should be noted that routing and flow control schemes must be coordinated, since each influences the behavior of the other, as described in [20].

PROBLEMS

7-1 For the network shown below, use Floyd's algorithm to determine the shortest path for each pair of nodes.

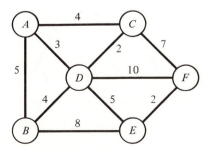

7-2 Derive Dantzig's algorithm and apply it to the above problem. (*Hint*: For each new entry of the matrix D^{m+1}, say, $d_{i,\,m+1}$, select $\text{Min}[d_{i,\,j} + d_{j,\,m+1}]$, $j = 1, \ldots, m$; similarly, for $d_{m+1,\,i}$. For each existing entry in matrix D^m, change it only if the path through the new node is shorter. See [14]).

7-3 For a given pair of network nodes, prove that if two routes are node-disjoint then they are also link-disjoint. Prove that the converse is not true.

7-4 Given the original ARPANET adaptive routing described in Sec. 7-4, and as-suming no bias, develop an example in which messages traverse in a loop. Routing updates occur every two-thirds of a second, and the link speed is 50 kbps. Assume a packet size of 1000 bits.

7-5 Discuss the problems associated with the backward-learning approach. Compare it to the ARPANET routing algorithm.

7-6 Find the maximum number of link disjoint and node disjoint routes from node x_1 to x_2 in the following network. (To obtain the maximum flow, you may use the labeling algorithm described in Sec. 6.3.)

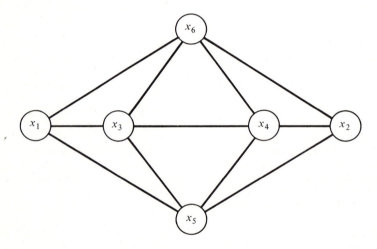

7-7 Write an essay on developing the interface between flow control and routing algorithms.

REFERENCES

1. D. R. Plane and C. McMillan, Jr., *Discrete Optimization—Integer Programming and Network Analysis for Management Decisions*, Prentice-Hall, Englewood Cliffs, N.J., 1971.
2. M. Schwartz, *Computer-Communication Network Design and Analysis*, Prentice-Hall, Englewood Cliffs, N.J., 1977.
3. F. Harary, *Graph Theory*, Addison-Wesley, Reading, Mass., 1972.

4. Network Analysis Corporation, *ARPANET: Design, Operation, Management and Performance*, New York, April 1973.
5. H. Frank and Ivan T. Frisch, *Communication, Transmission, and Transportation Networks*, Addison-Wesley, Reading, Mass., 1971.
6. R. G. Busacker and T. L. Saaty, *Finite Graphs and Networks: An Introduction with Applications*, McGraw-Hill, New York, 1965.
7. L. R. Ford, Jr., and D. R. Fulkerson, *Flows in Networks*, Princeton University Press, Princeton, N.J., 1962.
8. L. Kleinrock, *Communication Nets: Stochastic Message Flow and Delay*, Dover, New York, 1964.
9. J. M. McQuillan, "Routing Algorithms for Computer Networks—A Survey," *Proceedings of the National Telecommunications Conference*, 1977, pp. 28:1-1 to 6; reprinted in J. M. McQuillan and Vinton G. Cerf, *A Practical View of Computer Communications Protocols*, IEEE Computer Society, 1978, pp. 86–91.
10. L. R. Ford, Jr., and D. R. Fulkerson, "Constructing Maximal Dynamic Flows from Static Flows," *Operations Research*, vol. 6, 1958, pp. 419–433.
11. D. R. Fulkerson, "An Out-of-Kilter Method for Minimal-Cost Flow Problems," *Journal of the Society of Industrial and Applied Mathematics*, vol. 9, no. 1, March 1961, pp. 18–27.
12. L. R. Ford, Jr., and D. R. Fulkerson, "Maximum Flow through a Network," *Canadian Journal of Mathematics*, vol. 8, 1956, pp. 399–404.
13. B. Yaged, Jr., "Minimum Cost Routing for Static Network Models," *Networks*, vol. 1, December 1971, pp. 139–172.
14. E. Minieka, "On Computing Sets of Shortest Paths in a Graph," *Communications of the ACM*, vol. 17, no. 6, June 1974, pp. 351–353.
15. L. Kleinrock and F. Kamoun, "Hierarchical Routing for Large Networks: Performance Evaluation and Optimization," *Computer Networks*, vol. 1, 1977, pp. 155–174.
16. S. E. Dreyfus, "An Appraisal of Some Shortest-Path Algorithms," *Journal of the Operations Research Society of America*, vol. 17, 1969, pp. 395–412.
17. S. Even and R. E. Tarjan, "Network Flow and Testing Graph Connectivity," *SIAM Journal of Computing*, vol. 4, no. 4, December 1975, pp. 507–518.
18. A. A. Assad, "Multicommodity Network Flows—A Survey," *Networks*, vol. 8, 1978, pp. 37–91.
19. W. D. Kelton and A. M. Law, "A Mean-Time Comparison of Algorithms for the All-Pairs Shortest-Path Problem with Arbitrary Arc Lengths," *Networks*, vol. 8, 1978, pp. 97–106.
20. H. Rudin and H. Müller, "On Routing and Flow Control," *Proceedings of the International Symposium on Flow Control in Computer Networks*, Versailles, France, North-Holland, 1979, pp. 241–256.
21. V. Ahuja, "Approaches for Disjoint Routing in Communication Networks," *Proceedings of Trends and Applications*, Gaithersburg, Md., May 1979, pp. 36–40.
22. B. W. Boehm and R. L. Mobley, "Adaptive Routing Techniques for Distributed Communications Systems," *IEEE Transactions on Communication Technology*, vol. COM-17, no. 3, June 1969, pp. 340–349.
23. C. W. Brown and M. Schwartz, "Adaptive Routing in Centralized Computer Communications Networks with an Application to Processor Allocation," *Proceedings of the IEEE International Conference on Communications*, San Francisco, June 1975, pp. 47-12 to 47-16.

24. L. Fratta, M. Gerla, and L. Kleinrock, "The Flow Deviation Method: An Approach to Store-and-Forward Communication Network Design," *Networks*, vol. 3, 1973, pp. 97–133.
25. P. Baran et al., "On Distributed Communications," Rand Corporation, Santa Monica, Calif., August 1964. (Series of 11 reports.)
26. J. M. McQuillan, I. Richer, and E. C. Rosen, "An Overview of the New Routing Algorithm for the ARPANET," *Proceedings of the Sixth Data Communications Symposium*, Pacific Grove, Calif., November 1979, pp. 63–68.

CHAPTER
EIGHT

PERFORMANCE ANALYSIS

CHAPTER OUTLINE

Network performance pertains to measuring or estimating parameters that represent network behavior. The parameters of general interest are the number of messages per unit time through the network, the delay for transmitting a message through the network, resource (such as link or node processor) utilization, message queue lengths, and the like. In order to present techniques for estimating such parameters, some concepts in probability theory are required. In the preceding chapters, we have deferred detailed discussion of several analytic results, which are developed here. Thus, this chapter serves a dual purpose: to present the pertinent concepts of probability theory, and to use those concepts in describing approaches for estimating network performance.

8-1 PROBABILITY CONCEPTS

Probability theory pertains to the analysis of chance or random phenomena. The throwing of a die or the tossing of a coin are familiar examples of random experiments. Given any random experiment, there is a set of possible outcomes. For example, a throw of the dice results in one of six possible values. The tossing of a coin results in a head or a tail. The set of all possible outcomes is called the *sample space*. Note that the sample space can depend on the purpose of the experiment. In the random experiment of tossing two coins, it may be sufficient to consider only three events: both heads, both tails, and one head and one tail.

Given the sample space of an experiment, one is obviously interested in the chance that a specific event of the sample space occurs. Thus, we are tempted to assign numbers to the events. We can perform a sequence of repetitions of the same experiment, and count the number of times a given event occurs. Let f_a be the number of times that the experiment resulted in event a, such as a head in a coin toss. Then, the probability of that coin toss resulting in a head should be approximately f_a/n, where n is the total number of times that this experiment is conducted. As the number of repetitions increases, we expect the value of f_a/n to stabilize. Thus, the probability for the experiment to result in a should be

$$P(a) = \lim_{n \to \infty} \frac{f_a}{n}$$

The notation $n \to \infty$ implies that the result is valid when n approaches infinity.

We now describe three basic concepts in probability.

First, we define the probability for two events where their occurrence is independent of each other. Thus, the probability of occurrence of one event does not affect that of the other. In this case, the probability of occurrence of both events A and B, or $P(A \cap B)$, is the product of the probability of occurrence of A, or $P(A)$, times the probability of occurrence of B, or $P(B)$.

$$P(A \cap B) = P(A)\, P(B)$$

Next, we define the probability for two events where the occurrence of one event can affect the probability of occurrence of another event. Let A and B be two events such that $P(A)$ is greater than 0. Then, the conditional probability for event B given event A, written $P(B \mid A)$, is defined to be

$$P(B \mid A) = \frac{P(B \cap A)}{P(A)}$$

where $P(B \cap A)$ is the probability of occurrence of events A and B.

Finally, we define the probability for two events that cannot occur simultaneously. If two events are mutually exclusive, the probability of their union (occurrence of either one) is the sum of their probabilities. Thus,

$$P(A \cup B) = P(A) + P(B),$$

where events A and B are mutually exclusive. Here, $P(A \cup B)$ is the probability of occurrence of either event A or event B.

Example Suppose two perfectly balanced coins are tossed. What is the probability that at least one of them lands heads?

There are four possible outcomes of this experiment, as listed below.

Event	a	b	c	d
Coin 1	H	H	T	T
Coin 2	H	T	H	T

H = head; T = tail.

Since the coins are perfectly balanced, each outcome can occur with equal probability. Thus, $P(a) = P(b) = P(c) = P(d) = .25$. But events a, b, and c include a head. Also, the events a, b, and c are mutually exclusive. This is true since tossing two coins can result in only one of the above four combinations. Therefore, the probability that at least one coin lands with a head is

$$P(a \cup b \cup c) = P(a) + P(b) + P(c)$$

$$= .75$$

Before proceeding to describe some probability distributions of interest, we define the concept of a random variable and some related measures. Suppose that we wish to assign a number to each element of the sample space, which is similar to assigning each person his or her height or weight. Then, a rule that assigns a number to each sample point of an experiment is called a *random variable*. As such, a random variable is a function that assigns a number to each sample point in the sample space. Now, we can discuss the probability of occurrence of an event in terms of the random variable. Consider a perfect coin that is tossed twice. Let X be the random variable that counts the number of heads. Then, the random variable X can have a value of 0, 1, or 2, as listed below.

Toss		Number of	Probability
First	Second	heads (X)	P
Head	Head	2	.25
Head	Tail	1	.25
Tail	Head	1	.25
Tail	Tail	0	.25

Using this table, the probability that random variable X has a value of 0, 1, or 2 is .25, .5, and .25, respectively.

A random variable can be characterized by several measures. We briefly describe some commonly used measures. A *mean* or *expectation* of a discrete random variable* is defined by

$$E[X] = \sum_i x_i\, p(x_i)$$

---

* A random variable is discrete if it takes on discrete rather than continuous values. In this section, we are primarily concerned with discrete random variables. As such, unless otherwise stated, we will simply use the term *random variable* to represent a discrete random variable.

The function $p(x_i)$ provides the probability that random variable X takes on a value x_i.

Next, the *variance* of a random variable provides a measure of the spread of the distribution. If the distribution is concentrated close to $E[X]$, the variance is small; otherwise, it is large. This is shown in Fig. 8-1. The variance of random variable X is defined by

$$\mathrm{Var}[X] = E[(X - E[X])^2]$$
$$= \sum_i (x_i - E[X])^2 p(x_i)$$

It can be shown that

$$\mathrm{Var}[X] = E[X^2] - (E[X])^2$$

The *standard deviation (SD)* of a random variable is simply the value of the square root of the variance.

Example An experiment was conducted on a 2400-bps line to observe its transmission error rate. The experiment was run for 8 hours, and the number of errors observed at the end of each hour was 12, 6, 7, 3, 15, 10, 18, and 5. What is the mean error rate of the link? What is its standard deviation?

We assume that all the eight readings were independent and therefore equally likely. Thus, $p(x_i) = \frac{1}{8} = .125$, for $i = 1, \ldots, 8$. So

$$\mathrm{Mean} = E[X]$$
$$= \sum_i x_i p(x_i)$$
$$= .125 \, (12 + 6 + 7 + 3 + 15 + 10 + 18 + 5)$$
$$= .125 \times 76$$
$$= 9.5$$

$$\mathrm{SD} = \sqrt{\frac{[(12 - 9.5)^2 + (6 - 9.5)^2 + (7 - 9.5)^2 + (3 - 9.5)^2 + (15 - 9.5)^2 + (10 - 9.5)^2 + (18 - 9.5)^2 + (5 - 9.5)^2]}{8}}$$
$$= 4.87$$

The kth moment of random variable X is defined by the value

$$E(X^k) = \sum_i x_i^k p(x_i)$$

It can be seen that the first moment of a random variable is simply the mean of the random variable.

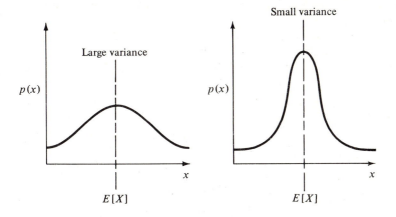

Figure 8-1 Variance of a random variable.

Probability Distributions

The *probability distribution* of a random variable gives the probabilities and the values that may be taken by the random variable. If random variable X assumes a set of values x_1, x_2, ..., x_k, with respective probabilities p_1, p_2, ..., p_k, where $p_1 + p_2 + \cdots + p_k = 1$, then we say that a discrete probability distribution for X has been defined. Let $P(X \leq x)$ define the cumulative probability that random variable X takes on a value less than or equal to x. Then, the distribution function of random variable X is defined by $F_X(x)$, or

$$F_X(x) = P[X \leq x]$$

Consider the case in which random variable X has a finite range a, ..., b, and the probability for each point is the same. This distribution, called the *uniform distribution*, is given by

$$F_X(x) = \begin{bmatrix} 0 & x < a \\ \dfrac{x - a + 1}{b - a + 1} & a \leq x \leq b \\ 1 & x > b \end{bmatrix}$$

The probability density function for the uniform distribution, which corresponds to the probability that the random variable takes on a given value (between a and b), is given by

$$p(x) = \begin{bmatrix} 0 & x < a \\ \dfrac{1}{b-a+1} & a \le x \le b \\ 0 & x > b \end{bmatrix}$$

The general shape of the uniform distribution is depicted in Fig. 8-2. The step function shows the increments with each discrete value.

Many applications of computer communication systems can be analyzed by considering them as a large group of experiments, with a fixed probability of occurrence of a given event in each experiment. One probability distribution used in such applications is the *binomial distribution*. This distribution applies to repetitive experiments, which often have two possible outcomes, and provides the probability that a given event occurs k times in N repetitions of the experiment. An example of this distribution is the determination of the number of transmission lines active at a given time, assuming that the probability for each line being active is the same.

Let the random variable X represent the number of successes out of N experiments. Then, the probability that the random variable has a value of k is given by

$$f(k) = \binom{N}{k} p^k (1-p)^{N-k} \qquad k = 0, 1, \ldots, N, \qquad (8\text{-}1)$$

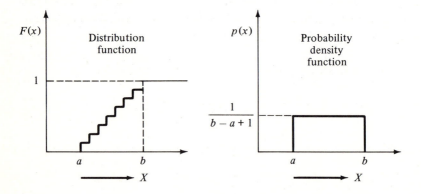

Figure 8-2 Uniform distribution and probability density function.

where p is the probability of occurrence of success in each experiment. The binominal distribution function is given by

$$F_x(J) = P(X \le J)$$

$$= \sum_{k=0}^{J} f(k)$$

$$= \sum_{k=0}^{J} \binom{N}{k} p^k (1 - p)^{N-k}$$

The above expression can be viewed as the probability that J or fewer lines out of N are active, given that the probability for each line being active is p. However, one may be interested in the probability of $J + 1$ or more lines being active simultaneously, which is given by $1 - F_x(J)$. For large values of N and small values of p, the above distribution can be approximated by the *Poisson distribution*. The Poisson density function with parameter λ is given by

$$f(k) = \frac{\lambda^k e^{-\lambda}}{k!} \qquad k = 0, 1, \ldots$$

It can be shown that the mean of a Poisson-distributed random variable is λ [2, p. 84]. Thus, if there are λ arrivals per second on the average, the probability that there are k arrivals in t seconds is given by

$$\frac{(\lambda t)^k e^{-\lambda t}}{k!}$$

We can now show the approximation of the binomial distribution by the Poisson distribution. The binomial probability density function is given by

$$f(k) = \binom{N}{k} p^k (1 - p)^{N-k} \qquad \text{from eq. (8-1)}$$

$$= \frac{N(N - 1) \ldots (N - k + 1)}{k!} p^k (1 - p)^{N-k}$$

By multiplying and dividing by N^k, we obtain

$$f(k) = \frac{1\left(1 - \dfrac{1}{N}\right)\left(1 - \dfrac{2}{N}\right), \ldots, \left(1 - \dfrac{k-1}{N}\right)}{k!} (Np)^k \left(1 - \frac{Np}{N}\right)^{N-k} \qquad (8\text{-}2)$$

Let N approach infinity in such a way that $Np = \lambda$. Then, each term in

$$1\left(1 - \frac{1}{N}\right)\left(1 - \frac{2}{N}\right) \cdots \left(1 - \frac{k-1}{N}\right)$$

approaches 1, while $(Np)^k$ approaches λ^k. Also,

$$\left(1 - \frac{Np}{N}\right)^{N-k} = \left(1 - \frac{\lambda}{N}\right)^N \left(1 - \frac{\lambda}{N}\right)^{-k}$$

approaches $e^{-\lambda}(1) = e^{-\lambda}$. Thus, eq. (8-2) reduces to

$$f(k) = \frac{\lambda^k e^{-\lambda}}{k!}$$

Example A multipoint line serves 200 stations. The probability that a given station has a message is .01. What is the probability that no station has a message?

Using the binomial distribution, the probability that no station has a message is given by

$$\binom{200}{0} .01^0 (1 - .01)^{200} = .1340$$

(The probability that there is at least one message is $1 - .134 = .866$).

Now, using the Poisson distribution, the probability that no station has a message is approximated by

$$\frac{e^{-2}2^0}{0!} = .1353$$

Note that $\lambda = 200 \times .01 = 2$.

Finally, an *exponential distribution* is used to develop models involving waiting times, such as the time to serve a customer. The exponential density with parameter λ is given by

$$p(t) = \lambda e^{-\lambda t}$$

When the input process is Poisson, the distribution of time intervals between two arrivals is exponentially distributed. Let the mean arrival rate be λ, so that the mean interarrival time T is $1/\lambda$.

Then, the probability that the mean interarrival time is less than t is

$$F(t) = 1 - e^{-\lambda t}$$
$$= 1 - e^{-t/T}$$

An interesting and useful property of this distribution is that the interarrival time between two given events (such as between nth and $n + 1$st arrivals) is independent of that of previous events (interarrival times between any two earlier arrivals, starting from 1st to $n - 1$st arrivals).

Note that the above distributions are useful when events are discrete, a property usually applicable in analyzing networks.

8-2 NETWORK PERFORMANCE ESTIMATES

The network performance measures of most common interest are network delay, throughput, node processor utilization, memory utilization, transmission link utilization, and the like. We first need to introduce a simple queuing system to derive some of these results.

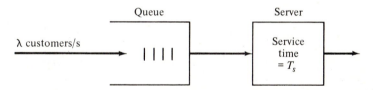

Consider a system in which there are random arrivals and a single random server, also called the *M/M/1 system*. We assume that random arrivals are characterized by the Poisson distribution. According to this distribution, the probability that there are k arrivals in t seconds is given by

$$\frac{e^{-\lambda t}(\lambda t)^k}{k!}$$

where λ is the average number of arrivals per second. For $k = 0$, the above probability reduces to $e^{-\lambda t}$. Thus, the probability that there are one or more arrivals in time t is

$$= 1 - \text{probability that there is no arrival}$$
$$= 1 - e^{-\lambda t}$$

By random service, we imply that the time to service an arrival is given by the exponential distribution function

$$Pr \text{ (service time} < t) = 1 - e^{-t/T_s}$$

where T_s is the mean service time.

Poisson arrivals usually provide a reasonable approximation, but the exponential service assumption is not very realistic. However, this assumption simplifies the analysis and usually provides adequate representation of real processes.

The queue size distribution for such a system is given by*

$$P_k = P_o(\lambda T_s)^k$$

where P_k is the total number of customers in the system, λ is the mean arrival rate per second, T_s is the mean service time in seconds, and P_o is the probability that the queue is empty. We can determine P_o as follows, by using the above expression for P_k and the fact that the sum of P_k, for $k = 0, \ldots, \infty$, must be 1. So,

$$\sum_{k=0}^{\infty} P_k = \sum_{k=0}^{\infty} P_o(\lambda T_s)^k = 1$$

Thus,
$$1 = P_o \sum_{k=0}^{\infty} (\lambda T_s)^k$$

$$= P_o \frac{1}{1 - \lambda T_s} \text{ (assuming } \lambda T_s < 1)$$

or
$$P_o = 1 - \lambda T_s \qquad (8\text{-}3)$$

Server utilization ρ can now be found from the probability that the queue is not empty, or

$$\rho = 1 - P_o$$

$$= 1 - 1 + \lambda T_s$$

$$= \lambda T_s$$

$$= \text{server utilization} \qquad (8\text{-}4)$$

---

* From [3, p. 8].

The queue size distribution can be described in terms of server utilization.

$$P_k = P_o(\lambda T_s)^k$$
$$= (1 - \lambda T_s)(\lambda T_s)^k \qquad \text{using eq. 8-3}$$
$$= (1 - \rho)\rho^k$$

Note that ρ is assumed to be less than 1. This is the geometric distribution, with mean queue size given by*

$$\sum_{k=0}^{\infty} kP_k = \frac{\rho}{1 - \rho}$$

Then, the mean waiting time is given by the service time multiplied by the mean queue size, or $\rho T_s/(1 - \rho)$. This waiting time is required before a given arrival is serviced.

Let us consider how often the queue length exceeds a certain value. For example, we want to establish the rth percentile for queue length k. This implies that the probability that k or fewer customers are in the queue is equal to $r/100$, that is, $P[X \leq k] = r/100$ for random variable X. Thus,

$$\frac{r}{100} = \sum_{i=0}^{k} (1 - \rho)\rho^i$$
$$= 1 - \rho^{1+k}$$

or
$$\rho^{1+k} = 1 - \frac{r}{100}$$

or
$$(1 + k) \log \rho = \log \left(1 - \frac{r}{100}\right)$$

or
$$k = \frac{\log \left(1 - \dfrac{r}{100}\right)}{\log \rho} - 1$$

Example At a switching center, messages arrive at the rate of 120/h. The message length is distributed exponentially, with a mean length of 144 characters. The speed of the link serving the switching center is 8 characters/s. Find the mean message waiting time and the link utilization.

* See [3, p. 9; 5, p. 172].

$$\text{Average arrival rate } \lambda = 120 \text{ messages/h}$$

$$= .033 \text{ messages/s}$$

$$\text{Mean service time } T_s = \frac{144}{8}$$

$$= 18 \text{ s}$$

$$\text{Average link (server) utilization } \rho = \lambda T_s$$

$$= .033 \times 18$$

$$= .6$$

$$\text{Mean waiting time } = \frac{\rho T_s}{1 - \rho}$$

$$= \frac{.6 \times 18}{1 - .6}$$

$$= \frac{10.8}{.4}$$

$$= 27 \text{ s.}$$

The 90th and 95th percentiles for the number of messages waiting are left as an exercise (see prob. 8-3).

Before proceeding to present results on network delays, let us review a useful equation first stated by Little.* According to Little, if t is the mean time spent by a customer in a system, and λ is the average arrival rate, then the mean number of customers in the system is λt. This is one of the more fundamental and commonly used results in queuing theory.

Now, we use the above results to derive an estimate of network delays. If $1/u$ is the average message size in bits, L_i the capacity of the ith link in bits per second, and λ_i the average number of messages on ith channel per second, then the average utilization of the ith link is λ_i/uL_i. Note that λ_i is the total message traffic resulting from all sources to the ith link. Using Little's result, the average number of messages in the ith link is $\lambda_i t_i$, where t_i is the average message delay in seconds on the ith link. But the average number of messages in the

---

* Little's result is described in several textbooks on queuing theory [1, p. 6; 6, p. 156].

system (assuming an M/M/1 system) is also $\rho_i/(1 - \rho_i)$, where $\rho_i = \lambda_i/uL_i$. Thus,

$$\lambda_i t_i = \frac{\lambda_i/uL_i}{1 - \lambda_i/uL_i}$$

or
$$t_i = \frac{1}{uL_i - \lambda_i} \qquad (8\text{-}5)$$

For a given link in a path, we wish to obtain the delay over each link, which requires the use of the Independence Assumption [1, p. 322]. According to this assumption, each time a message is received at a node within the network, a new length b is chosen independently from the probability density function

$$p(b) = ue^{-ub} \qquad b \geq 0$$

Thus, the assumption implies that the exponential distribution is used to determine the length of a message as it arrives at each node. Although this assumption is clearly false, its effect on message delays has been shown to be negligible for most interesting networks [1, p. 322].

Let γ_{jk} represent the average message traffic from node j to node k. Then,

$$\lambda_i = \sum_{\substack{j=1}}^{N} \sum_{\substack{k=1}}^{N} \gamma_{jk} \qquad (8\text{-}6)$$
$$\scriptstyle j, k: \text{link } i \text{ in } P_{jk}$$

where N is the total number of nodes and P_{jk} is the path from node j to node k.

Let T be the average message delay in the network. Then,

$$T = \sum_{j=1}^{N} \sum_{k=1}^{N} \frac{\gamma_{jk}}{\gamma} T_{jk}$$

where γ is the total message traffic in the network, and T_{jk} is the average message delay from node j to node k. Or

$$T = \sum_{j=1}^{N} \sum_{k=1}^{N} \frac{\gamma_{jk}}{\gamma} \sum_{\text{link } i \text{ in } P_{jk}} t_i$$
$$= \sum_{i=1}^{M} \frac{t_i}{\gamma} \sum_{\substack{j=1 \\ j,k:\text{link } i \text{ in } P_{jk}}}^{N} \sum_{k=1}^{N} \gamma_{jk}$$

where M is the total number of links.

Using eq. (8-6),

$$T = \sum_{i=1}^{M} \frac{t_i}{\gamma} \lambda_i$$

Using eq. (8-5),

$$T = \sum_{i=1}^{M} \frac{\lambda_i}{\gamma} \left(\frac{1}{uL_i - \lambda_i} \right)$$

We have used this measure throughout the book. The throughput of the network is simply

$$\sum_{j=1}^{N} \sum_{k=1}^{N} \gamma_{jk} = \gamma$$

Note that the above expressions provide the delays for a message to start on the link. It does not include the delay in processing a message through a node.

Example Consider the network shown in Fig. 8-3. We are interested in the average delay from node A to node D. The message rates are shown in Fig. 8-3. The link capacities are 4800 bps and the average message size is 200 bits. Then, using the above terminology,

$$\lambda_{(A-B)} = 6 + 4$$
$$= 10$$
$$\lambda_{(B-C)} = 6 + 4 + 2$$
$$= 12$$
$$\lambda_{(C-D)} = 6 + 2 + 3$$
$$= 11$$

$$L_i = 4800 \text{ bps for all } i$$

$$\frac{1}{u} = 200 \text{ bits}$$

So

$$uL_i = 24$$

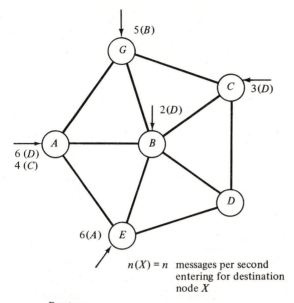

Routes
$G \rightarrow B$
$A \rightarrow B \rightarrow C$
$A \rightarrow B \rightarrow C \rightarrow D$
$B \rightarrow C \rightarrow D$
$C \rightarrow D$
$E \rightarrow A$
$G \rightarrow B$

Figure 8-3 A network configuration used to estimate message delays.

$$\text{Network throughput } \gamma \quad = \sum_{j=1}^{N} \sum_{k=1}^{N} \gamma_{jk}$$

$$= 6 + 6 + 4 + 5 + 2 + 3$$

$$= 26$$

Then, the average delay for a message from node A to node D is

$$= \sum_{i=1}^{M} \frac{\lambda_i}{\gamma} \left(\frac{1}{u L_i - \lambda_i} \right)$$

$$= \left(\frac{10}{26} \times \frac{1}{24 - 10} \right) + \left(\frac{12}{26} \times \frac{1}{24 - 12} \right) + \left(\frac{11}{26} \times \frac{1}{24 - 11} \right)$$

$$= .0985 \text{ s}$$

The average utilization of each link may be determined simply by $\rho = \lambda T_s$. For example, the utilization of link B–C

$$= 12 \times \frac{200}{4800}$$

$$= .5$$

SUMMARY

This chapter begins with an introduction to probability theory followed by a brief overview of queuing theory and its application to estimating network performance.

The above results provide an introduction to analyzing the performance of a computer communication network and its components. The binomial and Poisson distributions, and the extension to the M/M/1 queuing system, provide only the basis for some common problems. Detailed treatment of these topics appears in several textbooks [1, 3, 4].

PROBLEMS

8-1 Show that the variance of random variable X is $E[X^2] - (E[X])^2$, where $E[X]$ is the expected value of random variable X.

8-2 There are 150 terminals feeding a network node. Each terminal sends one transaction every 3 minutes, while the node can only process 60 transactions per minute. What is the probability that a transaction is processed as soon as it arrives? *Hint*: Determine the probability that there are no more than 60 transaction arrivals per minute. The large number of calculations may require writing a computer program.

8-3 For the example on page 273 (that determines average wait time), derive the 90th and 95th percentiles of the number of messages waiting for service. State clearly what these numbers represent.

8-4 A node receives messages from all other nodes at a total rate of 100 messages per hour. The node processor can forward messages at a rate of 120 messages per hour. Assuming an M/M/1 queuing system, find (*a*) the average processor utilization, (*b*) the mean service time, (*c*) the probability that the queue is empty, (*d*) the mean waiting time, (*e*) the average number of message buffers occupied in the node, and (*f*) the 90th percentile of the number of message buffers occupied.

8-5 For the example on page 276, find the average message delays from node A to C, node B to D, node C to D, node E to A, and node G to B. What is the average utilization of each link in the network? What is the average message delay for this network?

8-6 Consider the network topology shown below. Assume that each of the nodes A, G, C, D, and E sends and receives a fixed number k of messages to node B. The message size is exponentially distributed, with a mean of 200 bits, and each link operates at 2400 bps. Node B takes an average of .1 s to process a message. What is the maximum value of k such that a message and its response do not exceed a total of 1 min?

What is the maximum value of k such that the buffers required for each link do not exceed 200 bytes more than 5 percent of the time? *Hint*: Evaluate k so that the 95th percentile queue size does not exceed 8 messages in a link queue.

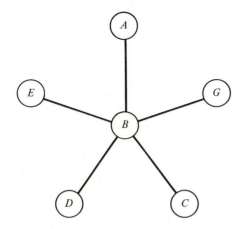

REFERENCES

1. L. Kleinrock, *Queueing Systems*, vol. II: *Computer Applications*, Wiley, New York, 1976.
2. P. G. Hoel, S. C. Port, and C. J. Stone, *Introduction to Probability Theory*, Houghton Mifflin, Boston, 1971.
3. IBM Corporation, "Analysis of Some Queuing Models in Real-Time Systems," No. GF20-0007-1, 1971.
4. L. Kleinrock, *Communication Nets: Stochastic Message Flow and Delay*, Dover, New York, 1964.
5. A. B. Clarke and R. L. Disney, *Probability and Random Processes for Engineers and Scientists*, Wiley, New York, 1970.
6. R. B. Cooper, *Introduction to Queuing Theory*, Macmillan, New York, 1972.

APPENDIX
A

NETWORKS AND NETWORK SERVICES

APPENDIX OUTLINE

In this appendix, we describe some existing or planned computer communication networks and network services. A large number of public and private networks have emerged in the past few years. In Europe, TRANSPAC, the Nordic Public Data Network, and EUR-ONET are either in operation or expected to be operating soon. In North America, TYMNET, TELENET, ARPANET, and DATAPAC are examples of operational networks that offer various services.

The first and perhaps the foremost packet-switching network is ARPANET, which was developed to provide resource sharing. The network began operation in 1969 with four nodes, and has since grown to more than 100 nodes (see Figs. 1-1 and 1-2). The network nodes, or interface message processors (IMPs), are Honeywell 516 and 316 computers that are connected by 50-kbps links. The network employs adaptive routing based on traffic patterns. We have addressed different aspects of this network throughout the book (Secs. 5-2 and 7-4), and several publications describe details of this network [1–16].

Here, we provide details on TYMNET and DATAPAC, followed by an overview of TELENET, the Nordic Public Data Network, and the TRANSPAC network.

A-1 TYMNET*

TYMNET is a centrally directed packet data communication network that has been in operation since 1971. TYMNET started with a 30-node network consisting of Varian 620 minicomputers and a central supervisor (with three backup supervisors) using an SDS 940 computer system. The central supervisor provides network management and routing. As of 1978, TYMNET had grown to 300 nodes, interconnected by leased synchronous voice-grade and digital lines ranging between 2400 bps and 9600 bps.

The network nodes consist of minicomputers that can be classified as *remote* or *base*. The software in remote accommodates all idiosyncrasies of different terminal types, while the software base handles several types of host processors. A remote, also called TYMSAT, provides the interface for low-speed dial-up (asynchronous) and high-speed (binary synchronous) access. A base offers an interface to

---

* The information in this section is derived from several publications on TYMNET [17–23]. Specific references are quoted where appropriate.

TYMSHARE's XDS-940, PDP-10, and IBM System/370 computers. TYMCOM, another type of base, interfaces to additional types of host processors. The supervisor originally ran on an XDS-940 connected through a base node, but has since been recoded to run on an Interdata 7/32 processor. Although one node operates as the supervisor at a given time, several other nodes are capable of operating as the supervisor.

TYMNET employs a useful feature to handle several transmission links that converge in a given location, such that one node cannot handle them all simultaneously. Providing more than one node at a given location requires establishment of node interconnections and entails overhead to manage the interconnections. To address this condition, TYMNET employs a *memory shuffler* [20] that copies the core of one node onto another without any intervention required by the node CPU. The transfer takes place over coaxial cables and is of the order of a million bits per second. Thus, the memory shuffler permits a cluster of adjacent nodes to function as if it were one node with a very large capacity.

A physical record transmitted over the link consists of a collection of logical records. Each logical record is associated with a virtual circuit (described later). The formats of a physical record and a logical record are shown in Fig. A-1. Characters are stored in *buffers*, and each buffer is identified by a unique number. A buffer does not contain the data; instead, it consists of a pointer to the location where the first byte of data and a count of the number of bytes are stored. Data is stored in a separate area that is allocated and freed as required.

Routing

The objectives of the routing philosophy are to minimize the probability of disruption, avoid congestion, balance loads, minimize response time for interactive users, and offer adequate bandwidth for high-speed users [20]. As we briefly described in Sec. 6-2, a circuit is selected based on the minimum cost, which is the sum of the costs of each link on the route. The supervisor establishes the path at log-on time. A cost table* is used to establish the route for a circuit. The load condition of a line is based on the time taken by a node to service a channel (user) on the line. If this time exceeds the threshold of .5 s, the node is considered overloaded (in that direction), and the supervisor is

---

* See Sec. 6-2 for cost table.

informed. The supervisor then increases the line cost. Similarly, when the service time falls below .5 s, the node is not overloaded and the supervisor reduces the line cost. The path selection algorithm used by the supervisor is an optimized version [20] of Floyd's algorithm (Sec. 7-2) that takes about 12 ms to select a circuit.

Routing is implemented through a table, called the *permuter table*, in each node. Each permuter table entry points to one buffer of a buffer pair. The buffer pair consists of a buffer each for incoming characters and for outgoing characters.

Centralized Control

The supervisor node controls the network and manages its resources. The supervisor software runs on an Interdata 7/32 computer. There are four nodes that have the capability to act as supervisor, while only

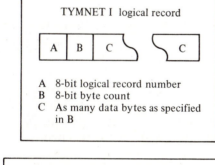

TYMNET I logical record

A 8-bit logical record number
B 8-bit byte count
C As many data bytes as specified
in B

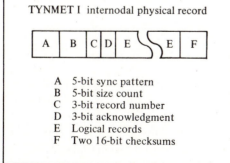

TYNMET I internodal physical record

A 5-bit sync pattern
B 5-bit size count
C 3-bit record number
D 3-bit acknowledgment
E Logical records
F Two 16-bit checksums

Figure A-1 TYMNET—record formats. (From J. Rinde, "Routing and Control in a Centrally Directed Network," *Proceedings of National Computer Conference,* 1977, AFIPS Press, vol. 46, p. 606.)

one is active at a time. In case of failure, a backup supervisor takes over automatically. The functions of the supervisor include:

Keeping track of topology, failures, and load conditions.
Establishing optimal paths for circuits initiating at any instant.
Collecting accounting and diagnostic information.

A primary function of the supervisor is to establish virtual circuits. A user logs on a remote along with a user name and password. The supervisor checks the user name and password, determines the host for the user, and selects a minimum-cost path, as described earlier. The permuter tables along the (chosen) route are updated to include routing information for the new circuit. The messages on the circuit are routed using the permuter table in each node.

Flow Control

The number of circuits passing a node is restricted, depending on the type of node and memory available in the node. It varies between 48 and 256. Furthermore, the maximum number of users (channels) on a given line is also restricted to 48 to 192, depending on the line speed [20].

TYMNET controls the average input-output rate to a node through a mechanism called *back-pressure* [21]. Periodically, every node examines the number of buffers associated with each input process. If a certain threshold is exceeded, the process is signaled to stop inputting until further notice.

An upgraded version, TYMNET II, is under development [20]. The nodes are taking over several of the local tasks, while the supervisor will only handle tasks of global importance. Besides path selection, the supervisor can also reroute a circuit automatically when an intermediate network element fails.

A-2 DATAPAC

The Canadian DATAPAC network is a public, packet-switched data communication network. The network began operation in November 1976, and first provided commercial service in June 1977. The network is operated by the Computer Communications Group of the TransCanada Telephone System and was developed by Bell-Northern Research. The following description is based on references [24–30].

The configuration of DATAPAC as of June 1977 is shown in Fig. A-2. Each node consists of an SL-10 Data Network Processor manufactured by Northern Telecom Limited. Each SL-10 is a multiprocessor consisting of a variable mixture of functional processors. Memory is divided into 64-byte blocks that are used for both messages and control blocks. The nodes are interconnected through 56-kb links. Each node is connected to at least two other nodes.

DATAPAC supports the protocols for CCITT recommendation X.25 [24, 25]. The network offers a call-based service with two types of calls: permanent or switched. Permanent call is analogous to a private line and requires no call setup or clearing procedures. Switched calls require call setup and call clearing (Sec. 5-2). Two levels of service are available. Priority service is appropriate for time-sensitive jobs, such as inquiry-response applications. Normal service is appropriate for jobs that are less sensitive to network delays, such as remote job entry applications. On each link, priority service packets

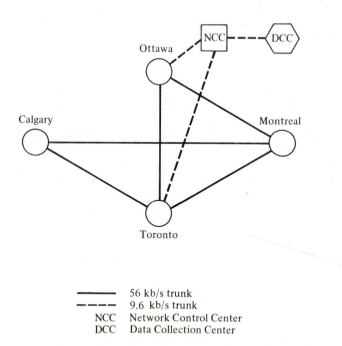

<table>
<tr><td>————</td><td>56 kb/s trunk</td></tr>
<tr><td>— — — —</td><td>9.6 kb/s trunk</td></tr>
<tr><td>NCC</td><td>Network Control Center</td></tr>
<tr><td>DCC</td><td>Data Collection Center</td></tr>
</table>

Figure A-2 DATAPAC configuration. (From C. I. McGibbon, H. Gibbs, and S. C. K. Young, "DATAPAC: Initial Experiences with a Commercial Packet Network," *Proceedings of the Fourth International Conference on Computer Communication*, Kyoto, Japan, September 1978, p. 103.)

are given preference over normal service ones. The maximum amount of data in a packet is 128 bytes for priority service and 256 bytes for normal service.

DATAPAC includes a Network Control Center (NCC), located in Ottawa, that is connected by 9.6-kb links to the Ottawa and Toronto nodes. The Data Collection Center (DCC) is connected to the network through NCC and provides off-line processing for network-generated statistics and accounting data [26, 28]. It also provides generation and distribution of network software and customer service data. NCC provides the network administration support by acting as the staging point for all data flow between the DCC and the network, such as for accounting and statistics. NCC also continuously probes

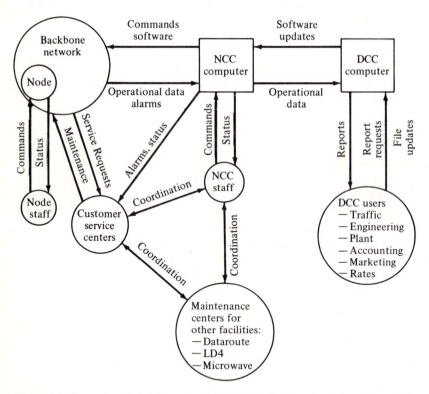

Figure A-3 Flow of control information in DATAPAC. *Note*: An "alarm" is raised when a network component fails. (From S. C. K. Young, and C. I. McGibbon, "The Control System of the Datapac Network," *Proceedings of the Third International Conference on Computer Communication*, Toronto, 1976, p. 140.)

and samples the network to provide real-time information to NCC operators on network performance, traffic, and failure situations. The flow of control information in DATAPAC is depicted in Fig. A-3.

Functional Layers

As shown in Fig. A-4, the internal structure of a DATAPAC node [30] consists of four layers. The *node nucleus* provides process creation and message transfer between processes. A *process* is a virtual or a logical processor that serves as the environment for program execution. The node nucleus manages the process states, such as "waiting for a message" or for a "processor." The nucleus layer ensures that messages between any pair of processes are maintained in sequential order. This layer exists within each node and has no knowledge of the nodes in the network.

The *packet subnet* permits a process in one node to send or receive packets from processes in another node, using links and a routing strategy. In this layer, it is possible that packets may be delivered out of sequence or, occasionally, lost or duplicated. The routing of packets in the packet subnet layer is accomplished through a routing table in each node. The routing table uses only node numbers. It contains the output route queue for each destination node. Each output route queue is serviced by one or more processes, such as a trunk process feeding packets to a specific trunk. The routing tables are maintained by a process in each node. Changes in routes are sent and propagated by these processes throughout the packet subnet. The route changes are intended to address failure conditions and not to provide adaptive routing based on monitored traffic patterns.

The main function of *process liaison* is to provide end-to-end error control and flow control to handle traffic between a single pair of processes. End-to-end error control is provided by the sender holding

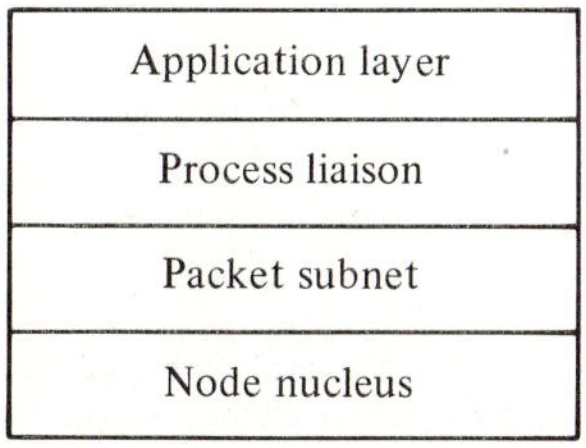

Application layer
Process liaison
Packet subnet
Node nucleus

Figure A-4 Functional layers in DATAPAC.

a copy of each dispatched packet until an acknowledgment is received. Flow control is provided by the receiver controlling the number of messages the sender can transmit to the receiver. The receiver derives this number based on its estimated rate of processing packets. A packet is considered to be processed after it has been received and dispatched to the subscriber out of the network. The receiver estimates its rate of processing packets by using the delay across the network, the rate of flow, and the buffer space available in the receiver.

The *application layer* uses process liaison to build user interface. Two main types of interfaces are provided: the interactive terminal interface for single-character terminals, and the standard network interface that allows multiple logical channels for a host computer. Details on the DATAPAC subscriber interfaces are given in [29].

DATAPAC has been designed to satisfy certain performance objectives. Let the transit delay through the network be defined by the time between receipt of the last bit of a packet at the source node and its complete reception (and processing) in the destination node. It includes the propagation delays, queuing delays, and service times incurred in traveling from node to node. It does not include the queuing delay for the destination access line. The average and the 90th percentile transit delay objectives (during peak busy hour of the year) are tabulated below.

	Delay, s	
Service	Average	90%
Normal	.36	.62
Priority	.13	.19

Source: W. W. Clipsham, F. E. Glave, and M. L. Narraway, "Datapac Network Overview," *Proceedings of the Third International Conference on Computer Communication*, Toronto, 1976, p. 134.

The availability objective, or the percent of time that the node can operate in full-duplex mode with any other destination node, is 99.963 percent.

A-3 TELENET

The TELENET packet-switching network was the first such commercial network in the United States. TELENET began operation in August 1975, and had grown to 81 switching nodes, called the TELENET Central Offices (TCOs), by June 1978. TCOs are divided into three classes. Class 1 TCOs are interconnected through at least three paths. Each Class 2 or 3 TCO is connected to a Class 1 TCO. Thus, the backbone of the network is an interconnected collection of Class 1 TCOs. Class 2 and Class 3 TCOs include microprocessor-based concentration equipment. Each TCO is the equivalent of an IMP in ARPANET. Each message from host computers or terminals is reorganized into packets, and then sent into the network. Packets are forwarded by a given TCO to the next TCO, according to a routing table stored in the TCO. Upon arrival at the destination node, packets belonging to a message are reassembled and then forwarded to the destination computer or terminal. Besides the above functions, each TCO also interacts with the network control computer for billing, traffic statistics, and line and equipment status.

TELENET supports the protocols for CCITT recommendation X.25 [33]. Each packet contains 128 characters of data and some control information. For interactive applications with unbuffered terminals, the average packet size is 20 to 40 characters. TELENET charges are based on the number of packets sent, without regard to the distance involved. The network is described in several publications [31, 34, 36]; references [33, 35] also address CCITT recommendation X.25; and references [32, 37] respectively address topics of packet switching and satellites for networks.

A-4 NORDIC PUBLIC DATA NETWORK

The Nordic Public Data Network is planned to satisfy the data communications needs of Denmark, Finland, Norway, and Sweden. The data network will consist of a set of data switching exchanges (DSEs) that are connected by 64-kbps links. The network is accessed by a DTE through a DCE.* The DCEs, in turn, are connected to DCCs.

---

* See Sec. 2-3 for a description of these terms and the functions these components perform.

Data circuit concentrators (DCCs) can be regarded as subscriber stages that have been moved out of the DSE. A DCC is connected to a DSE by at least two 64-kb/s circuits. The data multiplexers (DMX/RMX) are connected to concentrators or exchanges through 64-kb/s circuits. When a customer requires connection to several DTEs, a customer multiplexer (CMX) is placed on the customer's premises. The connections of these components are shown in Fig. A-5.

The Nordic Public Data Network offers use of several commands for operation and maintenance of the switching and transmission systems. These commands can be divided into several groups, such as charging functions (to administer charges), call tracing functions, traffic supervision functions (to supervise blocking, congestion and occupancy), and the like. The command language conforms to the man-machine language (MML) recommended by CCITT. The network will initially offer a circuit-switched service using CCITT recommendation X.21 (described in Sec. 2-3). Plans for offering the packet-switched service were under study at the time of writing [41]. Additional details on this network are given in [38–40].

A-5 TRANSPAC

TRANSPAC is the public packet-switched network of the French PTT (Post, Telephone and Telegraph Administration). The network began operation in 1978. In 1979, it grew from 4 to 12 nodes, as shown in Fig. A-6. It is expected to grow to 19 nodes in 1981.

The network supports CCITT recommendation X.25.* The primary service offered by TRANSPAC is full-duplex virtual circuits. A virtual circuit provides communication through the network for two logical channels. A logical channel is a connection from a user terminal or computer to the network. As in DATAPAC, two types of virtual circuits are offered: permanent and switched. A permanent virtual circuit is a permanent association between two terminals or computers through the network. It does not require a call-establishment or call-clearing procedure. The logical channel number is assigned at the time of subscription. A switched virtual circuit is a temporary association between two terminals or computers. Such terminals (or computers) can call different terminals (or computers) at different times. It requires call-establishment and call-clearing procedures. The logical channel number is assigned during the call-establishment phase.

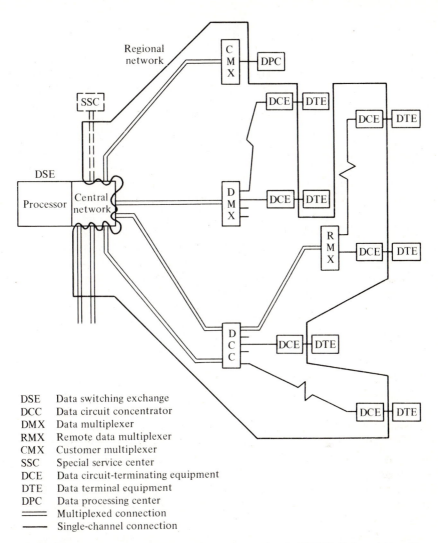

DSE	Data switching exchange
DCC	Data circuit concentrator
DMX	Data multiplexer
RMX	Remote data multiplexer
CMX	Customer multiplexer
SSC	Special service center
DCE	Data circuit-terminating equipment
DTE	Data terminal equipment
DPC	Data processing center
═══	Multiplexed connection
───	Single-channel connection

Figure A-5 Main components and their interconnection in NPDN. (Adapted from H. Svendsen, "The Nordic Public Data Network [NPDN]," *Proceedings of the Online Conference on Data Networks—Developments and Use*, London, June 1980, p. 191.)

At the time of circuit establishment, an appropriate route is chosen based on the message (packet) traffic. Each node on the route is updated with the identification of the new virtual circuit; each packet on the (new) virtual circuit follows the fixed route. TRANS-

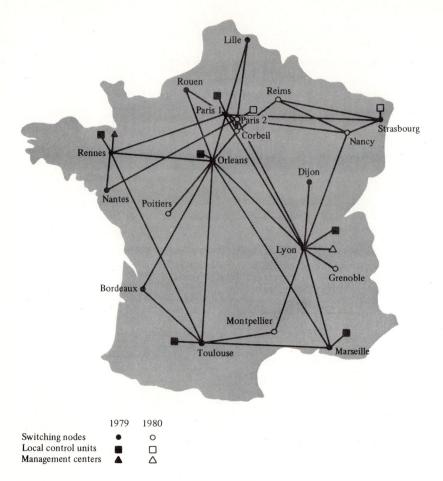

Figure A-6 Evolution of the configuration of TRANSPAC. (From R. Despres and G. Pichon, "The TRANSPAC Network Status Report and Perspectives," *Proceedings of the Online Conference on Data Networks—Developments and Use*, London, June 1980, p. 215.)

PAC employs at least two lines for each connected pair of nodes to provide reliability.

TRANSPAC network is accessed directly on packet-switching nodes for synchronous terminals. For asynchronous terminals, the network is accessed through a protocol adaptation service (teletype, IBM 2741-compatible terminals, and Telex terminals). The network service characteristics allow 24-hour operation seven days a week. The average transit time of a packet within the network is less than 150 ms at peak time.

Details on this network appear in [42, 43].

REFERENCES*

ARPANET

1. H. Frank and W. Chou, "Network Properties of the ARPA Computer Network," *Networks*, vol. 4, 1974, pp. 213–239.
2. S. M. Ornstein, F. E. Heart, W. R. Crowther, H. K. Rising, S. B. Russell, and A. Michel, "The Terminal IMP for the ARPA Computer Network," *Proceedings of the Spring Joint Computer Conference*, May 1972, pp. 243–254.
3. F. E. Heart, R. E. Kahn, S. M. Ornstein, W. R. Crowther, and D. C. Walden, "The Interface Message Processor for the ARPA Computer Network," *Proceedings of the Spring Joint Computer Conference*, May 1970, pp. 551–567.
4. L. Kleinrock, "Analytic and Simulation Methods in Computer Network Design," *Proceedings of the Spring Joint Computer Conference*, May 1970, pp. 569–579.
5. H. Frank, I. T. Frisch, and W. Chou, "Topological Considerations in the Design of the ARPA Computer Network," *Proceedings of the Spring Joint Computer Conference*, May 1970, pp. 581–587.
6. C. S. Carr, S. D. Crocker, and V. G. Cerf, "HOST-HOST Communication Protocol in the ARPA Network," *Proceedings of the Spring Joint Computer Conference*, May 1970, pp. 589–597.
7. L. G. Roberts and B. D. Wessler, "Computer Network Development to Achieve Resource Sharing," *Proceedings of the Spring Joint Computer Conference*, May 1970, pp. 543–549.
8. H. Frank, R. E. Kahn, and L. Kleinrock, "Computer Communication Network Design—Experience with Theory and Practice," *Proceedings of the Spring Joint Computer Conference*, May 1972, pp. 255–270.
9. S. D. Crocker, J. F. Heafner, R. M. Metcalfe, and J. B. Postel, "Function-Oriented Protocols for the ARPA Computer Network," *Proceedings of the Spring Joint Computer Conference*, May 1972, pp. 271–280.
10. R. H. Thomas and D. A. Henderson, "McROSS—A Multi-Computer Programming System," *Proceedings of the Spring Joint Computer Conference*, May 1972, pp. 281–294.
11. L. G. Roberts, "Extensions of Packet Communication Technology to a Hand Held Personal Terminal," *Proceedings of the Spring Joint Computer Conference*, May 1972, pp. 295–298.
12. S. R. Kimbleton and G. M. Schneider, "Computer Communications Networks: Approaches, Objectives and Performance Considerations," *ACM Computing Surveys*, vol. 7, no. 3, September 1975, pp. 129–173.
13. J. M. McQuillan, I. Richer, and E. C. Rosen, "An Overview of the New Routing Algorithm for the ARPANET," *Proceedings of the Sixth Data Communication Symposium*, Pacific Grove, Calif., 1979, pp. 63–68.

* *Note*: Some references pertain to networks in addition to those under which they are listed.

14. J. Davidson, W. Hathaway, J. Postel, N. Mimno, R. Thomas, and D. Walden, "The ARPANET TELNET Protocol: Its Purpose, Principles, Implementation, and Impact on Host Operating System Design," *Proceedings of the Fifth Data Communication Symposium*, Snowbird, Utah, 1977, pp. 4–10 to 4–18.
15. Network Analysis Corporation, *ARPANET: Design, Operation, Management and Performance*, New York, April 1973.
16. J. A. Payne, "ARPANET Host to Host Access and Disengagement Measurements," NTIS Report-78-3, Accession No. PB283554, U. S. Dept. of Commerce, Springfield, Va., May 1978.

TYMNET

17. M. P. Beere and N. C. Sullivan, "TYMNET—A Serendipitous Evolution," *IEEE Transactions on Communications*, vol. COM-20, no. 3, June 1972, pp. 511–515.
18. *TYMNET—Time-Tested Network Service*, Tymnet, Inc., Cupertino, Calif. (Brochures)
19. J. Rinde, "Routing and Control in a Centrally Directed Network," *AFIPS Conference Proceedings*, National Computer Conference, 1977, vol. 46, pp. 603–608.
20. A. Rajaraman, "Routing in TYMNET," *Proceedings of the European Computing Congress*, 1978.
21. J. Kopf, "TYMNET as a Multiplexed Packet Network," *AFIPS Conference Proceedings*, National Computer Conference, 1977, vol. 46, pp. 609–613.
22. *TYMNET: TYMCOM Bisynchronous Reference Manual*, Tymnet, Inc., Cupertino, Calif.
23. L. Tymes and J. Rinde, "The TYMNET II Engine," *Proceedings of the Fourth International Conference on Computer Communication*, Kyoto, 1978, pp. 109–114.

DATAPAC

24. M. L. Hess, M. Brethes, and A. Saito, "A Comparison of Four X.25 Public Network Interfaces," *Proceedings of the International Conference on Communication*, Boston, 1979, pp. 38.6.1–38.6.8.
25. A. M. Rybczynski and D. F. Weir, "DATAPAC X.25 Service Characteristics," *Proceedings of the Fifth Data Communications Symposium*, Snowbird, Utah, 1977, pp. 4–50 to 4–57.
26. C. I. McGibbon, H. Gibbs, and S. C. K. Young, "DATAPAC—Initial Experiences with a Commercial Packet Network," *Proceedings of the Fourth International Conference on Computer Communication*, Kyoto, September 1978, pp. 103–108.
27. W. W. Clipsham, F. E. Glave, and M. L. Narraway, "Datapac Network Overview," *Proceedings of the Third International Conference on Computer Communication*, Toronto, 1976, pp. 131–136.
28. S. C. K. Young and C. I. McGibbon, "The Control System of the Datapac Network," *Proceedings of the Third International Conference on Computer Communication*, Toronto, 1976, pp. 137–142.
29. D. A. Twyver and A. M. Rybczynski, "Datapac Subscriber Interfaces," *Proceedings of the Third International Conference on Computer Communication*, Toronto, 1976, pp. 143–149.
30. P. M. Cashin, "Datapac Network Protocols," *Proceedings of the Third International Conference on Computer Communication*, Toronto, 1976, pp. 150–155.

TELENET

31. *TELENET Communications Corporation—Packet Switching Network,* Auerbach Computer Technology Report, Auerbach Publishers Inc., 1978.
32. L. G. Roberts, "The Evolution of Packet Switching," *Proceedings of the IEEE,* vol. 66, no. 11, November 1978, pp. 1307–1313.
33. R. B. Hovey, "Packet-Switched Networks Agree on Standard Interface," *Data Communications,* May/June 1976, pp. 25–39.
34. S. L. Mathison, "A New Alternative for Corporate Data Networks," *Data Communications,* April 1979, pp. 83–93.
35. A. Rybczynski, B. Wessler, R. Despres, and J. Wedlake, "A New Communication Protocol for Accessing Data Networks—The International Packet-Mode Interface," *AFIPS Conference Proceedings,* National Computer Conference, 1976, pp. 477–482.
36. C. B. Newport and P. Kaul, "Communications Processors for TELENET's Third Generation Packet Switching Network," *Proceedings of the IEEE Electronics and Aerospace Systems Convention,* EASCON-77, September 1977, pp. 8-2A to 8-2L.
37. L. G. Roberts, "Dynamic Allocation of Satellite Capacity through Packet Reservation," *AFIPS Conference Proceedings,* National Computer Conference, 1973, pp. 711–716.

NORDIC PUBLIC DATA NETWORK

38. *The Public Data Networks in the Nordic Countries,* Telecommunications Administration of Denmark, Finland, Norway and Sweden, March 1978.
39. A. H. Kvist, "The Public Data Network in the Nordic Countries," *Proceedings of the Fourth International Conference on Computer Communication,* Kyoto, September 1978, pp. 201–206.
40. T. Larsson, "A Public Data Network in the Nordic Countries," *Proceedings of the Third International Conference on Computer Communication,* Toronto, August 1976, pp. 246–250.
41. H. Svendsen, "The Nordic Public Data Network (NPDN)," *Proceedings of the Online Conference on Data Networks—Developments and Use,* London, June 1980, pp. 189–207.

TRANSPAC

42. A. Danet, R. Despres, A. Le Rest, G. Pichon, and S. Ritzenthaler, "The French Public Packet Switching Service: The Transpac Network," *Proceedings of the Third International Conference on Computer Communication,* Toronto, 1976, pp. 251–260.
43. R. Despres and G. Pichon, "The TRANSPAC Network Status Report and Perspectives," *Proceedings of the Online Conference on Data Networks—Developments and Use,* London, June 1980, pp. 209–232.

INDEX